# VOODOO DOS

## TIPS & TRICKS WITH AN ATTITUDE

Second Edition

# VOODOO DOS

## TIPS & TRICKS WITH AN ATTITUDE

Second Edition

Kay Yarborough Nelson

Ventana Press Voodoo™ Series

**Voodoo DOS: Tips & Tricks With an Attitude, Second Edition**
Copyright © 1993 by Kay Yarborough Nelson
Ventana Press Voodoo™ Series

All rights reserved. This book may not be duplicated in any way without the expressed written consent of the publisher, except in the form of brief excerpts or quotations for the purposes of review. The information contained herein is for the personal use of the reader, and may not be incorporated in any commercial programs, other books, databases or any kind of software without written consent of the publisher or author. Making copies of this book, or any portion for any purpose other than your own, is a violation of United States copyright laws.

Library of Congress Cataloging-in-Publication Data
Nelson, Kay Yarborough
    Voodoo DOS : tips & tricks with an attitude/Kay Yarborough
  Nelson. -- 2nd ed.
      p.  cm.
    Includes bibliographical references and index.
    ISBN 1-56604-046-9 : $21.95
    1. Operating systems (Computers)  2. PC-DOS (Computer File)
3. MS-DOS (Computer File)   I. Title.
QA76.76.063N44   1993
005.4'469--dc20                                                            93-15446
                                                                         CIP

Book design: Karen Wysocki, Brian Little
Cover Illustration: Lynn Tanaka, Lynn Tanaka Illustration
Cover design: Thea Tullose, Tullose Design; John Nedwidek, Sitzer:Spuria
Editorial staff: Charles Hutchinson, Virginia Phelps, Pam Richardson, Cabell Smith
Production staff: Rhonda Angel, John Cotterman, Brian Little, Karen Wysocki
Technical review: Brian Little

Second Edition  9 8 7 6 5 4 3 2
Printed in the United States of America

Ventana Press, Inc.
P.O. Box 2468
Chapel Hill, NC 27515
919/942-0220
FAX 919/942-1140

**Limits of Liability and Disclaimer of Warranty**

The author and publisher of this book have used their best efforts in preparing the book and the programs contained in it. These efforts include the development, research and testing of the theories and programs to determine their effectiveness. The author and publisher make no warranty of any kind, expressed or implied, with regard to these programs or the documentation contained in this book.

The author and publisher shall not be liable in the event of incidental or consequential damages in connection with, or arising out of, the furnishing, performance or use of the programs, associated instructions and/or claims of productivity gains.

# Trademarks

Trademarked names appear throughout this book. Rather than list the names and entities that own the trademarks or insert a trademark symbol with each mention of the trademarked name, the publisher states that it is using the names only for editorial purposes and to the benefit of the trademark owner with no intention of infringing upon that trademark.

# About the Author

Kay Yarborough Nelson, author of a couple of dozen computer books, knows how to extract the essence from complex programs and operating systems and present it to readers in simple, plain English. Kay Nelson is the author of the acclaimed *Voodoo Windows*, *Voodoo WordPerfect for Windows* and *Voodoo Mac*, published by Ventana Press. She has also written encyclopedias and macro handbooks for advanced readers (Sybex's *Encyclopedia WordPerfect* and *WordPerfect 5.1 Macro Handbook*) instant references for all audiences (Sybex's *DOS Instant Reference* and *WordPerfect Instant Reference*) and beginner books like Peachpit Press's *The Little DOS 5 Book* and *The Little Windows Book*, and *Friendly Windows* and *Friendly WordPerfect* from Bantam Books. Her books have been translated into many languages, including French, German, Spanish, Italian, Portuguese, Dutch and Swedish.

She has an irreverent attitude about computers.

# Acknowledgments

Nobody works all alone with DOS. I owe a great deal of gratitude to the authors of all the books and magazine articles I've read over the years while struggling with that old devil DOS, and to all the co-workers and technicians and folks I've conversed with. Unfortunately, I can't give credit everywhere it's due; the sources for all the tips I've picked up have blended into memory. If you see your favorite trick here, one that you thought you came up with yourself—well, somebody else did, too, and it probably wasn't me. I most likely picked it up somewhere along the way.

I am grateful to James S. Forney's book, *DOS 5 Demystified*, for showing me how to get the current date in a batch file. That one, at least, I can remember—because I never could have thought of it myself.

Most heartily I thank Robert Lorincz of Computer West Computer Systems of Santa Clara, CA, for building my computer, repairing it when necessary, removing the cat hair from it and sharing some voodoo with me.

And to my husband, Ray, I appreciate more than I can ever say all the hours you spent reading over these tricks and trying them out before we sent them off.

At Ventana Press, I'd like to thank Elizabeth Woodman for not saying "What DOS?" when a strange lady called her about doing an unusual series of books. Thanks also to Joe Woodman, Fran Phillips, Diane Lennox, Laura Wenzel and all the other marketing wizards at Ventana who worked to send this series off with a bang. (Although I still think we could do a T-shirt.)

Special thanks to Chuck Hutchinson, my project editor, to technical reviewer Brian Little and to production manager Karen Wysocki.

# TABLE OF CONTENTS

## Introduction .................................................. xv
What's inside .................................................. xvi
How to use this book .......................................... xviii
Use the index! ................................................. xix
Software versions ............................................. xix
Your favorite trick? .......................................... xix

## Chapter 1: Beyond Magic .............................. 1
Setup tips ..................................................... 2
Once you've installed DOS ..................................... 13
Help! .......................................................... 17
Customizing DOS ............................................... 23
Running lean & mean ........................................... 34

## Chapter 2: Shell Secrets ............................ 37
The Shell interface ........................................... 37
Shell voodoo .................................................. 42
Switching from the Shell to the command line .................. 47
Finding what you're looking for ............................... 49
Selecting files ............................................... 51
File attribute tricks ......................................... 59

## Chapter 3: Working with Programs .............. 63

Running programs from the Shell ........................................ 64
Switching between programs ............................................. 66
Setting up program groups .................................................. 69

## Chapter 4: Command-Line Tricks ................. 83

Command-line basics ........................................................... 83
Editing commands ................................................................ 85
Bailing out of commands ...................................................... 87
Miscellaneous command-line tricks ...................................... 88
The new, improved DIR command ......................................... 99
Wildcard tips & traps .......................................................... 104
Special symbols & commands ............................................. 107

## Chapter 5: Disk & Drive Magic .................. 111

The usual cautions & then some ......................................... 111
Formatting disks ................................................................. 112
Tricks for undeleting files ................................................... 119
Miscellaneous disk tricks .................................................... 124
Organizing your disk files ................................................... 139
Copying tricks ..................................................................... 141
Logical drives ...................................................................... 144
Using the disk utilities ........................................................ 146
Working with your hard disk ............................................... 148

## Chapter 6: A Miscellany of Alchemy .......... 153

Tips for deleting files .......................................................... 153
AUTOEXEC.BAT arts ............................................................ 156
Backup tricks ...................................................................... 162
Copying tricks ..................................................................... 174
Tricks for finding things ...................................................... 178
Tricks for printing from DOS ............................................... 180

## Chapter 7: Batch Files ....................................... **185**
Tips for using the Editor ........................................................ 185
Batch file tips ........................................................................ 191
What a batch file can do ...................................................... 200

## Chapter 8: DOSKEY Revealed ..................... **209**
Giving several commands at the same time ........................ 210
Recalling previous commands .............................................. 211
Editing DOSKEY commands ................................................ 213
Using DOSKEY for macros ................................................... 215
Macros versus batch files .................................................... 216
Saving macros ...................................................................... 217

## Chapter 9: Arcane Commands ................... **223**

## Chapter 10: Managing Memory ................. **237**
Using a disk cache & a RAM drive ...................................... 255

## Index ................................................................ **269**

# INTRODUCTION

If you're like me, you don't want to plow through thousand-page encyclopedias or work through tutorial exercises that in all likelihood won't tell you what you need to know, anyway. *Voodoo DOS*—one book in a series of Ventana Press Voodoo™ books—enables you to *use* your computer. Browse through the book; you'll find a wealth of information that you can use today. Come back to it later, when you're ready to discover even more.

*Voodoo DOS* offers you a new bag of tricks, whether you're a beginning or an experienced hand at the computer.

All the "tips" and "traps" in this book are short and relatively easy. They're *voodoo* because they get quick results for you. Don't waste time trying to understand theories and applications in long, boring books when you can quickly find new and better ways to use your computer. You'll also discover how to do a few things you probably never thought possible.

You don't have to be a DOS expert to use these tricks. They're for "the rest of us." There's nothing on DEBUG or QBasic or batch files that will turn your computer into an appointment book, for example. These are *user tricks*, not programmer magic.

If you upgraded to DOS 5 or 6, you probably did so to get more memory for your programs. Well, you'll get more than that.

Microsoft added a lot of new features to DOS and improved many of the old ones, and you'll find lots of tricks for using them all.

If you haven't upgraded to DOS 6 yet, do it! DOS 6 is a trickster's delight. It comes with all sorts of new utilities. In addition to a built-in disk compression program that freed up 85 megabytes of space on my hard disk (really!), a memory optimizer and disk defragmenter, several new commands and all sorts of neat tricks you can do with your CONFIG.SYS and AUTOEXEC.BAT (like making your own startup screen and setting up different configurations on the same machine), DOS 6 comes with three new utilities for command line and Windows users, too. There's no reason not to upgrade. The installation program is painless.

## WHAT'S INSIDE

Here's a quick preview of *Voodoo DOS*, to help you find the chapter of immediate interest to you.

### Chapter 1: Beyond Magic

Upgrading to a new DOS version and stuck with an installation problem? Help is here. Or, if you've installed DOS with no problems whatsoever, you'll learn how to customize it to your liking. You can even create custom Help for yourself, if you know where to look. With DOS 6, you can even start your machine interactively so that you can proceed through your CONFIG.SYS step by step or turn off your AUTOEXEC.BAT to see where problems lie in the startup routine. Look in Chapter 1.

### Chapter 2: Shell Secrets

The Shell game started with DOS 4 but improved, beginning with DOS 5. This chapter holds the beginning of a repertoire of skills to get you quickly productive with the Shell.

### Chapter 3: Working With Programs

Continuing with tricks you can do through the Shell, this chapter also enables you to get the most from your programs, set up program groups, switch between programs, use keyboard shortcuts for programs and more.

### Chapter 4: Command-Line Tricks

You can't get away from it, and maybe you don't want to. If you don't use the Shell (and even if you *do*), you'll surely use the command line. Maximize what you can do at the DOS prompt.

### Chapter 5: Disk & Drive Magic

Dealing with disks is a daily chore. Here are maneuvers for getting around some boring day-to-day routines, as well as tips about the new Quick Format command, copying disks and dealing with your hard disk. In DOS 6, all sorts of new utilities let you optimize your hard disk, do backups and increase the amount of space on an already full disk. You'll see tricks for all these, too.

### Chapter 6: A Miscellany of Alchemy

This chapter is a mixed bag for all sorts of things from getting screen dumps to searching for files. If you can't find what you're looking for in another chapter, look here.

### Chapter 7: Batch Files

Meet the new DOS Editor. Or get acquainted with batch files and what they can do for you.

### Chapter 8: Doskey Revealed

Macros? In DOS? Yes, with Doskey. If you like batch files, you'll appreciate getting to know DOS's macro facility.

### Chapter 9: Arcane Commands

Isn't it maddening that some DOS commands can use wildcards and some can't? That some can be abbreviated and not others? That some have really obscure switches and options that no one can figure out?

This chapter puts you back in charge of commands like the much-misunderstood RESTORE and more of your favorites! You'll see commands that are new with DOS 6, too.

### Chapter 10: Managing Memory

You probably bought DOS 5 or 6 to get more memory. Find your path through the memory maze with short, concise tips that are relevant to your computer. By all means, get DOS 6 if you haven't got it yet and see how painless managing memory can be with the new MEMMAKER command.

## HOW TO USE THIS BOOK

To get the most out of this book, you at least ought to know the DOS basics, like how to enter commands, but you certainly don't have to be an advanced user. If you've used DOS even a little bit, you're ready for *Voodoo DOS*. If you see something you don't understand or really want to know more about, you can always look it up in the DOS manual.

The examples presented here assume that you have a hard drive, and that it's drive C. If it's not—if it's drive D or E or something else—just remember to use *your* drive letter. Likewise, I usually call the floppy drive "drive A"; substitute the letter you use for your floppy drive. I also assume that your DOS files are stored in a C:\DOS directory, where the Setup program normally puts them.

A word or two about the conventions used here: what you type in is shown in **boldface**. You can usually use either all capital letters or all lowercase letters, or a mixture of the two; DOS doesn't care. I use lowercase letters because it saves you (and me) from having to press the Shift key. If you have to use a shifted character, I'll tell you.

DOS commands DIR and BACKUP and such are in capital letters to distinguish them from Shell commands like Backup Fixed Disk that are in capital and lowercase letters. That's the way they appear on the Shell menus, and those of us who have struggled with DOS for so many years are just plain used to seeing them that way.

## USE THE INDEX!

Tips and traps on certain topics are grouped together, but because DOS has so many commands that let you do so many things, check out the index to locate a particular topic. Suggestions for handy batch files, for example, are scattered throughout the book as well as concentrated in Chapter 7, "Batch Files."

## SOFTWARE VERSIONS

This book has something for every DOS user, but the higher the version, the more sorcery you'll discover. All the tips and traps herein apply to DOS 5 and 6; but lots of tricks work with DOS 3.3, too.

*Voodoo DOS* will show you new ways to use old commands. You'll learn lots of ways to tweak many of the DOS commands secrets not readily apparent in the manual (but then, what *is* readily apparent in a manual, anyway?).

By the way, we mean no disrespect to anyone's religion or politics. These "voodoo" books are fun. They get your attention and are full of magic tricks! Anything I don't understand completely is magic, and I'll never understand computers. I just try to get some work out of them and probably you do, too.

## YOUR FAVORITE TRICK?

If you've got a favorite trick that's not covered here, send it to Ventana or to me, and we'll try to get it in the next edition. If we include your trick, the next edition is yours free. Be sure to include your name and address.

If you like this book, stay on the lookout for other Ventana Press Voodoo™ books. They're designed to help you make magic with the most popular software on the market today.

You can write to Ventana Press, P.O. Box 2468, Chapel Hill, NC 27515, (919) 942-0220 or fax (919) 942-1140, or get me on CompuServe (72000,1176) or America Online (KayNelson).

*—Kay Nelson*

# Chapter 1
# BEYOND MAGIC

Let's begin at the beginning. If you're having trouble installing DOS, you'll find some voodoo here that will help. Normally, all you have to do is put Disk 1 in drive A and type **a:setup**. The instructions on the screen will guide you through the process.

If you've already installed DOS, you'll probably want to customize it, and this chapter features lots of tips on doing just that. For example, you can create a custom prompt, change the screen colors (if you've got a color monitor) and redefine the function keys. You'll also find tricks for creating your own Help screens as well as for freeing space on your hard disk by deleting parts of DOS you'll never use.

But to get the most out of this book, you should know a couple of fairly basic things before you begin:

- *PATH*. Your files are stored in a system of directories and subdirectories. To let DOS know where they are, you use a notation—called a *path*—in which subdirectories are separated by backslashes. For example, C:\WP51\DOCS\VOODOO shows the path to a VOODOO subdirectory from the *root directory* (where it all begins, the very first level) on drive C.

- *AUTOEXEC.BAT*. You have an AUTOEXEC.BAT file in your root directory that executes when you start your computer. If you didn't create it, DOS automatically did—as part of the Setup installation program. That file should have a line beginning with PATH (either uppercase or lowercase; it doesn't matter), indicating which directories hold your most frequently used programs. At the very least, that line should look like this:

```
path=c:\;c:\dos
```

Your favorite programs ought to be in it, too, something like this:

```
path=c:\;c:\dos;c:\wp51;c:\windows
```

Once a program is in your path, just type the command used to start it from any subdirectory on your hard disk.

- *CONFIG.SYS.* There's also a special CONFIG.SYS file in your root directory that contains information about the components of your system. (Chapter 7, "Batch Files," has tips for viewing and editing these important files.)

Now you've graduated from a short course in DOS! Those concepts are basic for getting some mileage from the tricks that follow in this chapter and in the whole book.

## SETUP TIPS

Check out the tips in this section if you're having trouble installing DOS 5 or 6. If it's running and everything's working just fine on your system, skip to the next section of this chapter.

**Upgrading to DOS 5 or 6 from a previous version.** If you're upgrading to DOS 5 or 6 from DOS 3.3 or 4, be sure to use the Setup program on the DOS Disk 1. Because DOS files are compressed, you can't just copy all the files onto your hard disk as you could with earlier versions.

**Installing DOS 5 on a brand-new hard disk.** If you're installing DOS 5 on a brand-new hard disk that doesn't have a version of DOS on it, you'll need to use a set of "OEM version" disks (OEM stands for original equipment manufacturer). You can get these disks from your dealer or from Microsoft (202-882-8080). The main difference between the upgrade version and the OEM version is that the latter erases whatever system files it finds whereas the former (which you're probably using) preserves your old version of DOS so you can get it back later if you want to.

**An alternative to using the OEM version.** If you had to reformat your hard disk, there won't be any version of DOS on it. You don't want to haul your computer in to your dealer; you just want to install DOS so the thing will run again. This sneaky trick gets around having to use those OEM disks: install your *old* version of DOS (3.3 or 4); then install DOS 5 or 6.

**New monitor? Just install DOS again.** If you purchase a new monitor after installing DOS 5 or 6, the manual tells you that you need to get your original DOS disks out, expand two compressed files that are appropriate for your new monitor and then either create a DOSSHELL.INI file or edit your old one. That's pretty complicated. Instead, just install DOS 5 or 6 again, and it will read what your system consists of and set itself up for your new monitor. It takes a little longer, but saves a big headache.

**Start the Shell automatically if you're a new user.** If you're relatively new to DOS, you'll find you can do most everyday things through the Shell, and it's a lot easier to use than the command line because you don't have to memorize commands. To start the Shell automatically each time you turn on your computer, add **dosshell** as the last line in your AUTOEXEC.BAT file.

**Check disk space before installing DOS.** You'll need at least 2.8mb of free space on your hard disk for DOS 5; DOS 6 needs even more space—about 6mb—but it checks for you. Installation doesn't replace your previous version of DOS but stores it in a directory called OLD_DOS.1 so you can get it back later if you want to. Issue the CHKDSK command to see how much free space you have; it will tell you near the bottom of the listing how many bytes are free, and that number should be bigger than 2,800,000. You'll need over 7mb to install DOS 6 if you install both the DOS and Windows utilities.

**Bad drive A? Use ASSIGN or SUBST before installing DOS 5.** If you have a flaky drive A and a good drive B, or if you have installation disks that will only fit in drive B, or if for some other reason you don't want to use drive A during Setup, **assign a:=b:** or **subst a: b:** before you install DOS 5 so DOS will think drive B is drive A. Setup will ask you to insert a disk to use as the Uninstall disk in drive A, and it will look for that disk only on that drive. Switch the drives before you start installing; then type **a:** to change to drive A and type **setup** to start installing (don't Ctrl-Alt-Del to restart your computer). DOS 6 lets you install from either drive A or drive B.

**Repartitioned your disk? You may need to change your AUTOEXEC.BAT file.** In some cases you'll need to repartition your hard disk (divide it into smaller logical drives) before installing DOS. If the drive where you intend to put DOS doesn't have enough room for it, if you have more than four logical drives, or if you originally used certain incompatible third-party software to partition your disk, you may need to repartition your disk with the FDISK program supplied with DOS.

If you repartitioned your hard disk *before* you put DOS on it and you didn't use the same number of drives that were there before, any statements in the AUTOEXEC.BAT file that called for files on a drive you deleted won't work unless you edit the AUTOEXEC.BAT file to use the right drives. (DOS insists on calling your first hard drive "C" and assigning drive letters from there.)

Also, if you moved files from one logical drive to another *after* installing DOS, you may need to make changes to your path statement in the AUTOEXEC.BAT file. And, if you're running Windows, you may need to make sure your program items still have valid startup commands.

In addition, if you stored DOS in a directory other than the one the Setup program suggested, check your AUTOEXEC.BAT and CONFIG.SYS files to make sure they refer to the right directory. In the Shell, just highlight these files one at a time and press F9 to see what's in them. If you need to make changes, you can use the built-in Editor (see Chapter 7).

**Possible partitioning problems with Setup.** If you partitioned your hard disk with something other than FDISK, DOS's partitioning program, you may have difficulty installing DOS. In fact, you may find that DOS can't read your drives. This can happen because some partitioning programs, like SpeedStor or SuperStor, let you create logical drives that are larger than 32 Mb by using unconventional methods (at least unconventional to DOS). Microsoft recommends that you back up your hard drive (since repartitioning destroys the information on it), remove the partitions with the original partitioning program and then repartition the hard drive with FDISK.

You'll need to make a floppy disk version of DOS (with **setup /f**). Once you've backed up your files and removed the old partitions, boot from the floppy and also run FDISK from it to create your new logical drives. Then format each partition with the FORMAT command, restore your files (use the program you backed them up with) and, finally, install DOS with the Setup program.

If you've got one of many third-party disk partitions, such as a Priam, Everex, Novell, UNIX or Disk Manager partition, or if you have a Syquest or Bernoulli hard drive, DOS 6 enables you to install it without repartitioning the disk. For example, you can sometimes install DOS 6 "manually" (see the tip "Installing DOS 6 manually"), or you can run the Setup program with the /U switch. In other cases you'll need to call your hard disk's manufacturer. See the DOS 6 manual for details, if you get an "incompatible hard disk or device driver" message.

**Keep that Uninstall disk handy.** If your hard disk ever fails, you can use the Uninstall disk that's created during the installation process as an emergency startup disk. It has a copy of your AUTOEXEC.BAT file on it. In fact, it has all you need if you ever have to reconstruct your file allocation table (FAT), as you did when

you installed DOS 5 or 6. It even has a program called
UNINSTAL.EXE, which lets you uninstall DOS 5 or 6 and go back
to whatever version of DOS you were using before.

To use the Uninstall disk as a bootable floppy, put it in drive A and
turn on your computer. When you get the Uninstall screen, press F3
and type **Y** to get back to the previous version of DOS.

**The Uninstall disk gets you back to your previous DOS version.**
If you should ever want to go back to DOS 3.3, 4 or 5 (although I can't imagine why), restart your computer with the Uninstall disk in drive A and follow the instructions on the screen.

**A secret /G switch lets you bypass making an Uninstall disk.**
You can type **setup /g** to install DOS 6 without making an Uninstall disk. You can't easily go back to your previous version of DOS without an Uninstall disk, though. But if you're planning to compress your disk with DOS 6's new DoubleSpace program, you won't have any use for an Uninstall disk anyway. Once a disk has been compressed, you can't uninstall DOS 6.

**Upgrade to Windows 3.1 if you're running 3.0.** Several features in DOS 6, such as the Anti-Virus program, aren't compatible with Windows 3.0. If you're running Windows 3.0, it's way past time to upgrade anyway, so I won't bother telling you how to avoid the incompatibilities. Upgrading is the sure way.

**You can't start your computer with DOS program disks.** You used to be able to jump-start your computer from the DOS disks if the hard disk wasn't working. But you can't do that with DOS 5 and 6 because of their compressed files. Use the Uninstall disk instead, or make a system disk (**sys a:** on a blank formatted floppy in drive A or **format a: /s** on an unformatted floppy). You don't have to copy COMMAND.COM onto this disk like you used to; DOS 5 and 6 will do it for you.

## Chapter 1: Beyond Magic    7

However, you won't be able to use the Uninstall disk as a bootable disk if you reformatted, repartitioned or compressed your hard disk after installing DOS. So it's a good idea to have another emergency system disk around.

**Make a special DOS 6 startup disk.**   DOS 6 lets you make a disk you can use to restart your computer if anything goes wrong during installation *before* it makes the Uninstall disk. You can also use this disk if you need to install DOS 6 manually (see the tip "You may need to install DOS 6 manually.") Assuming you have a previous version of DOS on your computer before you install version 6, here's how to make that disk.

Put Setup Disk 1 in drive A (or B) and, at the command line, type **a:setup /f** (or **b:setup /f**). Then follow the on-screen instructions.

Now, if anything goes wrong during setup, you can restart with that floppy disk.

**Other neat things to put on a bootable floppy.**   Once you make a system disk to use in an emergency, you can make it even more useful by copying some other DOS files onto it. Put your AUTOEXEC.BAT and CONFIG.SYS files on it to configure your system as usual when you start up with the disk. Put CHKDSK.EXE on it to check the hard disk that's causing trouble. Put FORMAT.COM on it if you ever need to reformat (shudder) your hard disk. You can copy BACKUP.EXE and RESTORE.EXE on it, too, in case you can save some files from the bad hard disk.

**Don't use a previous DOS version as a boot disk.**   If you're ever tempted to use an old bootable floppy with a previous version of DOS on it to start your computer, don't. You can damage the information on your hard disk that way. Go on a witch hunt now: find all your old emergency startup disks and label them clearly (use the VER command to check which version they are if you're not sure). Then put them somewhere out of the way or reformat them for something else. Don't keep them handy. If your hard disk fails, it's too easy to panic and reach out for the closest disk; you don't want one that has the older system files on it.

> **You don't have to back up the hard disk before installing DOS.**
> The DOS documentation and the Setup program both tell
you to back up your entire hard disk before installing DOS. It's up to you—I've never done it and have never, ever, lost anything, even when installing and working with early beta versions of DOS 5 and 6. If you have (and want to keep) copies of your program disks and recent copies of the work you've been doing, save yourself some time and don't back up everything first. But if you *don't* have copies of what you want to keep, you're playing with fire; sooner or later something will go wrong with your hardware or software.

I copy each day's work onto a floppy disk (and copy over it the next day) and keep disk copies of my programs—and that's all. When a chapter is near completion, I make an extra backup copy and store it at another location. This strategy works for me. Other folks like to do a "real" backup with the BACKUP command (or Backup Fixed Disk in the Shell). Some use a utility program like Norton Backup, which takes a snapshot of the entire hard disk. It all depends on how you like to work. If I had a tape drive, I'd do a "real" backup.

If you have to repartition your hard disk before installing DOS (see the previous tricks), you must do a backup because repartitioning destroys any and all information on your hard disk.

> **You can expand those compressed files individually.** Don't
> panic if you get a disk error message while you're installing
DOS on your hard disk. I know firsthand this can happen, because it happened to me at the spot on the floppy disk that contained DOSSHELL. There's a way to uncompress those compressed files "manually."

Just use the EXPAND command to uncompress the compressed file. Compressed files have an underline (_) as the last character in their extension. For example, DOSSHELL.EX_ is the compressed version of DOSSHELL.EXE. So, to expand it from its compressed version on the disk in drive A into your DOS directory on drive C, enter

    expand a:dosshell.ex_ c:\dos\dosshell.exe

**A packing list that comes with DOS 6 can help you find files.**
If you don't know which disk a DOS 6 file is on—one that you need to decompress, for example—you can find it easily. Open the file PACKING.LST that's on Setup Disk 1 in any word processing program, and you'll see a list of what's on which disk.

**Conserve disk space with a minimal install.** If your hard disk doesn't have the space needed for DOS (and you'll need a lot more room than that if you plan to save any of your work), you can do a minimal installation of DOS 5. This approach is really effective only with DOS 5 because DOS 6 wants most of its commands to be on your hard disk. To save disk space with DOS 6, you can choose not to install the utility programs, and you can delete a few other files. See the tip "Delete DOS files to free more disk space" later in this chapter for which commands you can delete.

First, install DOS 5 onto floppy disks by running the Setup program as **setup /f**. The screen will give you all the instructions you'll need. Then, disable any lines that start memory-resident programs (also called TSRs, or terminate-and-stay resident programs) running from your AUTOEXEC.BAT file. Begin those lines with REM to disable them. Use a text editor if your AUTOEXEC.BAT is long; if it's short (just a couple of lines long) simply COPY CON AUTOEXEC.BAT and reenter your AUTOEXEC.BAT file from the keyboard. See Chapter 7, "Batch Files," if you need help with this.

Put the DOS Disk 1 (the one you made) in drive A and type **a:setup /m**. This minimal install will automatically include the following commands, among others: COPY (for copying files), DIR (for viewing contents of directories), ERASE or DEL, PATH (for quick access to frequently used directories), TYPE (for viewing contents of text files), RENAME (for renaming files), MD and RD (for making and removing directories) and CLS (for clearing the screen).

A minimal install includes all the internal DOS commands, which are automatically loaded in memory when you start your system. If you want any of DOS's external commands, such as CHKDSK.COM and FORMAT.COM, copy them from the floppy disks.

Then use the following lines to rename the AUTOEXEC.NEW and CONFIG.NEW files AUTOEXEC.BAT and CONFIG.SYS, respectively:

```
ren c:\autoexec.new autoexec.bat
ren c:\config.new config.sys
```

When you're done, remove all the floppy disks and press Ctrl-Alt-Del to restart your computer.

When you think of all the work this is going to be, you may reconsider getting rid of some of that old stuff you thought was vital to keep on your hard disk. After all, you can always copy it onto floppies.

**You may need to install DOS 6 manually.** The DOS 6 installation program has been improved over the one that comes with DOS 5, but there's always the possibility that you may need to bypass the automated setup program and install DOS 6 "manually," especially if you've used third-party partitioning programs on your hard disk.

If your DOS 6 disks will go in your drive A, put Disk 1 in drive A and restart. If you have 3.5-inch DOS disks and drive A is a 5.25-inch drive, look back at the tip "Make a special DOS 6 startup disk" and make a startup floppy that will fit in your drive A. When that's done, restart with either Disk 1 in drive A or the startup floppy you made in that drive. Then type **sys c:**.

Put Disk 1 in either drive A or B and type **a:setup /q** (use **b:setup /q** if you're using drive B). Follow the onscreen instructions.

As a last check, look at the contents of your AUTOEXEC.BAT and CONFIG.SYS files and make sure everything's OK—that device drives are referred to in the correct directories, that your PATH statement includes the DOS directory and so forth. If you're not sure how to look at what's in these files, see the tip "Are you getting a "Bad command or file name" message?" later in this chapter.

## Chapter 1: Beyond Magic    11

That's it. Take any floppy disks out of your drives and restart. You've installed DOS 6 manually. Don't do this unless you have to; the automated installation program is so much easier!

**A couple of pitfalls when installing DOS 6.**   You're gonna love DOS 6! But there can be some conflicts between what you've already got on your system when you install it. So turn off any third-party disk-caching, anti-virus, or undelete programs that you may have put on your computer before you try installing DOS 6. It's OK to have the DOS 5 equivalents of these things running, though (such as SMARTDrive for disk caching and MIRROR for undeleting). Also, if you're on a network, turn off anything that might in-terrupt you while you install DOS 6, such as a message facility that lets you know when your print job's done or tells you there's something wrong in the print queue.

And it should go without saying that you shouldn't be running Windows when you install DOS 6.

**Run DoubleSpace!**   While you're installing DOS 6, you may notice a message telling you to use DoubleSpace to compress the files on your hard drive. Do it! (Be sure to run DEFRAG first.)

DoubleSpace is slightly misnamed because in some circumstances it can even *triple* the size of your hard disk. Testimonial: I had 3mb of free space on my hard disk before running DoubleSpace; after, I had 85mb of free space.

The process takes a while, so start it running and go do something else. If I remember correctly, it took a little less than two hours on my system, which has a 200mb hard drive and, as you've seen, was literally full of files.

**But if I compress my disk, what do I have to do after that?**   If you use DoubleSpace to compress your hard disk, the only difference you'll see is that you have more room. I wondered about this, too—whether I'd have to decompress each file as I wanted to use it, whether I could copy files to floppies and have them be usable, whether I could install new programs and have to run DoubleSpace to compress them, too—but the answer is that everything works just fine without your having to do anything else. At least it does on my system. So far.

If you don't let compress your disk immediately after setup, you can still do it later. You can't run DoubleSpace from Windows or from the DOS Shell. Go to the command line before you type **dblspace** to start the program running. You'll be prompted through the whole process.

See Chapter 5, "Disk & Drive Magic," for more neat new DOS 6 tricks for compressing and defragmenting your disks.

### If you're running Windows, install the DOS 6 Window utilities.

DOS 6 comes with Microsoft Anti-Virus, Backup, and Undelete for Windows. During Setup, DOS 6 detects whether you have Windows on your system and, if you do, installs the Windows versions of these programs (if you let it). If you aren't watching the screen carefully, you may think that you're getting both the DOS and Windows versions, but you may not be getting both.

By default, Setup will install just the Windows version. You'll need to specifically tell Setup to install both, which I imagine is what most folks want. Instructions are on the screen, but they go by pretty fast. If they zip past you, you can go back and install the DOS versions of Anti-Virus, Backup, and Undelete (or the Windows versions, if you didn't have Windows when DOS 6 was installed and you add Windows to your system later) by running Setup again.

Put the Setup Disk 1 in drive A (or B) and at the command line type **a:setup /e** or **b:setup /e**. Then follow the on-screen instructions. If you're installing the Windows versions, Setup creates icons for them as well as a new Microsoft Tools group in the Program Manager.

### Not enough room to install both the DOS and Windows versions of the new utilities?

Here's how to get around that. If Setup reports that it can't install both versions of the new utility programs, go ahead and let it install whichever version it wants to—Windows or DOS. Then use DoubleSpace to compress your disk after DOS 6 is installed. You'll probably have plenty of room for the other version then. To install it, run **setup /e** as described in the preceding tip.

## ONCE YOU'VE INSTALLED DOS

After you've installed DOS, the adventure is just beginning. In the following pages, you'll find advice to help you on your way.

**Your computer is locked up.** If your computer freezes up after you run Setup, the AUTOEXEC.BAT file may be automatically loading a TSR. Setup doesn't like TSRs and won't coexist with them. Go back and enter **type autoexec.bat** at the C:\> prompt and see if there's a line in there that starts a TSR (like SideKick) running. If there is, put **rem** at the beginning of the line. See Chapter 7 if you need help editing your AUTOEXEC.BAT file.

When you've saved the changed AUTOEXEC.BAT file, press Ctrl-Alt-Del to restart your computer.

**DOS isn't running in high memory.** Sometimes DOS doesn't run in the high memory area (HMA), where it's supposed to. You can check to see if DOS is where it belongs by entering **mem** at the DOS prompt. If you don't see a message that DOS is in the high memory area, check to see that your CONFIG.SYS file has these lines:

```
device=c:\dos\himem.sys
dos=high
```

If both lines are there and HIMEM.SYS is in your DOS directory (better check that, too), you may be using some kind of hardware that Setup can't figure out. Try looking at the README.TXT file in your DOS directory to see if it has any hints about exotic (to DOS) hardware. You can do a type **readme.txt | more** or an **edit readme.txt** to read that file.

**Are you getting a "Bad command or file name" message?** If you're getting "Bad command or file name" messages as you use DOS, the directory that holds your DOS files may not be specified accurately in the path statement in your AUTOEXEC.BAT file. The Setup program will put your DOS directory in that statement if it isn't already there. (Having your DOS directory in your path lets you execute DOS commands from any directory; it tells DOS to check each directory specified in the path whenever you give a command.)

If you're running the Shell, the easiest way to check whether your DOS directory is in your path is to highlight AUTOEXEC.BAT (it's in your root directory) and press F9. Otherwise, at the command line, enter

```
type c:\autoexec.bat
```

If the path to the DOS directory is somehow not right, you can use the Editor to change it (there's more on this in Chapter 7).

**Don't have too long a path.** If your path statement requires DOS to search several drives and hundreds of files, your computer can slow down considerably. Keep your path lean for maximum performance. Remember, DOS only cares about executable (program) files, not data files. Keep program files in separate directories like C:\WP51 and keep data files in subdirectories like C:\WP51\DOCS. Then just put your program directories in your path, as shown in the example below for DOS, Windows and WordPerfect:

```
path=c:\dos;c:\windows;c:\wp51
```

Notice that there aren't any spaces in this sample path—DOS stops reading a path when it comes to a space.

**Trouble at startup? Bypass your CONFIG.SYS and AUTOEXEC.BAT files.** If you're having startup troubles, the most likely culprits are the lines in your AUTOEXEC.BAT and CONFIG.SYS files. DOS 6 lets you bypass them or step through them line by line.

## Chapter 1: Beyond Magic

- To bypass the AUTOEXEC.BAT and CONFIG.SYS files entirely, press F5 when your computer displays the "Starting MS-DOS..." message.

- To step through the CONFIG.SYS file line by line and tell DOS to bypass the AUTOEXEC.BAT, press F8 when your computer displays the "Starting MS-DOS..." message.

These tricks are really useful to know about, but you should be aware that if you bypass these normal startup files, your computer won't work as it usually does. No device drivers (such as your mouse) will be loaded, for example, and you'll see only the C> prompt instead of the one that shows the path to the current directory.

Here's how these tricks work in real life. Say that you can't start your computer. The power works, but DOS doesn't start. To check if the problem's somewhere in memory management (a likely culprit), press Ctrl-Alt-Del to restart. When you see "Starting MS-DOS..." press F8. You'll be prompted for each line that's in your CONFIG.SYS. Press Y for all of them, but when you're asked about the device named EMM386.EXE, press N. When you're asked whether to run AUTOEXEC.BAT, press Y. If your computer starts, the problem may be with the EMM386 memory manager. To try to fix this problem, run MemMaker (type **memmaker** at the DOS prompt).

If running MemMaker doesn't fix the problem, try again. Restart your computer, but this time, press F5 at the "Starting" message. DOS will start without running your AUTOEXEC.BAT or checking your CONFIG.SYS files. If your computer starts, it's probably one or the other of these files that's causing the problem, and you can test some more to see which it is. If your computer still doesn't start, call Microsoft! You get 90 days' free support with DOS 6; why not use it? The number is 206/646-5104.

If you're not on the phone by now, you've decided that you need to test CONFIG.SYS and AUTOEXEC.BAT. To locate the exact problem, press Ctrl-Alt-Del to restart. This time, press F8 when you see the "Starting" message. You'll be prompted for each line that's in your CONFIG.SYS. Press Y for all of them, but when you're asked about whether to run AUTOEXEC.BAT, press N. Now, if your computer doesn't start, you know the problem's in CONFIG.SYS, not AUTOEXEC.BAT.

Assuming that your computer starts (so CONFIG.SYS is the culprit), you'll need to test each line in the CONFIG.SYS file. Restart your computer and press F8 at the "Starting" message. Type N for every line in your CONFIG.SYS file except the one you're testing, and type Y for the lines that have these commands in them (your system needs them so it will work):

```
HIMEM.SYS
EMM386.EXE
DOS=HIGH,UMB
SHELL=
```

If you've added any fancy hard disk drivers that are required for you to access your hard disk, don't disable them by marking them with REM. See the manual that came with your hard disk if you need to figure out what these lines are.

If everything started OK, the problem wasn't the line you tested. Do the startup procedure again and test a different line in the CONFIG.SYS. When your computer doesn't start, the problem is in the line you just tested. Don't stop now! You may have a problem with more than one line. Test them all; then open CONFIG.SYS in the Editor and put a REM statement at the beginning of each line that's causing problems. Save CONFIG.,SYS and restart your computer. If everything runs OK, you can forget about doing anything else. If not—say that your mouse doesn't work because you had to disable the line that has its device driver—call the manufacturer of the device that isn't working any more and see if they can help you. You may need to update your device driver. The problem will usually be in your CONFIG.SYS file, but if it's not and is in the AUTOEXEC.BAT, testing it is a little more complex. Restart your computer with the F8 key trick, type Y for each line in the CONFIG.SYS, and then type Y to run the AUTOEXEC.BAT. If your system doesn't start and you've debugged CONFIG.SYS, your problems are in the AUTOEXEC.BAT.

Restart again, bypassing the AUTOEXEC.BAT, and then open it in the Editor. Begin each line with a REM statement except one line (the one you're testing) and any lines that have these commands in them:

```
@ECHO OFF
PROMPT
PATH
```

Now, to figure out which line is the culprit, save your AUTOEXEC.BAT and restart with the F8 trick, typing Y to run the AUTOEXEC.BAT. Keep testing one line at a time until you can't start your computer. That last line you tested is the one that's causing the trouble. If you can run your computer without it, delete the offending line to prevent further trouble. If not, call the manufacturer of the program that's causing the problem.

## HELP!

One of the neatest things about DOS 5 was its online help facility. DOS 6's help facility is even better! You can get help in several different ways, either in the Shell or at the command line, and you can even make custom Help text.

**Get Help at the command line.** Now you don't have to remember what those obscure switches used with commands mean. Just enter the command you want help with, followed by /?. Or type **help** followed by a space and the command you want help with. For instance, for help with the ERASE command, you'd type **erase /?** or **help erase**.

**New Help with DOS 6.** DOS 6 cleaned up Help quite a bit and made it easier to understand. Now Help screens are complete with notes and examples (see Figure 1-1). In addition, DOS 6 added a more concise version of Help that lets you see just the command syntax. To get full Help on a command, type **help** at the command line, followed by the command's name. For the quick version, type **fasthelp** plus the command's name, or type the command's name plus /?.

**18   Voodoo DOS**

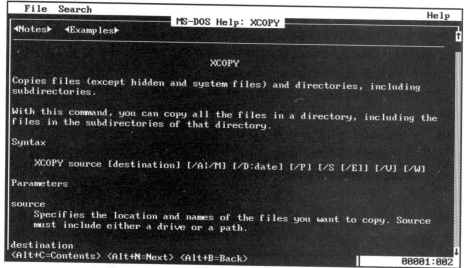

*Figure 1-1:* A new, improved DOS 6 Help screen.

To see a list of all the commands in DOS 6, type **fasthelp** just by itself. The question mark version of getting Help is ever so slightly faster than the FASTHELP version.

**Order the MS-DOS 6 Resource Kit to get a command reference.** If you'd like a printed Help manual (all these Help screens, just printed out), turn to the back of your user's guide to find the coupon to send in. It's easy to overlook because it's at the back of the manual—and who reads it anyway?! You'll also get a Supplemental Disk containing the commands that were in DOS 5 but not in DOS 6, and a few other goodies. Of special note is the AccessDOS program that's on the Supplemental Disk; it makes DOS easier to use by people who are physically challenged. For example, it has utilities that change the keyboard layout to one that's easier to use if you type with only your right or left hand.

**Get Help in the Shell.** If you're in the Shell, just press F1. This gets you context-sensitive help (help on whatever's currently selected). If you don't want help on what's selected but want to use the Help index to select another topic of help, press

Alt-H or click on the Help menu. This doesn't bring up context-sensitive help but lets you choose whether you want the Help index, help on the Shell's basic procedures, help on commands, help about procedures or simply help on using the Help system.

**Most Help text doesn't fit in the first window you see.** Most Help screens have more text than you can see in the first window they display. If the scroll bar on the right is darkened and the slider box is at the top, as in Figure 1-2, there's more to see.

*Figure 1-2:* Most Help screens offer more than one window.

**Making custom Help screens for program groups.** When you create a program group for the Shell (you'll see some Shell tricks in Chapter 2, "Shell Secrets"), you can add Help text specifying what it does, who owns it or whether it contains sensitive information—or anything you like—in the Add Group dialog box. This is good to do if you're setting up program groups for other people to use; everybody can be reminded of what each group is for and of any peculiarities each might have. You can enter as many as 255 characters, including spaces. If you need to force a line break, type ^m (a caret and an m, not a Ctrl-m) where the line is to break. Your Help message will be displayed for any selected group when you press F1. You can do this for each program item you add. The only difference is that you have to use a different dialog box. Click on the Advanced button in the Add Program Item Properties dialog box and type in your 255-character-maximum Help text. The ^m trick works here, too, for breaking lines.

**Making custom Help screens for yourself.** You can use a custom group Help screen like the one in the previous tip to make custom Help screens for techniques you have trouble remembering. The trick is simply to create an empty group and name it whatever the help is about. For example, I can never remember which switches to use with XCOPY if I'm copying a bunch of files that I know won't fit on one floppy disk. I made a new group called "Copying Trick" and put the procedure in the Help part of the Program Group Properties dialog box (see Figures 1-3 and 1-4). Whenever I'm ready for a big copying job, I highlight the Copying Trick group and press F1.

**Copy files onto more than one floppy disk if necessary.** This is a neat trick to know. Isn't it annoying to get the message that the floppy disk is full when all the files you want to copy haven't been copied yet? You don't want to make a list of the files still to be copied and compare it to the files that aren't copied yet; that could take a long, long time. Here's how to get around the problem. Turn on the archive attributes for all the files you want to copy. To do this, use **attrib +a \*.\*** for all files in the directory (or **attrib +a \*.\*** /s for all files in any subdirectories) or use the File menu's Change Attributes command in the Shell. Then use XCOPY with the /M switch, which tells DOS to copy each file whose archive attribute is on. The archive attribute is turned off after each file is copied. When your first floppy disk fills up, put a new blank disk in the drive and keep on XCOPYing with the /M switch. Because only the files that haven't been copied yet still have their archive attributes on, they will copy onto the next floppy. You can see why I have trouble remembering this procedure!

*Figure 1-3:* You can make your own Help screens.

*Figure 1-4:* All you have to do is press F1 when your topic is highlighted.

**Making batch Help files.** If you want to use the command line and wouldn't be caught dead using the Shell, you can make yourself custom on-line Help messages. Use the Editor or your favorite word processing program to write down those procedures you always forget. Save the file as a text-only file (ASCII format). Give each file a name you can remember and store them all in a C:\HELP directory. For example, you could call the XCOPY trick in the previous example XCOPYTRK.BAT. Put C:\HELP in the path statement in your AUTOEXEC.BAT file. Then create a batch file called HELPME.BAT, containing just this line:

```
type c:\helpme\%1.BAT
```

The %1 indicates that you can type the name of any of your custom Help batch files (without the .BAT extension) to see its text on the screen. For example, to get an on-line reminder of what to do for the XCOPY trick, type

```
helpme xcopytrk
```

**Keep your DOS help handy.** If you'd like to be able to keep handy Help on hot keys in DOS and other programs, make a file that contains the key combinations and what they do. For example, Gil Arroyo of Seattle, Washington, created a file like this for shortcuts in frequently used programs:

```
copy con c:\ref keyref.dat
printer control alt+p
thesaurus ctrl+t
dictionary ctrl+w
setup config ctrl+alt+esc
^Z
```

This text created the file KEYREF.DAT in an existing directory named REF. Now, whenever Gil needs to check a hot key combination, all he has to do is TYPE his KEYREF.DAT file so that it appears on the screen. No more looking all over the disk for several different help files for various programs! (Check out Chapter 7 if you're not familiar with creating batch files like this one.)

*Thanks to Gil Arroyo, Seattle, WA.*

**Getting help elsewhere.** There's also specialized help, different than what's available in the Shell or at the command line, in the Editor and in Qbasic. In fact, DOS 5 has four kinds of Help: DOSSHELP.HLP, DOSSHELL.HLP, EDIT.HLP and QBASIC.HLP. DOS 6 adds FASTHELP, as you've seen, along with several other specialized .HLP files..

## CUSTOMIZING DOS

DOS can be customized in many ways. If you have a color monitor, you can change the screen colors, tweak the preset Shell color schemes, set different colors in the Editor and create custom-colored prompts. If you don't have a color monitor, there are plenty of other things you can do, such as changing the graphics display, creating custom prompts and reassigning your function keys.

**Switching to a graphics display.** The Shell is normally in text-only display, but you have other options if you've got a graphics card. If your computer supports graphics mode, you'll probably prefer it. Graphics display (see Figure 1-5) is a lot prettier with a graphics card, and your directories look like Windows' little folders. Also, in graphics mode, the mouse pointer is an outlined arrowhead; in text mode, it's a solid rectangle.

To switch modes, choose Display from the Options menu and experiment until you find a display you like (scroll to see more choices). The choices you'll get depend on what kind of video card your system has; Figure 1-6 shows the beginning of a list for a VGA card screen display (some choices aren't visible because you have to scroll to see them). You may not want to choose a high-resolution option, though. I find the screen harder to read when there are so many lines on it. Click Preview to see a sample of each mode.

```
                    MS-DOS Shell
   File  Options  View  Tree  Help
   C:\
   [=]A   [=]B   [=]C   [=]D

        Directory Tree                        C:\*.*
   [📁] C:\                        [📄] CONFIG   .SYS     216  07-26-91
        [📁] ANEW                  [📄] AUTOEXEC.BAT     436  05-20-91
        [📁] BATCH                 [📄] DOTOPS            30  04-13-91
        [📁] DOS                   [📄] NOTOPS  .BAT      41  04-13-91
        [📁+] DR11                 [📄] WINA20  .386   9,349  04-09-91
        [📁] FRACTINT              [📄] COMMAND .COM  47,845  04-09-91
        [📁] HJ2                   [📄] HJ      .BAT      34  04-03-91
        [📁] HSG                   [📄] MIRROR  .FIL  62,464  04-03-91
        [📁+] MIRROR               [📄] MIRROR  .BAK  62,464  04-03-91
        [📁] MOUSE                 [📄] CONFIG  .OLD      77  02-23-91
        [📁] MOUSE1                [📄] AUTOEXEC.BAZ     396  02-23-91
        [📁] OLD_DOS.1             [📄] AUTOEXEC.OLD     396  02-23-91
            Main                          Active Task List
   [ ] Command Prompt
   [ ] Editor
   [ ] MS-DOS QBasic
   [■] Disk Utilities
   [ ] WordPerfect
   [■] Smokey
   [■] Copying Trick
```

*Figure 1-5:* Directory listings in graphics mode.

```
                  Screen Display Mode
   ┌─────────────────────────────────────────────┐
   │    Current Mode: Graphics (30 lines)        │
   │  Text       25 lines    Low Resolution      │
   │  Text       43 lines    High Resolution 1   │
   │  Text       50 lines    High Resolution 2   │
   │  Graphics   25 lines    Low Resolution      │
   │  Graphics   30 lines    Medium Resolution 1 │
   └─────────────────────────────────────────────┘
       (  OK  )      ( Preview )     ( Cancel )
```

*Figure 1-6:* Your graphics mode choices depend on which video card you have.

> **Text mode is a bit faster.** If speed is a concern and you use the Shell a lot, see if you can live with text mode. It's a bit faster than graphics mode. But if you don't use the Shell much, it won't matter anyway. Go for the pretty interface.

**The DOSSHELL.INI file.** If you've worked with Windows, you may be aware of the text files (WIN.INI and SYSTEM.INI) that you can edit to make Windows behave as you want. There's also a DOSSHELL.INI file.

Bring it into the Editor with **edit dosshell.ini**. The file looks pretty cryptic, but you can read it. Each section begins with a word in brackets, followed by a list of each setting for that section. You can do things like change the wording of the Help messages, specify shortcut keys for switching among your programs (more on this in Chapter 3, "Working With Programs") and reset the color schemes (Hot Pink and Emerald City could use a little tweaking).

**Name your colors correctly.** By the way, if you change the colors, use a color that's already listed in DOSSHELL.INI. The color brightwhite isn't the same as white, for example, and the "pinks" in Hot Pink are called *brightmagenta* and *magenta*. Here are the colors you can use:

   red and brightred
   white and brightwhite
   blue and brightblue
   black and brightblack
   green and brightgreen
   brown and brightyellow
   cyan and brightcyan (blues)
   magenta and brightmagenta (pinks)

It's much easier to edit an existing color scheme than to create a new one.

**Editing DOSSHELL.INI.** You can edit DOSSHELL.INI with any text editor that can handle lines with more than 256 characters and, like the the Editor, can save files as ASCII files. To make sure you don't change anything vital, make a copy of DOSSHELL.INI before you start and rename it something like DOSSHELL.BAK so you can get the original back if necessary.

**Use SYSEDIT instead of the Editor.** If you're running Windows, you have an undocumented System Configuration Editor (SYSEDIT.EXE) you can use to edit .INI files, CONFIG.SYS files and AUTOEXEC.BAT files. It's quick and easy and also makes automatic backups with a .SYD extension. Having those backups can be handy.

To run SYSEDIT, enter **sysedit** in the Windows Run dialog box. It will automatically bring up your AUTOEXEC.BAT and CONFIG.SYS files (and your Windows .INI files), all in different windows. You can rearrange the windows to see them all at once.

**Customize the colors in the Editor.** If you have a color monitor, you can change the colors the Editor uses. (To get to the Editor, type **edit** at the DOS prompt or choose Editor from the Shell's Main group.) Select Display from the Options menu and experiment until you find a combination you like. The box to the left of the color choices will change to reflect your selections. Some aren't very readable, but white on blue is always a good standby. The Editor automatically saves your choice when you click OK. Chapter 7 has more Editor tricks.

**Make your own startup menu.** With DOS 6, you can have one CONFIG.SYS file for different system configurations. For example, you might want to have one set up for yourself and another for your wife, husband, significant other or office mate who shares the same computer. Or you might want to have one configuration with network settings and another without. Or you can just make yourself a neat startup screen to personalize your computer. You'll be editing your CONFIG.SYS file, so for safety's sake, copy it onto a floppy disk so you can get the original version back if anything goes wrong while you're experimenting.

DOS 6 comes with several new specialized commands that let you set up startup menus. They're MENUITEM, MENUCOLOR, SUBMENU and MENUDEFAULT, and they're all used inside your CONFIG.SYS file.

A picture's worth a thousand words, so look at this example:

```
[MENU]
MENUITEM=KAY, Kay's System
MENUITEM=RAY, Ray's System
MENUCOLOR=15,1
MENUDEFAULT=KAY, 60
NUMLOCK=OFF
[COMMON]
BUFFERS=20
FILES=10
STACKS=9,256
DEVICE=C:\DOS\HIMEM.SYS
DEVICE=C:\DOS\EMM386.EXE NOEMS
DOS=HIGH,UMB
[KAY]
LASTDRIVE=E
[RAY]
LASTDRIVE=G
DEVICEHIGH=C:\DOS\INTERLNK.EXE
[COMMON]
```

In this example, a startup menu appears when you start your computer. It has two choices, KAY and RAY. The [KAY] part of the file holds the commands that will be put in effect when you select KAY from that startup menu. If you select RAY, the commands after [RAY] go into effect (the last drive letter is set to G, and INTERLNK.EXE—a command that connects two computers when you attach a cable in each one's parallel or serial port—takes effect). The [COMMON] area applies to either setup (a maximum of 20 buffers, 10 files, DOS, HIMEM.SYS, and EMM386.EXE loading high; see Chapter 10 for more about these commands).

The [COMMON] block is at the end of the file for safety's sake. Some programs go into your CONFIG.SYS file and append commands to the end of it. If you put an empty [COMMON] block there, those commands will be in effect no matter which configuration you select.

The MENUCOLOR item set the background screen color to blue (1) and the displayed text to bright white (15). Sixteen colors are possible:

| | |
|---|---|
| 0 | black |
| 1 | blue |
| 2 | green |
| 3 | cyan |
| 4 | red |
| 5 | magenta |
| 6 | brown |
| 7 | white |
| 8 | gray |
| 9 | bright blue |
| 10 | bright green |
| 11 | bright cyan |
| 12 | bright red |
| 13 | bright magenta |
| 14 | yellow |
| 15 | bright white |

Experiment with your favorite color combinations, such as red text on a black background or vice versa (devilish!).

The MENUDEFAULT item specifies that KAY is the default configuration. For a nice touch, a timeout value of 60 seconds is set so that if the user doesn't select either menu item, KAY goes into effect after one minute.

If all you want is a neat startup screen, use your text message (such as "This is Kay's computer. Everybody else: hands off.") as the startup menu and set a timeout of ten seconds or so.

When you've edited your CONFIG.SYS file to set up your message, save the file as CONFIG.TST, for instance. Don't save it as CONFIG.SYS; otherwise, you'll overwrite the CONFIG.SYS that you know is working. Then rename CONFIG.SYS as CONFIG.OLD, rename CONFIG.TST as CONFIG.SYS, and restart your computer. If all is well, your menus will work; if not, you can rename CONFIG.OLD as CONFIG.SYS, restart your computer, and try again.

**Customize CONFIG.SYS so it prompts you.** DOS 6 adds a new capability to CONFIG.SYS. If you insert a ? (question mark) in a line in your CONFIG.SYS file, when you start your computer, it will ask you if you want that command to be executed. For example, if you'd rather have control over when DOS is to be loaded into high memory and when it isn't, you'd set up the DOS=HIGH line in CONFIG.SYS this way:

```
DOS?=HIGH
```

See Chapter 10, "Managing Memory," for the mystery of why and how to load DOS in high memory.

**Customize your prompt.** DOS 5 and 6 change the basic prompt from C to C:\>, indicating that it will show the path to the current directory. You can change this prompt quite easily. For example, to produce the current time at the prompt instead of the path, enter

```
prompt $t$g
```

Maybe you'd like the time and the date. To get "Today is Sun 2-16-1993," for instance, enter

```
prompt Today is $d$g
```

Or, for a two-line prompt with lots of information in it, enter prompt

```
Today is $d$_The current directory is $p$g
```

You'll get the following prompt (the $_ characters in the above line force a line break):

```
Today is Sun 2-16-1993
The current directory is c:\wp51\docs
```

Get creative. Here's a list of the available symbols and their effects:

| Symbol | Effect |
| --- | --- |
| $ | Used with all the following options |
| _ | Start a new line |
| b | Produce a bar (for a pipe command) (\|) |
| d | Display the date |
| e | Esc character |
| g | Produce greater than (>) |
| h | Backspace one character |
| l | Produce less than (<) |
| n | Display the current drive |
| p | Display the current drive and directory |
| q | Produce an equal sign (=) |
| t | Display the time |
| v | Display the DOS version line |

To get the standard prompt back, enter **prompt $p$g** at the command line.

Experiment until you find a prompt you like. Put it in your AUTOEXEC.BAT to make it your standard prompt—just replace the prompt line that's already there with your custom prompt line.

**Want a really weird blinking prompt? Change the video attributes.** There are more things you can do with the prompt and the screen. Put the following line in your CONFIG.SYS file. (It may already be there.) You can put it anywhere you like as long as it's on a line by itself.

```
device=c:\dos\ansi.sys
```

If you want the Shell to come up automatically when you start your computer, though, make sure that DOSSHELL is the last line in your AUTOEXEC.BAT.

Want a reverse-video display? Use this line:

```
prompt $p$g $e[7m
```

Here's how to get a reverse-video display that blinks, too (you may have to press Enter twice):

```
prompt $p$g $e[5;7m
```

Here are the rules for changing the video characteristics. Start with **$e** (lowercase), which tells DOS to notice that you're going to use ANSI codes. Then, between a bracket ([) and a lowercase m, type all the codes you want to use from the following list. Separate each one with a semicolon if you use more than one.

- 0   Turn off all attributes
- 1   Bold (intensified)
- 4   Underline (not supported on color monitors)
- 5   Blink
- 7   Reverse video

You can get text, too, by combining these attributes with the previous trick ("Customize your prompt"). For example, to get a blinking "At your service" prompt, enter this:

```
prompt $e[5m At your service$g
```

To get the nonblinking prompt back, enter this:

```
prompt $e[0m
```

Put combinations you like in your AUTOEXEC.BAT.

**Another neat prompt combination.** This one shows the current time (hours and minutes), the current date and the current directory:

```
prompt The time is $t$h$h$h$h$h$h on $d. $_The →
current directory is $p$g
```

All those $h characters backspace over the long time format so that all you see is hours and minutes.

**Change both the screen and prompt color.** If you have a color monitor, you can have fun resetting both the screen color and the prompt color as well as setting up your prompt with video attributes and custom text. Here are the background and foreground color combinations and their codes:

| Color | Foreground | Background |
|---|---|---|
| Black | $e[30m | $e[40m |
| Red | $e[31m | $e[41m |
| Green | $e[32m | $e[42m |
| Yellow | $e[33m | $e[43m |
| Blue | $e[34m | $e[44m |
| Magenta | $e[35m | $e[45m |
| Cyan | $e[36m | $e[46m |
| White | $e[37m | $e[47m |

Type the following line to get yellow characters on a blue background:

```
prompt $e[33m $e[44m$p$g
```

If it looks muddy on your screen, try adding high intensity with this line:

```
prompt $e[1m
```

For a high-intensity yellow prompt on a blue background, with text that goes back to regular intensity for your input, try this:

```
prompt $e[33m $e[44m $e[1mAt your service$g$e[0m
```

Try out various combinations and put your favorite as a line in your AUTOEXEC.BAT. To get back to the standard prompt, use the following line and then clear the screen (with CLS):

```
prompt $e[0m$p$g
```

**Lost your prompt altogether?** It's easy to lose your prompt as you experiment with various combinations if you set both the foreground and background to the same color. If this happens, you can get your standard prompt back by entering prompt

```
$e[0m$p$g
```

Or, you can reboot with Ctrl-Alt-Del.

**Customize the keyboard.** If your CONFIG.SYS file has that **device=c:\dos\ansi.sys** line, you can redefine the function keys on your keyboard. If you want to start the Shell by pressing a key instead of typing **dosshell**, you can assign it to F12 (if you have an extended keyboard) like this:

```
prompt $P$g$e[0;134;"dosshell";13p
```

To reassign the function keys, start with **$e[0;** and enter the code for the key you want to reassign, followed by a semicolon. Then type the command the function key will carry out, enclosed in double quotation marks and followed by another semicolon. Type **13p** (the code for pressing Enter). Got it?

Here's another example. You can assign FORMAT B: to F8, like this:

```
prompt $e[0;66;"format b:";13p
```

Amaze your friends. Assign a wide directory listing to F7, like this:

```
prompt $e[0;65;"dir /w /p";13p
```

Look up the codes for the keys in Figure 1-7. To keep a key assignment, put the prompt line in your AUTOEXEC.BAT.

| Key | Code | Key | Code | Key | Code | Key | Code |
|---|---|---|---|---|---|---|---|
| F1 | 59 | Shift-F1 | 84 | Ctrl-F1 | 94 | Alt-F1 | 104 |
| F2 | 60 | Shift-F2 | 85 | Ctrl-F2 | 95 | Alt-F2 | 105 |
| F3 | 61 | Shift-F3 | 86 | Ctrl-F3 | 96 | Alt-F3 | 106 |
| F4 | 62 | Shift-F4 | 87 | Ctrl-F4 | 97 | Alt-F4 | 107 |
| F5 | 63 | Shift-F5 | 88 | Ctrl-F5 | 98 | Alt-F5 | 108 |
| F6 | 64 | Shift-F6 | 89 | Ctrl-F6 | 99 | Alt-F6 | 109 |
| F7 | 65 | Shift-F7 | 90 | Ctrl-F7 | 100 | Alt-F7 | 110 |
| F8 | 66 | Shift-F8 | 91 | Ctrl-F8 | 101 | Alt-F8 | 111 |
| F9 | 67 | Shift-F9 | 92 | Ctrl-F9 | 102 | Alt-F9 | 112 |
| F10 | 68 | Shift-F10 | 93 | Ctrl-F10 | 103 | Alt-F10 | 113 |
| F11 | 133 | Shift-F11 | 135 | Ctrl-F11 | 137 | Alt-F11 | 139 |
| F12 | 134 | Shift-F12 | 136 | Ctrl-F12 | 138 | Alt-F12 | 140 |

*Figure 1-7:* Function key codes.

**Don't reassign function keys that have other uses.** The function keys F1 through F6, F9 and F10 have other uses in DOS, so you can reassign only F7, F8 and the extended-keyboard keys F11 and F12. Instead, use a shifted combination or an Alt or Ctrl key combination (don't take Alt-F1, Alt-F4 or Shift-F9, though).

**Lost? Reset your function keys back to their original meaning.** To reset a key to its original meaning, use this pattern:

```
prompt $e0;keycode;0;keycodep
```

**At last! No Num Lock.** DOS 6 comes with a NUMLOCK command that you can put in your CONFIG.SYS file and turn that pesky Num Lock feature off. Just put this line in the CONFIG.SYS file and save it:

```
NUMLOCK OFF
```

When you restart your computer, you can use the keys on the numeric keypad as arrow keys instead of having them enter numbers when you type them.

## RUNNING LEAN & MEAN

You need 2.8mb of unused space on your hard disk to install DOS 5 and about 6mb to install DOS 6 (more if you install both DOS and Windows versions of Microsoft Undelete, Backup and Anti-Virus; but once you install it, you can delete a lot of it to free up disk space.

**Delete your old DOS to gain disk space.** Once you're sure you love DOS 5 or 6 and it isn't causing problems, you can free space on your hard disk by running DELOLDOS. It just erases and deletes the OLD_DOS.1 directory, where your previous version of DOS is stored.

Before running DELOLDOS, make sure that nothing you want to keep, like a batch file or two, has strayed into that directory. DELOLDOS deletes itself when it finishes, so it's an auto-destruct command. Once you use it, it's gone.

## Chapter 1: Beyond Magic

**Delete DOS files to free more disk space.** You'll probably never use a lot of what DOS does; you can erase certain features from your hard disk to save yourself some space. And, if you have a laptop computer that has a small hard disk, clearing off unnecessary files from your DOS directory can be important.

Remember, you can always recall a file you've deleted, either from a backup copy or by using EXPAND.EXE to uncompress it from your distribution disk.

Here are some possibly unnecessary DOS files to erase:

- If you don't have a 386 (or higher) computer, nuke EMM386.EXE. It's a memory manager you can't use anyway.
- If you don't have a 286 (or higher) computer, get rid of HIMEM.SYS.
- If you don't have a 386 (or higher) computer and you're running DOS 6, delete all the MEMMAKER files (MEMMAKER.*) because MEMMAKER is for optimizing memory you don't have anyway.
- If you don't have extended or expanded memory, you probably won't be using a disk cache (created with SMARTDRV.SYS) or a RAM disk (created with RAMDRIVE.SYS), so you can erase them.
- If you're a Shell-hater and you know you'll never use it, delete DOSSHELL.COM, DOSSHELL.EXE, DOSSHELL.GRB, DOSSHELL.HLP, DOSSHELL.VID, DOSSWAP.EXE and DOSSHELL.INI.
- Likewise, if you'll never use QBasic, erase QBASIC.EXE and its Help file, QBASIC.HLP, as well as all the sample files that end in .BAS.
- A word of caution: if you delete QBASIC.EXE, you won't be able to use the Editor. If you're fond of using your word processing program as a text editor, however, you may never need the DOS Editor anyway. You can remove it (EDIT.COM) and its Help (EDIT.HLP). And *of course* you can get rid of EDLIN.EXE, it's not in DOS 6 anyway.
- You probably won't want DEBUG.EXE or EXE2BIN.EXE, either, if you're not a programmer.

- Read the README.TXT to see if anything pertains to you; then print it out, if you want to, and delete it from your disk. You can do likewise with APPNOTES.TXT.
- Look at the .CPI files (which hold font information) and delete any you don't need. For example, if you don't have EGA, you can get rid of EGA.CPI. If you don't have a laptop computer, you won't need LCD.CPI (for the liquid-crystal display). If you don't have an IBM ProPrinter, you can remove the 4201.CPI file; and if you don't have the IBM QuietWriter III printer, you can erase the 5202.CPI file.
- If you only use DOS in English, eliminate the multilingual support files, like DISPLAY.SYS (for code page switching), KEYB.COM (for selecting a different-language keyboard), NLSFUNC.EXE (for providing multinational display support and switching code pages), PRINTER.SYS (for changing character sets) and COUNTRY.SYS (for changing the date, time and other formats).
- A few other files can be deleted if you don't need them. For example, JOIN.EXE is normally used on systems that don't have hard disks, but you may have a dual-floppy-drive laptop that could use it. Go on a witch hunt to find more candidates for deletion. If you follow the above guidelines, you'll get most of the useless files out of your DOS directory; the rest don't really take up much space.

## MOVING ON

Now that you've learned a few tricks about using and customizing DOS, it's time to take a closer look at the magic you can do in the DOS Shell. Chapter 2, "Shell Secrets," shows you an assortment of tricks to use with DOS's new graphical interface.

If you prefer not to use the Shell, you may be interested in techniques for getting magic from the command line (see Chapter 4, "Command-Line Tricks") or fine-tuning your system to optimize memory usage (see Chapter 10, "Managing Memory").

# Chapter 2

# SHELL SECRETS

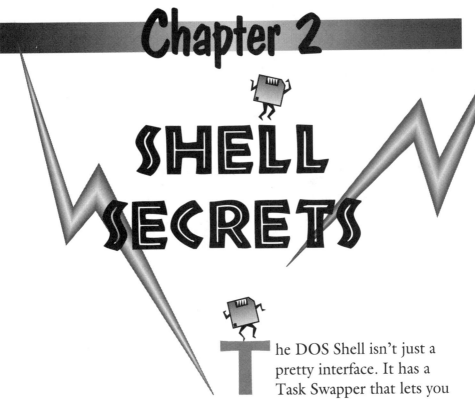

The DOS Shell isn't just a pretty interface. It has a Task Swapper that lets you switch among many programs and perform a lot of other neat tricks that you can't do at the command line—like rename directories and look at the contents of two directories or disks at once. A lot of the Shell's menu items even prompt you for those obscure switches so you don't have to remember them all. And the Shell lets you put programs and documents into groups that make sense to you and the way you work.

Why is it called the Shell? Well, because it "surrounds" DOS and protects you from the command-line interface (that enigmatic C:\>), where you have to remember things like which command does what, how to specify directories and little illogical niceties, such as using DEL for DELETE but not using ERA for ERASE.

This chapter shows you useful things to do with the Shell.

## THE SHELL INTERFACE

If you're not used to the Shell (see Figure 2-1), you may find it a little bewildering at first. Your Shell will undoubtedly look somewhat different from this one because this is my own Shell and I've added a few things to it. If your screen is in Text mode, you won't see tiny folder icons like the ones shown here. Look in Chapter 1 to see how to switch between Text and Graphics modes. But the basic parts are the same. Here's a *very* quick rundown of what's what, followed by a few basic Shell tricks.

*Figure 2-1:* Basic parts of the Shell in Graphic mode.

The Directory Tree area shows you the structure of directories and subdirectories on your hard disk. Normally, drive C, or your first hard drive, will be displayed. To see what's on another drive, such as a floppy disk in drive A or B, click on the drive icons just above the Directory Tree area. (You can press Ctrl and type the drive letter to do this, too.)

The File List is the area to the right of the Directory Tree. It lists the files that are in the selected (or highlighted) directory in the Directory Tree area. As you select different directories, you'll see what's in them in the File List.

The Program List at the bottom left of the screen shows you the groups of programs you've set up. I'll tell you how to set up program groups in Chapter 3. If you haven't set up any program groups, you'll just see the Main group—consisting of the command prompt, the Editor, QBasic and the Disk Utilities group (a really handy group to have, by the way).

If you turn on the Task Swapper from the Options menu to switch between programs, you'll see an Active Task List in the bottom right of the screen (not shown in Figure 2-1). It shows the programs you have running, and you can double-click on a program's name to go to it. (There are other ways to switch between programs, but I'm saving them for Chapter 3, "Working With Programs.")

To move from area to area, press the Tab key or click in the area you want to activate. Pressing Shift-Tab will move you counterclockwise. The highlight in the title bar will move to show you which area is active. If you have a color monitor, the title bar will change color.

In the Directory Tree area, a tiny plus (+) on a directory means that there are subdirectories underneath it and the directory is collapsed. To expand a directory to see what's in it, just click on it with your mouse or highlight it by typing the first letter of the directory's name and another +. There will be a minus (-) on it when it is expanded. To collapse it again, type a -. Remember, a tiny + on a directory means it's collapsed.

There are more tricks for viewing the contents of directories later in this chapter; these just get you accustomed to the Shell if you haven't had much experience with it.

**Menu shortcuts.** In the Shell, you choose commands from the menus at the top of the screen instead of typing them at the command line (the C:\ prompt). All menu commands have shortcuts. Some even have more than one; and some have hidden shortcuts.

If you see a key listed next to a menu item, you can use it instead of a command (see Figure 2-2, which shows the File menu). For example, instead of choosing Delete, you can press Del.

```
Move...              F7
Copy...              F8
Delete...            Del
Rename...
Change Attributes...
```

*Figure 2-2:* Many keyboard shortcuts are listed on the menus, but there are others, too.

You can also press Alt or F10 and type the first letter of a menu's name; then type the underlined letter of the command you want. For example, pressing Alt-F (for File menu) and typing **m** is the same as choosing Move from the File menu.

Don't forget these keyboard shortcuts! There are lots of them in the Shell. They can save you time: you don't have to take your hands off the keyboard to reach for the mouse. I'll mention keyboard shortcuts whenever they're appropriate in the following Shell tricks.

**Easy menu tricks.** You can back out of a menu by clicking anywhere else on the screen with your mouse or by pressing the Esc key, but if you want to keep the menu bar active, press Alt or F10 instead.

**Activating menu items.** Some menu items, like Select Across Directories and Enable Task Swapper, are toggles—they're either on or off. When a menu choice has a little bullet next to it, it's active (see Figure 2-3). Select it again to make it inactive. There's no other on-screen indicator for these, and they can be sneaky. Especially sneaky is Select Across Directories, which can cause problems (as you'll see later).

## Chapter 2: Shell Secrets 41

```
Confirmation...
File Display Options...
Select Across Directories
Show Information...
•Enable Task Swapper
Display...
Colors...
```

*Figure 2-3:* A bullet next to a menu choice means it's active.

**Dimmed menu items.** You can't select a menu item that's dimmed. For example, you can't choose Rename from the File menu if the File List isn't active and a file hasn't been selected.

**Disappearing menus.** The Tree menu on the main menu bar will sometimes mysteriously appear and disappear. It appears only when the Directory Tree or File List areas are active. It's not on the menu bar when the Active Task List is active or when you're in the Program List area.

**Dialog box tricks.** An ellipsis (...) next to a menu item indicates that there's a dialog box associated with that choice. For example, if you choose File Display Options (see Figure 2-3), you'll see the options you can select in a dialog box.

When you're in a dialog box, press Tab or use the arrow keys to move from area to area. You can move backward with Shift-Tab. Clicking with the mouse wherever you want to go is usually faster, though. It depends on whether you have to type text in a dialog box or choose buttons. If you're typing, using the keyboard is faster.

You can just press Enter to choose an OK button. Likewise, press Esc to choose a Cancel button.

If you have a mouse, you can often simply double-click on an item to select it and close the dialog box at the same time. This isn't true in all dialog boxes, though; you'll need to experiment.

If you don't have a mouse, you'll need to press the space bar to select items in a dialog box.

 **Canceling a dialog box.**  Click outside a dialog box or press Esc to cancel it, even if you already typed information into it.

 **Keeping your hands on the keyboard.**  Combining all these tricks, you can make your selections from menus and dialog boxes without reaching for the mouse at all. If you're the type who likes to keep on typing, here's a summary of ways to keep your hands on the keyboard:

- To select a menu, press Alt and the first letter of the menu's name.

- Type the underlined letter of the selection you want.

- Press Tab to move from area to area in a dialog box; press Shift-Tab to move backward.

- To select an item from a list in the dialog box, type the first letter of the item's name; type the letter again to move to the next item; or press PgUp and PgDn to scroll through the box.

- Press the space bar to toggle a button or check box on or off.

- Press Enter to choose OK; press Esc to cancel the box without making any selections.

## SHELL VOODOO

Now we can get into some Shell voodoo. As I mentioned earlier, the Shell can do things the DOS command line never dreamed of.

Which commands are easier in the Shell?

- ATTRIB, because you don't have to remember what's what. Just choose Change Attributes from the File menu when a file or group of files is highlighted and pick the attributes you want to change.

- BACKUP, because you can just choose Backup Fixed Disk from the Disk Utilities group. For RESTORE, use Restore Fixed Disk. These recommendations are made with reservations, however. I personally prefer using XCOPY to either BACKUP or the Disk Utilities Backup Fixed Disk command. However, DOS 6 alleviated the BACKUP and XCOPY confusion by providing a new Microsoft Backup utility. See Chapter 6, "A Miscellany of Alchemy," to find out more about backups. (See Chapter 6, "A Miscellany of Alchemy," to find out why and how.)

- COPY, for sure. To copy files, just press Ctrl and drag them, or use the F8 keyboard shortcut. Moving files is a lot easier, too: just drag them where you want them to go or press F7. The advantage to using F8 and F7 is that you can use wildcards to specify groups of files with similar names instead of selecting each one or each group of files.

- CD (CHDIR) and MD (MKDIR). Simply highlight a directory in the Shell to change to it (CD). Instead of making a directory with MD, choose Create Directory from the File menu.

- DIR. It's not necessary to use DIR at all in the Shell. Simply highlight the name of a directory to see what's in it. Choose Show Information from the Options menu to get detailed information about files and directories.

- DISKCOPY and FORMAT. Both commands are right there on the Shell menu in the Disk Utilities group; but they're just as fast or faster to enter at the command line if you're used to it. Enter FORMAT as **format /q** to do a quick format (a heavy-duty erase on a used floppy disk).

- TYPE and MORE. These two commands, used to view the contents of a text file, are outdated by the Shell. Press F9 to see what's in a file. It won't zip past, so you don't have to use MORE; press PgDn to see the next screen and Esc to get back to the Shell.

- UNDELETE. This depends on your personal preference. It's faster to perform this function at the command line. I usually enter **undelete /dos** to see *everything* that's been deleted instead of using the /LIST parameter that's the default in the Undelete dialog box. You don't save time using the Shell.

The Shell's Search option is also the hands-down winner for finding files. FIND at the command line only looks for specific lines in the text of a file; it doesn't help you find entire files, like Search does.

I'm not recommending you go to the Shell menu just to see a directory or copy a file if you're already at the command line. But if you're housecleaning your files—moving batches of files to other directories, renaming files and directories and so forth—you'll find the Shell much, much nicer and faster to use.

**Which commands are better at the command line?** This one's easy: all the commands for which there aren't any menu choices in the Shell, like XCOPY, are easier at the command line.

**To mouse or not to mouse?** If you're using the Shell, get a mouse. They're inexpensive. They're friendly. You can use the Shell without one but, my, it gets complicated! Here's an example. To select files that aren't directly next to each other, just Ctrl-click on them with a mouse. To select files with the keyboard, however, you must first press Shift-F8; then move to each item you want to select with the arrow keys; then press the space bar to select each one; then press Shift-F8 again when all items are selected. Here's another example. Using the keyboard to view a file, you have to press Tab to move from area to area. Next, you have to use the arrow keys to move to a particular file. Then you have to press the space bar to select the file before you can press F9 to see what's in it. These are a lot of keys to press when one mouse click would do.

**Keyboard shortcuts for viewing files in the Shell.** There are all kinds of keyboard shortcuts for viewing files in the Shell. In fact, there are so many that if I listed them all here you'd move on to another trick in a hurry. I'll break them down into categories for easier digestion, and you'll see them throughout this chapter.

Here are shortcuts to use for viewing files:

+     Expands the selected directory.
-     Collapses an expanded directory.
*     Expands the branch you're in.

Ctrl-*     Expands all folders in the window.

Use the gray +, - and * keys on the numeric keypad if you have one on your keyboard; they're faster than pressing Shift and using the keys on the upper row.

You can use the Tree menu if you prefer, but these keyboard shortcuts are a lot faster.

**Collapsing the entire tree.** OK, you expanded every single directory on your hard disk and now you have one b-i-g display. You know how to collapse each directory, but you don't want to collapse each one. You want to get back to the standard display quickly.

Voodoo. Select the root directory (pressing Home will do that in a hurry) and type a minus (-). Then type plus (+) to expand it one level, and you have the default display back.

**Choose how you want files to be displayed.** Normally, DOS alphabetizes your files, but if the files you usually work with begin with W, they may not always be readily visible in file lists in the Shell. There are two ways to get around this. Either choose another order of display with File Display Options from the Options menu (see Figure 2-4) or rename your favorite files and/or directories so they begin with a number (1WP51, for example)—that way, they'll always be at the top of an alphabetical list.

```
              ┌──────────── File Display Options ────────────┐
              │ Name:    [*.*_____]                          │
              │                                              │
              │                               Sort by:       │
              │   [ ] Display hidden/system files   ● Name   │
              │                                     ○ Extension │
              │                                     ○ Date   │
              │   [ ] Descending order              ○ Size   │
              │                                     ○ DiskOrder │
              │                                              │
              │      ( OK )      ( Cancel )     ( Help )     │
              └──────────────────────────────────────────────┘
```

*Figure 2-4:* The File Display Options dialog box lets you choose how you want directories to be displayed.

> **Quickly seeing which files you've just worked with.** Choose Date and Descending order as your file display options if you want to see the files you most recently worked with displayed at the top of the File List.

> **Displaying certain groups of files.** Enter wildcards at Name in the File Display Options dialog box to display sets of files that have similar names. This is a quick way to set up groups of files in your current directory to carry out various operations. For example, you might want to review all the files ending in .BAK so you can delete outdated backup files. Change the wildcard pattern in the dialog box to *.BAK and click OK.

Once DOS has shown you the list of all the .BAK files, click on the ones you want to select or, to select them all, choose Select All from the File menu (Alt-F S is the keyboard shortcut).

If you sort by Extension, you'll get a display of all the files in the directory sorted alphabetically by extension. (Files with no extensions will come first.)

If you sort by Name without changing *.* (the default), you'll get the normal alphabetical list of all the files.

**Don't leave Select Across Directories set to On.** Since we're looking at the Options menu to customize the Shell, be warned that if you leave Select Across Directories on, you're asking for all sorts of confusion when you next copy or move files. All the files recently selected in all the directories used will still be selected!

Turn on Select Across Directories only when you're doing mass moving or copying, and turn it off when you're done.

If Select Across Directories is on, a little bullet is next to it.

**Don't turn off Confirmation prompts.** Normally, the File Options Confirmation dialog box in the Shell has all three options set to On. This protects you from inadvertently overwriting or deleting a file when you move, copy or rename a file with the same name, or when you delete files. (The Confirm on Mouse Operation option tells DOS to show a dialog box whenever you move or copy with the mouse.)

You may be tempted to save yourself time by turning off prompts, but it's a good idea to leave them on. The Undelete feature in DOS 5 and 6 can get back deleted files, but files you've overwritten, like Humpty Dumpty, can't be put together again.

## SWITCHING FROM THE SHELL TO THE COMMAND LINE

You may not always want to stay in the Shell. If you've used DOS for a while, you may be more comfortable with the command line until you experiment with some of the things you can do in the Shell. There are a couple of ways to exit easily from the Shell and take it out of memory, or to exit temporarily to the DOS command line.

**Exiting from the Shell.** If you're planning to return to the Shell after using the command line, exit to the command line with Shift-F9 or choose Command Prompt from the Main group. If you exit from the Shell with F3 or Alt-F4 (or choose Exit from the File menu), the Shell gets taken out of memory and DOS has to read the entire hard disk again when you come back to the Shell. This can take a while.

**Getting the Shell back.** If you exited temporarily to the command line from the Shell (see the previous trick), you can return to the Shell by typing **exit** at the command prompt. Sometimes you'll see a message saying you can press any key to return to the Shell.

Don't worry: you can still exit temporarily to the DOS prompt while you're running a program from the Shell if your program, like WordPerfect, has an option that allows it.

If you removed the Shell from memory, you can press any key till the cows come home and you won't get back to the Shell. The trick is to type **dosshell** at the command line.

**Don't type dosshell at the command line if the Shell is still in memory.** If you exited temporarily to the command prompt without removing the Shell from memory and you type **dosshell** again, you'll run another copy of the Shell. If there's not enough RAM to do this, you'll get a message that DOS is unable to load the Shell.

If you're not sure whether the Shell is in memory, use this trick: type **exit** at the DOS prompt. If the Shell is in memory, it'll start. If it's not, nothing will happen and you can type **dosshell** to start it.

**Use Run instead of exiting the Shell.** The File menu's Run feature has the same effect as exiting temporarily to the command line. When you use Run, you get a dialog box in which you enter what you'd normally enter at the command line; that way, you have access to all the DOS commands through the Shell.

Run is good to use when you want one of the DOS commands, like XCOPY or MEM, that aren't built into the Shell. But if the Shell has the same built-in command, it's usually easier to use it instead. For example, there's no reason to choose Run from the File menu *and* issue the FORMAT command when it's in the Disk Utilities group, but either way will work. Run usually just takes you out to the command line.

Run is also useful for running programs that you don't use very often. Put the programs that you use most often into a program group (see Chapter 3, "Working With Programs") if you want to get the most from the Shell.

**Refreshing the screen.** It affects your file structure to exit to the command line and run a command or two, like deleting or renaming files, and the changes you made won't show up in the Shell's file lists when you return. Choose Refresh from the View menu (or press F5) to tell DOS to read your hard disk again and get those changes in there.

**Refreshing versus repainting the screen.** Don't confuse refreshing the screen with repainting the screen. When the screen is refreshed (with F5), DOS reads your entire hard disk and updates it with the changes made at the command line. (It automatically updates the changes made in the Shell.)

Repaint the screen (with Shift-F5) when you exit from a TSR and it's still visible on the screen; it gets the extraneous display off your screen.

## FINDING WHAT YOU'RE LOOKING FOR

The Shell has all sorts of built-in shortcuts for locating the files and directories you need. You'll find that it's a lot more straightforward than getting a directory listing at the command line or even using the TREE command that lets you see the structure of what's on a disk.

**Navigating through lists quickly.** Want to get back to the first file in a list or to the root directory in the Directory Tree window? Just press Home.

Pressing End will take you to the last item in a list.

Typing the first letter of a file or directory's name takes you straight to the first item that starts with that letter in the active window.

Don't forget the PgUp and PgDn keys; they'll move you quickly through lists, too.

**Scrolling tricks.** Click on the scroll arrows to scroll one item (line) at a time. Click on a scroll arrow and hold the mouse button down to scroll slowly. For the fastest scrolling, drag the scroll bar up and down.

**Use Search to find things.** Instead of doing a lot of scrolling through and opening of directories to find what you're looking for, use the Shell's Search feature. It's on the File menu. Just enter the name of the file you want in the Search File dialog box.

**Use wildcards with the Search feature.** Put wildcards in the Search File dialog box to search for a file even if you only know part of its name. Remember, an asterisk (*) stands for any number of characters, and a question mark (?) stands for a single character. So, if you know you're searching for a file named REPO something or other, enter **repo*.*** in the Search File dialog box (see Figure 2-5) and DOS will locate every file that begins with REPO and ends with anything, like REPORT2.TXT or REPORT.DOC, for example.

Once all the files have been located, press F9 to see what's in each one of them.

*Figure 2-5:* The Search File dialog box locates files more quickly than scrolling through directories.

> ⚡ **Don't search for \*.\*** The Search File dialog box comes up with the \*.\* pattern in it. Don't search for \*.\* because it means "everything"! If you don't enter a name or a wildcard pattern, DOS will search for everything, and you'll be right back where you started.

> ⚡ **Don't search through your whole hard disk.** Searching a big hard disk (over 80mb or so) can take a while. If you're pretty sure what directory the file you want is in, it's faster to highlight only that directory, uncheck the Search Entire Disk check box and search the highlighted directory.

> 💡 **Capitalization doesn't count.** When you use Search in a program like WordPerfect or Microsoft Word, you have to capitalize the words you're searching for exactly as they appear in the files. DOS doesn't care; it will find the file named REPORT.TXT, for example, even if it's typed rePOrt.TXT.
>
> You can tell the Editor to distinguish between uppercase and lowercase, however. Chapter 7, "Batch Files," has more information about working with the Editor.

## SELECTING FILES

Selecting files is another basic task in the Shell and, sure enough, there are all sorts of tricks for selecting files quickly.

> 💡 **Selecting several files.** Shift-click to select files that are next to each other; Ctrl-click to select files that aren't next to each other.

> 💡 **Selecting groups of files.** You can also select groups of files that aren't adjacent to each other. With both Ctrl and Shift held down, DOS selects everything between what's been selected and where you click. (Ctrl-click just selects each file you click on.)

So, select the first group of adjacent files by Shift-clicking; then select the *first* file in the next group with the Ctrl key down; then select the *last* file in the next group with both Ctrl and Shift down. Repeat this Ctrl-click, Ctrl-Shift-click process for the rest of the groups you want to select. Got it? It's easier to do than to describe. You can add selections to nonadjacent groups this way instead of clicking on each and every file you want.

**Use Help if you don't have a mouse.** What, no mouse? Check out Help. There are all kinds of keyboard workarounds for selecting without a mouse, but they're pretty complicated. For example, to select nonadjacent files, you have to press Shift-F8 to turn on Add mode; use the arrow keys to move to each item you want; and press the space bar to select each one. When you've selected all the items you want, you must press Shift-F8 again. See what I mean?

**Selecting files in different directories and on different disks.** Here's how to select files that are in different directories (and even on different disks). It takes two preliminary steps.

First, turn on Select Across Directories and then choose Dual File Lists from the View menu. Click on the directory names you want, or on the icons of the disk drives you want, and go right ahead and select your files.

When Select Across Directories is on, DOS keeps track of whatever you select, even if you're not viewing the contents of that disk or directory on the screen. You can select from as many directories and drives as you like; choose hundreds of files if you want!

Be sure to turn off Select Across Directories when you're through, however, or the next time you select you'll find you've just added to the cumulative list of selections. It's too bad there's nothing onscreen to indicate that Select Across Directories is on. The only way to tell is to see if that tiny diamond is next to the Select Across Directories choice on the Options menu.

**Selecting and deselecting everything.** Although they're not listed on the File menu, there are keyboard shortcuts for Select All and Deselect All.

Ctrl-/ selects all the files in the current directory.

Ctrl-\ deselects all the files in the current directory except for the last file you selected.

**Deselecting demystified.** OK, you've chosen a group of files but find there are a couple you really don't want. You don't have to deselect them all and start over again; just Ctrl-click on the ones you don't want. If you're using the keyboard, stay in Add mode (you'll be in Add mode because you just selected a group of files). Use the arrow keys to move the highlight to each one you don't want and press the space bar (or Ctrl-space bar) when each one is highlighted.

If you're not in Add mode and don't have a mouse, move to the single selected file with the arrow keys and press Ctrl-space bar to deselect it.

**Copying and moving files.** Drag to move files; press Ctrl and drag to copy them. The keyboard shortcut for COPY is F8; MOVE is F7. In this instance, a keyboard shortcut is better than a mouse because you can use wildcards for files that have similar names. This helps in big directories, where you can't see all of the files at once, or where the files you want have different names but similar extensions (like 123.WK1, OCT.WK1, SALES.WK1 and so forth).

Also, the keyboard shortcut lets you rename a file when you copy it into a new location (just put the new name in the To box), whereas you can't rename and copy at the same time with the mouse.

Remember, when you rename a file, you wind up with one file; when you rename and copy a file, you wind up with two files.

**Moving and copying several files at once.** The mouse doesn't limit you to moving and copying files one at a time. You can select several files and move or copy them at once. The icon that appears when you drag the mouse changes to a tiny stack of papers if more than one file is selected.

To see into the directories the files are coming from and going to, keep the Dual File List display on when you move and copy files. Yes, you can turn on Select Across Directories and select files from several different directories, but be sure to turn it off again when you're done.

For copying or moving large numbers of files, you may find it easier and less confusing to highlight the files you want to move or copy, press F7 (to move) or F8 (to copy) and type the directory name that the files are to be moved to. Either way—dragging or keyboard shortcuts—will work, however. Remember to Ctrl-drag with the mouse to copy; if you just drag, you move the file(s).

**Use a path name when copying.** If you're using the COPY or MOVE commands instead of dragging files with the mouse, be sure to include the full path name of where you want to copy or move files. It's easy to forget to specify a drive letter if you're copying files onto another drive.

**Making duplicates of files.** To make a duplicate of a file quickly, copy it into the same directory under another name, maybe with a .BAK extension so you know it's a duplicate. When you choose COPY or press F8, the original file name will be in the From box; put a new name in the To box to make a copy in the same directory. For example, to make a quick copy of your AUTOEXEC.BAT file, put AUTOEXEC.BAK in the To box. The original file remains unchanged.

That duplicate is not a true backup, however, and I don't want you to think so. I'll harp on the topic of backups—what they are and what they aren't—in Chapter 6, "A Miscellany of Alchemy."

**Turn off Confirmation dialog boxes when file housecleaning.** Suppose you're deleting all your outdated .BAK files, or copying newer versions of large groups of files over their older versions on floppy disks. It can get really maddening to have to respond to those "Do you really want to do that?" dialog boxes. Turn them off temporarily (choose Select Confirmation from the Options menu); turn them back on when you're done. (DOS will turn them back on for you when you restart your computer, if you forget.)

**You can't COPY CON with the Shell's Copy command.** You have to use the command line to copy from the console (the keyboard), which is a way of creating short batch files (see Chapter 7).

**Using XCOPY may be better than copying.** If you're copying large numbers of files or files that are in different directories, you may find it more efficient to use XCOPY at the command line (or via the Run command) instead of using the Shell. Because you can specify the date, it's faster than sorting files by date and then copying them. See Chapter 6 for XCOPY tricks.

**Quickly erasing everything on a disk.** To very quickly erase everything on a disk in drive A, click on the drive A icon; press Ctrl-/ (the quick way to select all the files on the disk—as long as they're in one directory); and press Del.

**Renaming a file as you move it.** You can rename and move a file at the same time by specifying a new name for it at the end of the path. For example, to rename the file DOC.TXT as DOC.RPT and move it to your C:\WORD\DOCS directory, enter word\docs\doc.rpt in the To part of the Move File dialog box. (The C:\ will already be there.)

You can't do this at the command line, but you can with DOS 6. DOS 5's RENAME command will only let you rename files in the same directory, but DOS 6 has a new MOVE command (see Chapter 4, "Command-line Tricks").

**Gang-renaming files in the Shell.** Obviously, you rename a file with the Shell's Rename command. But what's neat about this feature (and not obvious at first glance) is that you can use it to rename a bunch of files at once. Just select all the files you want to rename; DOS will prompt you for the new name of each one.

**Renaming a directory.** You can also rename a directory in the Shell (but not at the command line). Just select the directory, choose Rename and type the new name. (The REN command doesn't work on directories at the command line.)

**Seeing what's in a file.** The Shell allows you to see into a file by highlighting it and pressing F9 instead of typing the file name. If it's a text-only file, you'll be able to read it; but if it's a program file (an executable file), you'll see it in hexadecimal mode, with lots of garbage characters to the right. If it's a file created by a word processing program, you'll see all sorts of strange things (formatting characters), but you'll able to read part of it.

Once you're looking at a file's contents, press the PgUp and PgDn keys to see more of it. If you're using a mouse, click on the PgUp, PgDn and arrow symbols to scroll through the file.

The Shell can show you what's in a file in either ASCII mode (the default) or hexadecimal (hex) mode. To see a file in hex mode (base 16), press F9 when you're looking at the file in ASCII mode. Press F9 again to toggle back.

**Looking at garbage?** If you see garbage when you look into a file from the Shell, start the program that created it and retrieve the file to see what it contains. The Run command on the File menu is handy for this. If the file you want to look into is a Microsoft Word file, choose Run and enter **word** *filename* to start Word and open the file at the same time. (You'll have to specify a path to where these files are located if the directory that holds Word isn't in the path statement in your AUTOEXEC.BAT file.)

Or you can drag the icon of the file onto the program that created it and "drop" it. This will start the program and open the file.

**Getting information about a file.** To get detailed information about a file, select it and choose Show Information from the Options menu. You can also select several files and choose Get Information to get information about each one, one at a time.

Checking the Show Information window (see Figure 2-6) is a quick way to see the size of a group of files that you're ready to copy or move onto a floppy disk. If you're planning to copy or move the whole directory, look in the Show Information window under Directory to see its size.

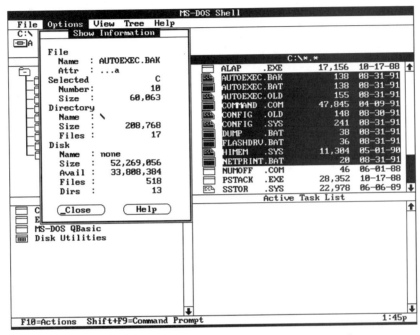

*Figure 2-6:* Check the Show Information window to get file information quickly.

The available space on the disk is listed next to Avail under Disk in the box on the left; it will tell you if there's enough room on the disk for the files you want to put on it.

If the files are too big to fit on one floppy disk, use the XCOPY trick described in Chapter 1.

**Choose All Files to see everything on a disk.** This command (on the View menu) lets you see all the regular files on a disk (see Figure 2-7). It also shows you the same information as the Show Information window. As you choose different files, you'll see information about each one, which is handy for checking a large number of files. To see which directory a file is stored in, look under Directory in the box on the left.

```
                              MS-DOS Shell
   File  Options  View  Tree  Help
   C:\QPRO
    A    B    C    D
                              *.*
                      1-README .CLP     968  03-11-91   3:00a
   File                 123    .MU  234,669  03-11-91   3:00a
     Name : 1-README.CLP 123   .RF    3,751  03-11-91   3:00a
     Attr : ...a        3270   .TXT   9,058  05-01-90   3:00a
   Selected          C  4201   .CPI   6,404  04-09-91   5:00a
     Number:         1  4208   .CPI     720  04-09-91   5:00a
     Size :        968  4ARROWS.CLP   1,482  03-11-91   3:00a
   Directory            5202   .CPI     395  04-09-91   5:00a
     Name : QPRO        8514A  .VRS   4,861  03-30-90  12:00p
     Size : 3,627,666   ACCESSOR.GRP  7,159  08-31-91   9:11a
     Files:        116  ADDEVICE.BAT    383  06-06-89  12:04p
   Disk                 AIRPLANE.CLP    442  03-11-91   3:00a
     Name : none        ALAP   .EXE  17,156  10-17-88   2:10a
     Size : 52,269,056  ALAP   .EXE  17,156  10-17-88   2:10a
     Avail: 29,200,384  ALTOFF .EXE     996  06-08-91  10:09a
     Files:        695  ALTON  .EXE     995  06-08-91  10:04a
     Dirs :         18  ALTRNAT.WPK     919  03-30-90  12:00p
                        ALTS   .WPM      73  08-31-91  10:48a
                        ALTT   .WPM      81  08-31-91  10:55a
                        ALTX   .WPM      67  08-31-91  10:36a
                        ALTY   .WPM      82  08-31-91  10:56a
                        ANSI   .SYS   9,029  04-09-91   5:00a
                        APLASIIN.PRS 40,273  08-31-91   8:41a
                        APPEND .EXE  10,774  04-09-91   5:00a
                        APPNOTES.TXT  9,701  04-09-91   5:00a
                        ARROW  .CLP     306  03-11-91   3:00a
                        ARROW-22.WPG    187  03-30-90  12:00p
   F10=Actions   Shift+F9=Command Prompt                10:20a
```

*Figure 2-7:* The All Files view is the fastest way to see all the normal files on a disk at once.

**All Files doesn't really show all files.** Despite its name, the All Files display doesn't show hidden files. To see hidden files, issue the following command at the command line:

    dir /a:h

**All Files can show several files with the same name.** When the All Files display is on, all the files on the disk are shown alphabetically, so you may see several files that have the same name. Check the Directory portion of the area on the left to see which directory each file is in.

**Viewing programs only.** If you're not working with files or doing disk housecleaning, you can see only the programs in the current program group by choosing Program List from the View menu. This option often gets overlooked, but it's nice for those of us who like a clean screen.

**Remembering the view.** You can set a preferred way of looking at the Shell screen because the Shell remembers the view you were looking at last and shows you that view again when you restart the Shell.

## FILE ATTRIBUTE TRICKS

In DOS, every file has four attributes, or special characteristics that tell DOS exactly what type of file it is and how it's being used. All these attributes are toggles: they're either on or off. Here is a list of what the four attributes do when they're on:

- *Archive* means that a file has been written to lately (usually since the last backup).
- *Hidden* means that a file won't appear in a directory listing.
- *Read only* indicates that a file can't be changed.
- *System* means that a file is a DOS system file.

The Shell lets you change a file's attributes easily; so, you can do a couple of tricks with them. Some of the following ideas may be especially valuable if you share a computer with others.

**Protecting files.** If there are files that you don't want changed—like your program files or your favorite batch files—you can make them all read-only files (files that can't be changed or deleted). Executable files end in .COM, .EXE or .BAT, so choose File Display Options from the Options menu, enter *.COM in the Name box and click OK. Then choose All Files from the View menu, and you'll see all the files on the disk that have a .COM extension. Choose Change Attributes from the File menu and simultaneously change all your .COM files into read-only files.

Repeat this process for your .EXE and .BAT files, and all of your program files will be protected from being changed or deleted by mistake. Neat, huh?

Other files you may want to make read-only files include document templates (if you use them for boilerplate), last year's budgets that you want to keep a record of or anything else that you don't want to be saved with changes.

**Protecting a file doesn't hide it.** If you think protecting a file means other folks can't see what's in it, you're wrong. They can still see into the file; it's just that, like you, they can't change it or delete it from the disk unless they turn off the read-only attribute.

**Hide a file you want to camouflage.** If there's a file you don't want other folks poking around in, give it the hidden attribute and it won't normally show up in directory listings, in the Shell or at the command line. (You had better remember it's there if you want to use it again, though.)

There's an even sneakier way to hide file names by using extended ASCII characters (described in Chapter 6).

**The Shell will delete read-only files.** If you try to delete a read-only file at the Shell, it will warn you that it's a read-only file, but then it will go ahead and happily delete the file if you tell it to. Be careful.

**Generally leave the system and archive attributes alone.** Leave the system attribute alone. DOS needs to know which files are system files.

There are times when you may want to change the archive attribute, however, to keep track of which files have been copied and which haven't, as you'll see in the next tip.

**Archive attribute tricks.** You may want to change the archive attribute with the /M switch when you do a backup. Normally, when you choose Backup Fixed Disk from the Disk Utilities, you'll see that the dialog box has been filled out with these switches:

    c:\*.* a: /s

This tells DOS to back up everything on your C drive, plus everything in all the subdirectories (/S) to drive A. Add the /M switch to back up only the files that have been changed since the last backup, like so:

```
backup c:\*.* a: /s /m
```

There's also a suggestion in Chapter 1 for using the XCOPY command with the /M switch; this turns the archive attribute off so you don't fill up a floppy disk and then have to figure out which files didn't get copied.

**Changing file attributes at the command line.** To change file attributes at the command line, use the ATTRIB command as **attrib** followed by **+r** or **-r** (to turn the read-only attribute on or off); **+a** or **-a** (to turn the archive attribute on or off); **+h** or **-h** (to turn the hidden attribute on or off); followed by the file name. To make a hidden file named TEST.TXT visible again, for example, you'd enter the following:

```
attrib -h test.txt
```

## MOVING ON

Now that you've explored these Shell techniques, it's time to really put the Shell to work for you by creating your own program groups and running programs from them. Chapter 3, "Working With Programs," continues to survey the Shell for voodoo to use in your daily work.

# Chapter 3
# WORKING WITH PROGRAMS

DOS 5 and 6 have a Shell that enables you to run several programs simultaneously and to switch between them. This can really help if you're writing a report with your word processing program, say, and you want to refer to your database to get names and addresses or go out to a spreadsheet program and do some quick budget recalculations. You don't need a fancy computer to do this: you can switch back and forth between programs even with an old XT or clone. In fact, DOS 5 and 6 give you a lot of the benefits of Microsoft Windows without your having to buy Windows, learn how to use it and buy a computer sophisticated enough to run it well.

With DOS's Task Swapper, programs aren't all in memory at the same time, like they are with Windows. They're listed as active tasks, but only the one you're working with is really active. Instead, the memory "snapshot" of each program started is saved as a disk file, and when you switch to a different program, DOS loads it back into RAM again.

The tips and traps that follow are useful for working with programs or setting up program groups to use through the Shell.

## RUNNING PROGRAMS FROM THE SHELL

If you use the Shell instead of the command line, you'll find all sorts of ways to start programs. You can use the Task Swapper from the Shell, too, while you can only run one program at a time from the command line.

 **Different ways to run a program.** There are at least six different ways to run a program in the Shell:

- Use the File menu's Run command.
- Run it from the Active Task List.
- Run it from the File List.
- Run it from the Program List.
- Open a file that has an extension associated with the program.
- Drag a data file onto its program and "drop" it (this is a neat trick).

There may even be more ways to run a program, in fact. And you can always go out to the command prompt (choose it from the Main group or press Shift-F9) and run a program from there.

To run a program from one of the Shell's lists, either double-click on it with a mouse or highlight it with Tab and the arrow keys, press Alt-F and type O to open it.

To run a program with the File menu's Run command or from the command prompt, however, you need to enter the command used to start the program, including the path to the directory where it's stored (if it's not already in the path statement in your AUTOEXEC.BAT file).

**The DOS external commands are programs, too.** The DOS external commands (like CHKDSK and MEM) are really just mini-programs. Because they all have .EXE or .COM as their extension, you run them from the Shell just as any other program; you don't have to exit to the DOS prompt. Double-click on CHKDSK in your DOS directory for a demonstration.

## Chapter 3: Working With Programs 65

**Associate files with programs to open them quickly.** If you tell DOS that "all the files ending in .XXX are associated with program YYY," for instance, you can just double-click on a file's name both to open it and to start the program running at the same time, even if the file and the program are in different directories. For example, you might want to associate Lotus 1-2-3 Release 3 with files that have the extensions .WKS, .WK1 and .WK3, since it can use them all.

To do this, highlight one of the files that has the extension you'd like to associate with a particular program and choose Associate from the File menu. In the dialog box that appears (see Figure 3-1), type the command that starts the program, including its path (if it is not already in your path).

*Figure 3-1:* You can associate files that have a particular extension with a certain program.

If you want to associate several different extensions with a single program, highlight the program, choose Associate and type in the dialog box all the extensions you want associated with the program. (*Don't type the period that comes before the extension.*) This is faster, of course, than associating files one by one. You can associate up to 20 extensions with any one program.

**What *not* to do when associating files and programs.** Don't associate files with programs that don't allow options as part of their startup command.

Don't enter COM, BAT or EXE as associated extensions. These extensions indicate executable files.

Don't have a bunch of different files selected when you associate files. Turn off Select Across Directories if it's on. Press Ctrl-\ to deselect all the files in the current directory except the last one you selected. You can then pick a file that has the extension you want to associate.

**Using associated files with other programs.** Associating a file with a program doesn't mean you always have to use it with that program only. To use an associated file with a different program, start the other program first and retrieve the file into it (assuming the other program can read it, of course).

## SWITCHING BETWEEN PROGRAMS

The Shell enables you to quickly switch between the programs you're running, which DOS never let you do. Because the programs aren't kept in RAM but are stored as temporary disk files, you can even do this on a machine that has only 640k or less of RAM.

**Turn on the Task Swapper first.** You can't switch between programs unless there's a tiny diamond next to the Task Swapper in the Options menu, indicating that it's on. (It's a toggle; choose it to turn it on and off.)

You can tell that the Task Swapper is on because a special area called the Active Task List appears in the lower-right corner of the Shell screen (see Figure 3-2) when you're looking at the Program/File Lists view. It lists all the programs you've started.

## Chapter 3: Working With Programs 67

*Figure 3-2:* When the Task Swapper is on, an Active Task List appears.

**Don't start multiple copies of a program running.** Once a program is running, it's listed in the Active Task List area of the Shell. Choose it from that area to return to it if you've used another program. If you choose your program from the Program List area (in the lower-left part of the screen), you'll start another copy of it running.

**Keyboard shortcuts for switching between programs.** If you find that these shortcuts are confusing at first, make a little chart and keep it on your keyboard for a while.

To start a program and add it to the Active Task List without leaving the Shell, highlight its name and press Shift-Enter. This is the fastest way to set up a bunch of programs you want to be able to switch among.

To return to the DOS Shell from a program, press Ctrl-Esc.

To switch to the next program you've got running, press Alt-Esc. (Save your work first, just in case something happens.) *If you're only running two programs,* this is faster than returning to the Shell and selecting the next program from there.

To cycle among programs you're running, hold down the Alt key and press the Tab key until you see the name of the program you want at the top of your screen. Release the Alt key when you see it. *If you're running several programs*, this is faster than returning to the Shell and selecting the next program you want from there.

**Look at program lists only and keep your screen clean.** Select Program List from the View menu to see only your program groups and the Active Task List. It's not as cluttered a screen as the Program/File List view (which is the default), and you can see what's going on better. If you're running programs instead of doing file housekeeping, you'll find this view handy. If this was the last view you displayed, DOS will remember it and show it to you again the next time you start the Shell.

**Be sure to exit normally from your programs.** Don't just switch back to the Shell and shut down your computer with programs still in memory! Use the program's Exit or Quit command as you normally would. When you exit from a program, its name is deleted from the Active Task List.

**Program hung up?** If a program freezes on you and you can't exit from it normally, go back to the Shell (with Ctrl-Esc), highlight the name of the frozen program in the Active Task List and press Del.

Then go back and exit from all the other programs you've got running and reboot your computer, just to make sure that there aren't any other problems lurking somewhere in memory.

**You can use the command prompt even though programs are running.** Pressing Shift-F9 from the Shell screen will take you out to the command prompt even if you're running programs in the Active Task List.

Remember to type **exit**, not **dosshell**, to return to the Shell.

**Returning to the Shell from Windows.** Pressing Ctrl-Esc won't return you to the Shell from Windows; it brings up the Task List in Windows. To return to the Shell from Windows, exit from Windows (double-clicking on the Program Manager's Control icon in the upper-left corner of its window is the fastest way) and then press any key.

## SETTING UP PROGRAM GROUPS

You can create your own groups in the Shell for programs that you use often, like your favorite word processing program. You can also put documents in these groups. That way, the things you work with most frequently are readily accessible.

Putting a program in a group gives you a new way to start it. It does not physically move the program into a different directory or copy it or change anything about it. Even if you have the same program in several different groups, there's still only one copy of the program on your hard disk, wherever you stored it.

For example, if you want to organize your work by project or client, you'd put your word processing, spreadsheet and graphics programs in a group along with all the documents related to that client's job. You'd create another group for the next client, and so forth. Program groups let you customize your programs and files beyond the limitations of DOS's hierarchical directories.

 **Here's how to set up a program group of your own.**

- Open the group to which you want to add the new group. This will usually be the Main group, but you can also add subgroups to groups. For example, different categories of clients could be grouped under a Client group.
- Choose New from the File menu.

- Choose Program Group from the New Program Object dialog box (see Figure 3-3).

- Fill out the Add Group dialog box (see Figure 3-4). You can use up to 23 characters, including spaces, for the group's title. That's what will appear on the screen. (You'll see more tricks about adding Help text and passwords later.)

Creating a group doesn't automatically put programs in it. You'll have to add the programs you want your new group to have. If you add a group to the Main group, however, you'll always be able to get back to the Main group because it will be listed in your new group.

To add an item to a group, open the group. Then choose Program Item instead of Program Group when you get the New Program Object dialog box. In this case, you'll get an Add Program dialog box (see Figure 3-5) to fill out. Here's where the magic begins: although you *can* put other programs in a group (perhaps a favorite utility program), you can also put batch files, DOS commands and even documents in a group as program items.

Let's see how to fill out the Add Program dialog box to put different things in groups.

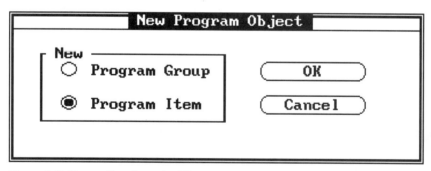

*Figure 3-3:* Choose New from the File menu to get the New Program Object dialog box.

## Chapter 3: Working With Programs    71

```
┌─────────────────── Add Group ───────────────────┐
│                                                  │
│  Required                                        │
│                                                  │
│    Title . . . .    [Status Reports_        ]   │
│                                                  │
│  Optional                                        │
│                                                  │
│    Help Text . .    [                       ]   │
│                                                  │
│    Password  . .    [                       ]   │
│                                                  │
│                                                  │
│       ( OK )      ( Cancel )      ( Help )      │
│                                                  │
└──────────────────────────────────────────────────┘
```

*Figure 3-4:* Use the Add Group dialog box to give your group a descriptive title.

```
┌─────────────────── Add Program ──────────────────┐
│                                                   │
│  Program Title . . . .  [WordPerfect_        ]   │
│                                                   │
│  Commands  . . . . . .  [wp                  ]   │
│                                                   │
│  Startup Directory . .  [c:\wp51\docs        ]   │
│                                                   │
│  Application Shortcut Key   [ALT+W           ]   │
│                                                   │
│  [X] Pause after exit      Password . . [    ]   │
│       ( OK )  ( Cancel )  ( Help )  ( Advanced...) │
└───────────────────────────────────────────────────┘
```

*Figure 3-5:* Use the Add Program dialog box to add a program or a document to a group.

**Filling out the Add Program dialog box.** The trick to adding an item to a group (and getting it in the right group) is to make sure that the group you're adding to is open before you choose New from the File menu. Just highlighting the group name doesn't work; it needs to be at the top of the Program List, in the shaded bar.

Type in the Program Title dialog box what you want to see on the screen. This isn't where you put the command to start the program.

In the Commands box, type the exact command used to start the program, including the path to where the program is stored, if it's not in the path statement in your AUTOEXEC.BAT file. If you want to use several commands, separate each one with a semicolon and a space.

The Startup Directory box lets you specify the directory you want to switch to when your program starts. If you're using a program like WordPerfect, which lets you specify the directory where you want your documents stored, you can just leave this box blank. But say you store your spreadsheet program files in a directory named SPREAD and your spreadsheet data files in a subdirectory named SHEETS: specify C:\SPREAD\SHEETS in the Startup Directory box, and when you save a spreadsheet it'll go to your SHEETS subdirectory.

**Make yourself a keyboard shortcut.** This can be a real time-saver. If you use a program frequently, assign it a keyboard shortcut. Then you can just press that key combination to switch to that program, once it's running. You won't have to press Alt-Tab to cycle through all your running programs or go back to the Shell and choose the program from the Active Task List.

Don't use a key combination that's already used. Move to the "Application Shortcut Key" box and press F1 to get Help. You'll see a list of the combinations that are taken. You have to use a Ctrl, Alt or Shift combination. I use Alt-W for WordPerfect, for example, because it's easy to remember.

**You can edit a program item later, too.** If you find out later that you want to change something about the way you set up a program item (for example, if you discover a keyboard shortcut has been used and you want to change it), you can come back to the Add Program dialog box by highlighting the program item and choosing Properties from the File menu.

## Chapter 3: Working With Programs 73

**Keep Pause After Exit checked.**  Normally, there's a slight pause when you switch from a program to the Shell and vice versa. It gives DOS a chance to display an error message if there's a problem. If you uncheck Pause After Exit, the error message will go by too quickly for you to see it.

When Pause After Exit is checked, you'll get a message telling you to press any key to return to the Shell after you exit from a program that you started from the Shell.

**Assigning passwords.**  Yes, you can also password-protect a group or an individual program item. You can use up to 20 characters, and some of them can be blank spaces. Once you have assigned a password, only the folks who know it can open the group or run the program. (They can start a program or open a document in one of the many other ways, though. To really protect a file, make it read-only, as described in Chapter 2, "Shell Secrets.")

Capitalization *does* count with passwords. This is one of the few places in DOS where uppercase and lowercase mean something. If you assign the password in all caps, you'll have to enter it in all caps.

**Sneaky password tricks.**  Here are a few suggestions for tricks to use when assigning a password:

- Deliberately misspell a word. I use *psuedo* instead of *pseudo*, for instance.
- Use a foreign word, like the capital of Tuva (Kyzyl).
- Use a mix of characters and symbols, like *could?be*.

**Don't forget your password!**  But if you do, here's how to find it. Call up DOSSHELL.INI and look up the group's password= line.

**Put documents in groups, too.**  If there are documents that you work with regularly, put them in your program groups. If, for example, you have a weekly report that you add to each day, stick it in the program group you run your word processing program from.

To put a document in a group as an item, include in the Commands part of the Add Program dialog box the command that's used to start the program and the path to where the document is located. In Figure 3-6, the item Weekly Report starts WordPerfect and opens the document WKRPT, stored in C:\WP51\DOCS\REPORTS. Figure 3-7 shows the results of adding these items to a group.

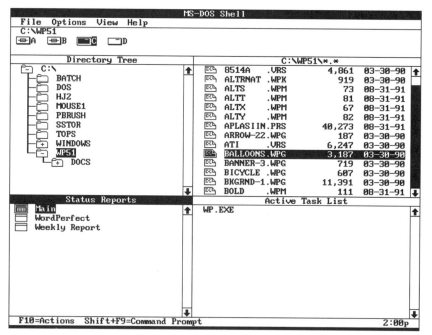

*Figure 3-6:* To add a document to a group, use the command that starts the program and show the path to the document.

*Figure 3-7:* Now there's a Status Reports group that contains a couple of program items.

**Don't put too many documents in a program group.** Each time you open a program item that starts a program, you run another copy of the program (if you've turned on the Task Swapper). Put only the document you like *to start up with* in a program group. Once you finish working with a document and save it, you can go to another document while still in the program without exiting to the Shell and running another copy of the program.

**Copy program items into different groups.** Once you put a program or a document into a group, it's faster to copy it into another group than to go through the whole dialog box rigmarole again. Open the group that contains the item you want to copy and select that item. Then choose Copy from the File menu. This is one place where you can't drag or use the F8 Copy keyboard shortcut.

**Copy an item even if you don't want it to be exactly the same.** It's faster to copy a program item and then modify its Program Item Properties dialog box to give the item a different name and prompt message, for example, than to set it all up from scratch. Whenever you can, just copy and then edit the item's dialog box. Choose Properties from the File menu to go straight to the dialog box.

**Copying an item doesn't make a new copy of it.** When you copy a program or a document into a different group, DOS doesn't really make a new copy of it on your hard disk (so you won't fill up your disk by making several copies of something). Using a copy of a program just gives you a different way to start it. (But be careful not to start more than one copy of it running, as you saw in the trap, "Don't start multiple copies of a program running," on page 69.)

**Give your program items descriptive names.** The name you give a program item can be a lot more descriptive than the name of the program or the name of the document. In the example above, for instance, Weekly Report is a lot more understandable than WKRPT, yes?

In fact, if you use the program name for all your program items, you'll get a list like this:

```
WordPerfect
WordPerfect
WordPerfect
```

That's not much help when each one starts a different document!

**Make sure your programs don't use reserved keys.** The Shell reserves these key combinations for its own use: Alt-Esc, Alt-Tab and Ctrl-Esc. You can't use those key combinations in both the Shell and one of your programs. If your program has another op-tion, use it. If not, check the appropriate Reserve Shortcut Keys box on the Advanced Property Options dialog box (highlight the program item, choose Properties from the File menu and click Advanced to see it).

Once you've checked this box, that key combination is disabled in the Shell, so use it with caution. For example, if you disable Alt-Tab, you won't be able to cycle among all the programs you've got running; you'll have to use Ctrl-Esc to go back to the Shell and pick the next program you want.

Screen capture programs seem to use these key combinations a lot, but they usually offer you several alternatives to use instead.

**You can prevent switching between programs.** If you *don't* want to be able to switch to a different program when a certain program is running, put an X in the Prevent Program Switch box on its Advanced Property Options dialog box. (Highlight the program's name in the Program List and choose Properties from the File menu; then click the Advanced button.)

If a program causes trouble when you switch, you might want to prevent the ability to switch to it; then you won't do it by mistake.

**Reorder program items to put the most frequently used ones at the top.** The Reorder command (on the File menu) lets you rearrange the items in a program group. Select the item you want to move, choose Reorder, select the new location and press Enter or double-click.

**You can put batch files in program groups, too.** You can put batch files you use a lot in program groups as separate items. For example, I have a batch file called DUMP.BAT that prepares my printer to receive screen dumps (it's an Apple LaserWriter connected to a "foreign" DOS machine). It's convenient to have this as a batch file in the Shell because it includes all sorts of alphabet soup I can never remember.

Just be sure the directory in which your batch files are stored is named in your path; then put the batch file's name as the command in the Commands part of the Program Item Properties dialog box.

**You can execute a batch file before or after a program starts.** If you want to execute a batch file before a program starts, put it in the Commands box, preceded by a CALL command, and separate the commands with semicolons. For example, my laser printer is connected via an AppleTalk network and a special card. If I want to print documents I've created in WordPerfect (or any other program, for that matter), I have to execute a batch file (which I named NETPRINT.BAT) that changes to the TOPS directory and tells the net to get ready to handle print jobs. So the line

```
call netprint; wp
```

executes NETPRINT.BAT and starts WordPerfect.

**Create a custom startup prompt.** If you use replaceable parameters (like %1) in the Commands box, you'll be asked, when you finish filling out the dialog box, if you'd like to display a prompt when it's time for the user to provide the information the %1 stands for.

For example, WordPerfect lets you specify a file name as part of your startup command. If you'd like to be prompted for this information when you start the program (or if you're setting up a group for somebody who's less experienced than you), put this in the "Commands" box:

```
wp %1
```

You'll get a Program Item Properties dialog box to fill out (see Figure 3-8) that lets you create a custom dialog box. Whatever window title you use will appear at the top of the box. Whatever you put as program information (up to 106 characters) will show up under that title (see Figure 3-9). You can put some descriptive information here if you're setting up groups for others to use (for temporary workers, for example, who have been hired to update or purge mailing lists in a database program).

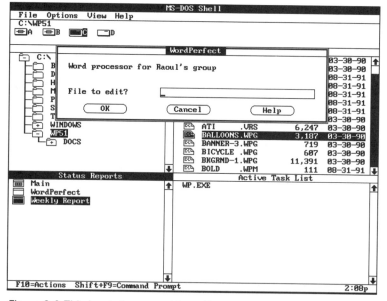

*Figure 3-8:* You can create custom dialog boxes that appear when you start a program.

*Figure 3-9:* This is what you would see if you started the program.

You can use more than one of these replaceable parameters (%0 through %9), and you can create a custom dialog box for each one.

**Create custom Help for your programs.** With that Add Program dialog box on the screen, check out some Advanced options (click the Advanced button). Here's where you can add custom Help text, up to 255 characters long, for your program item (see Figure 3-10). Type ^m wherever you want a line break (a caret and an m, not a Ctrl-m). Whenever you highlight the program item and press F1, the Help text is displayed (see Figure 3-11).

*Figure 3-10:* You can create custom Help screens for program items.

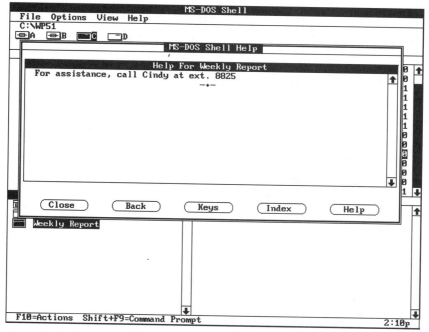

*Figure 3-11:* Here's the Help screen that appears.

**Add items to the Disk Utilities group.** Just because the Disk Utilities group is already created for you doesn't mean that you can't customize it by adding other utilities to it. For example, you might want to create an item for formatting a 720k disk in a 1.44mb drive B. To do this, you'd probably want to call the item something like Small B Format (or whatever helps you remember it) and enter

```
format b: /f:720
```

in the Commands box as the command to be carried out. Remember, you can put %1 at the end of that line to create a custom dialog box for this item, too (see previous tricks in this chapter for details about using replaceable parameters like %1). You might want to create a prompt like "Insert 720k disk in drive B:" to remind yourself that this is what your program item does. (See Chapter 5, "Disk & Drive Magic," for more disk tricks.)

The MEM command is also a nice utility to add to your Disk Utilities group. And, if you've purchased a separate utilities package such as the Norton Utilities or PC Tools, you can put your favorite utilities in this group, too. You can also create prompts that tell you how to use these programs.

**Deleting items from groups.** To delete a program item from a group, just highlight it and press Del. Don't worry; this doesn't delete it from your hard disk, just from the group.

To delete a group, you first have to delete all the items in it.

To delete an item or a group, you'll have to supply the password, if one's been assigned. (See the earlier tips about passwords if you've forgotten how.)

## MOVING ON

Now that you've explored the DOS Shell, it's time to examine the true nature of DOS: the command line. Chapter 4, "Command-Line Tricks," has all sorts of tips for getting the most from the cryptic and sometimes bewildering C:\> (and all its variations).

# Chapter 4
# COMMAND-LINE TRICKS

The Shell contains only a few of DOS's many, many commands. DOS commands are accessible through the command prompt, that familiar A> or B> or C> that tells you DOS is ready to do your bidding—*as long as you don't make a single mistake in what you type*. That's the catch. If you do, you'll see the "Bad command or file name" message staring back at you.

The ideas in this chapter will (I hope) help you avoid that dreaded but universal message.

## COMMAND-LINE BASICS

A few tricks are pretty basic, but you can't use them if you're not aware of them!

**A shortcut for going to the command line.** If you're in the Shell when you open the Main group, the command prompt choice will usually be highlighted. Just press Enter to go to the command line.

**Run a DOS command instead of exiting the Shell.** You can use the File menu's Run command to run any DOS command as though you were at the command line. Alt-F R is a keyboard shortcut for Run.

**To DOS, uppercase and lowercase don't count.** DOS doesn't care whether you enter commands in caps, lowercase letters or a mixture of the two. To DOS, DIR is the same as dir is the same as Dir is the same as DIr.

**But other things do count.** DOS does care about how you enter parameters (which tell the command what it will act on) and optional switches (which tell the command specifically how you want it to behave). If you don't get these exactly right, you'll get a "Bad command or file name," or some other error message.

If you're not sure what switches can be used with what commands, get help. Don't try to memorize all the switches and commands or to look them up in a big, fat book. It's much simpler to ask for help.

To get help on a command and all its switches, type **help** plus the command name at the command line. You can also type the command and **/?** to get help. These two lines, for instance, do the same thing:

```
help xcopy
xcopy /?
```

The following list of switch definitions that can be used with XCOPY is an example of the kind of help you'll get in DOS 5 (or with DOS 6's FASTHELP command); for a sample of DOS 6's improved HELP command, look back in Chapter 1, page 17.

```
Copies files (except hidden and system files) and directory
trees.

XCOPY source [destination] [/A | /M] [/D:date] [/P] [/S [/E]]
[/V] [/W]
  SOURCE       Specifies the file(s) to copy.
  DESTINATION  Specifies the location and/or name of new
               files.
  /A           Copies files with the archive attribute set,
               doesn't change the attribute.
```

| | |
|---|---|
| /M | Copies files with the archive attribute set, turns off the archive attribute. |
| /D:date | Copies files changed on or after the specified date. |
| /P | Prompts you before creating each destination file. |
| /S | Copies directories and subdirectories except empty ones. |
| /E | Copies any subdirectories, even if empty. |
| /V | Verifies each new file. |
| /W | Prompts you to press a key before copying. |

**Canceling a command.** To cancel a command before you've pressed Enter, press either Esc or Ctrl-C.

**Switching between the Shell and the command line.** This repeats a previous tip, but it's relevant here, too. To exit temporarily to the command line from the Shell, use the Shift-F9 shortcut. To exit the Shell and take it out of memory, use F3 or Alt-F4.

If you exit the Shell and remove it from memory, though, DOS will have to read your whole hard disk when you start the Shell again. This can drive you nuts. For a temporary exit to the command line, visit with Shift-F9.

Likewise, don't type **dosshell** to return to the Shell from the command line if the Shell is already in memory. But you may not know whether it's in memory; so try typing **exit** first. If nothing happens, it isn't in memory and you can type **dosshell** to start it. Voodoo!

## EDITING COMMANDS

There are several keyboard shortcuts for repeating the last command you issued, or part of it. Although these function-key shortcuts take a little getting used to, they can definitely save you time if you'll be issuing similar commands over and over again.

**Repeating a command.** To repeat the last command you entered at the command line, press F3. The exact same command will be carried out. This is handy for doing things like making copies of files on several floppy disks. For instance, suppose you've just done a COPY *.* A:. You can take out the disk that has the copied files on it, replace it with a blank disk and repeat the same command again: you'll have two sets of backup files.

**Instead of retyping, display the last command and edit it.** If you want to use a command similar to the last one you issued, press F3 to get it on the screen to edit. It's usually faster than typing it all over again, especially if there are lots of switches and colons and semicolons, as in a long path name. And it prevents typos, too.

**You can't use a mouse at the command line.** The mouse only works in the Shell, so it can't be used to edit commands at the command prompt. Too bad.

**You can use function keys at the command line, though.** Several function keys work as editing keys at the command line. DOS automatically remembers your previous command and stores it as a template in memory; you can use these keys to call back all or part of this template.

As you saw in a previous tip, you can press F3 to get an entire command back. Here are some more function keys that affect DOS command entries:

- Press F1 repeatedly to get the previous command back character-by-character.

- Press F2 to retype all the characters in the template, up to the character you type next. For example, if the previous command was

    ```
    type doc.txt | more
    ```

    and you press F2 and type **c**, you'll get **type do**.

- Press F4 to delete part of the template, beginning with the character you type next. This is the opposite of pressing F2.

Using the same example above, press F4, type **c** and then press F3 to get the template on the screen. You'll get

```
c.txt | more
```

- Press F6 to get a Ctrl-Z character in the command line, which is useful for writing batch files at the command line (it indicates the end of the file).
- Some of these function-key "shortcuts" are decidedly awkward, but using F3 to produce the last command, F1 to retype the previous command one character at a time, and F6 to produce a ^Z are useful tricks to remember.

**Repeating groups of commands.** Usually you can repeat only the last command entered at the command line. Starting with DOS 5, there's a new Doskey utility that remembers quite a few commands and lets you repeat them. Chapter 8, "Doskey Revealed," demonstrates how to put this new macro facility to work.

## BAILING OUT OF COMMANDS

A couple of tricks can be used for *stopping* commands as well as starting them.

**Pausing commands.** Many commands produce results that zip past you on the screen. Stop the scrolling by pressing Ctrl-S or the Pause key. Press any key to start scrolling again.

Use MORE to see screen displays one screen at a time. Unless you have the reflexes of a test pilot, this is a surer way of getting to read what's on the screen. To read a text file named TEST.TXT, for example, type either of these two lines:

```
type test.txt | more
more < test.txt
```

I'll show you other ways to use special symbols with commands such as MORE at the end of this chapter.

> **Canceling a command.** To stop a command that's already running, press Ctrl-C or Ctrl-Break. This won't automatically undo what's been done up to that point, though.

## MISCELLANEOUS COMMAND-LINE TRICKS

The following tricks defy categorization, but you'll undoubtedly find magic in them.

> **You have a screen-saver program.** Sometimes your screen gets too cluttered with commands. CLS will clear the screen. It's also handy for preventing screen burn-in if you'll be away from your computer for a while but aren't running Windows—and don't have one of those nifty screen-saver programs with little winged toasters that fly around on your screen, like After Dark.

> **Without DOS in your path, you may have difficulty running some commands.** Some DOS commands are internal: they are always available because they're stored in memory. Others are external: they're stored on disk.

Normally, the Setup program puts the path to your DOS directory in your AUTOEXEC.BAT file. If it's not there, or if it gets deleted by mistake, DOS won't be able to execute an external command because it won't be able to locate it.

DOS is usually stored in a directory named C:\DOS; make sure it's in your AUTOEXEC.BAT file if you get a "Bad command" message when you issue commands.

Chapter 6, "A Miscellany of Alchemy," details other ways to jazz up your path statement.

> **You can't press F1 for help at the command line.** If you're used to the Shell, you may also have gotten used to pressing F1 to get help. That won't work at the command line, but help *is* available there. Remember, type **help** plus the name of the command

you want help with, like **help attrib**. Or type the command and follow it with **/?**, as in **attrib /?**.

**You can create short batch files at the command line.** I say "short" because you can't edit the file, so if you make a mistake in a line and don't realize it until after you press Enter, you'll have to start over from scratch.

To make batch files at the command line, use the COPY command and tell DOS to copy from the CONsole (the fancy name for the keyboard). Once you type **copy con** and give a file name, DOS will put whatever you type into the named file until you press Ctrl-Z to signal the end of the file. Here's an example of a very simple batch file that changes you to a directory buried way down in a file structure, so you don't have to type a long path name when you want to change to the WORD subdirectory:

```
copy con word.bat
cd c:\wordpro\docs\progs\word
^Z
```

Press Enter at the end of each line. When you press Enter after Ctrl-Z (F6 will generate that ^Z for you), DOS tells you that one file has been copied. From then on, just type **word** at the DOS prompt to go immediately to your WORD subdirectory.

**Forbidden file names.** DOS reserves some device names for its own use. Don't use the following as your file names:

```
AUX     CLOCK$  CON     COM1
COM2    COM3    LPT1    LPT2
LPT3    NUL     PRN
```

**The command-line shortcut (\) to the root directory.** There's a shorthand notation that takes you immediately to the root directory from any subdirectory. Just type \ (a backslash), all by itself, after the CD command at the command line.

Suppose you're in a subdirectory. To go immediately to the root directory on drive C, just type **cd \**.

**The .. (dot dot) shortcut.**   The .. (dot dot) shortcut brings you up to the next-higher directory level. If you're in C:\WP51\DOCS\VOODOO\CH1, typing **cd ..** takes you up one directory to C:\WP51\DOCS\VOODOO.

This is very helpful when you want to move up through your directory hierarchy one level at a time.

You can also use .. as a shortcut in long path names. To change to a directory two levels up in the same path you're in, use

    cd ..\..

For instance, if you're in C:\WP51\DOCS\VOODOO, entering

    cd ..\..

takes you two levels up to \WP51.

With a little practice, you'll amaze your friends as you zip through long path names.

Entering **cd ..** at your root directory has no effect because there's no directory above it.

**The mysterious . (period) shorthand.**   The . (period) stands for the directory you're in, so for a listing of the current directory, type

    dir .

It's the same thing as

    dir *.*

**Path shortcuts.**   You don't always have to type the whole path, as in C:\WP51\DOCS\VOODOO\CH4. You can leave out information as long as both you and DOS know that what you leave out refers to the current drive and directory.

For example,

    copy a:*.*

copies all the files on a floppy in drive A into your current directory, since DOS assumes that's the destination.

To copy all the files in the current directory onto a floppy disk in drive A, use

```
copy . a:
```

You can use *.* if you're not comfortable with the period, but they mean the same thing.

To copy all the files from the \WORDPRO directory to your current directory, enter

```
copy \wordpro\*.*
```

Just remember that DOS assumes you want to copy to the current drive and directory unless you tell it otherwise.

Also, you don't have to use the whole path notation with commands if the directory you're referring to is under your current directory. For example, you can switch from the directory C:\WP51\DOCS to C:\WP51\DOCS\VOODOO by just typing

```
cd voodoo
```

In fact, if you type **cd \voodoo**, you'll get an "Invalid directory" message because DOS will search for it on another branch.

You *can* use the backslash (\) at the root directory, though: for example, both **cd wp51** and **cd \wp51** will change you to the WP51 directory from the root (C:\).

To get to a subdirectory on another path, you'll have to use the backslash notation. For example, to switch to C:\WORD\TEXT from C:\WP51\DOCS, you have to type

```
cd \word\text
```

(leave out the C: because it's on the same drive).

**Some commands make sense only at the command line.** A handful of commands make sense only at the command line and not in the Shell, because they're either unnecessary or irrelevant in the Shell. These commands are CD (or CHDIR) for changing directories, RD (or RMDIR) for removing directories, CLS for clearing the screen, and MORE and TYPE (for seeing what's in a file).

**Other command-line commands have Shell equivalents.** The list below shows command-line commands and their Shell equivalents.

| Command Line | Shell |
|---|---|
| ATTRIB | Choose Change Attributes from the File menu. |
| BACKUP | Choose Backup Fixed Disk from the Disk Utilities (XCOPY is even better, although it isn't available in the Shell). In DOS 6, you can use the new MSBACKUP features (described in Chapter 6). |
| COPY | Drag the selected file or press F8 in the Shell. |
| DIR | Directory listings show automatically. |
| DISKCOPY | Choose Disk Copy from the Disk Utilities. |
| FORMAT | Choose Format or Quick Format from the Disk Utilities. |
| MORE and TYPE | Press F9 to see file contents. |
| REN | Choose Rename from the File menu. |
| RESTORE | Choose Restore Fixed Disk from the Disk Utilities. |
| UNDELETE | Choose Undelete from the Disk Utilities. |

**New commands in DOS 6!** DOS 6 adds the new commands DELTREE and MOVE (as you'll see in the next tricks), but it *doesn't* include a few commands that were in DOS 5, such as BACKUP, because they're replaced by improved commands (in this case, MSBACKUP). If you need those commands, you can get the Supplemental Disk (see Chapter 1 for how).

**The new MOVE command lets you rename directories!** To rename a directory, use the MOVE command, which is new in DOS 6. Just give the old name first and then the new name:

```
move c:\oldname c:\newname
```

## Chapter 4: Command-Line Tricks    93

**You can't create a new directory with the MOVE command.**
You can rename a directory with the MOVE command (see the previous tip), but you can't create a new directory that doesn't already exist. You still have to use CD for that. If you try to create a new directory with MOVE, by specifying the path to a nonexistent directory, you'll get a "Cannot move C:\XXXX - no such file or directory exists" message.

**You can't move a directory to a different level in your directory system.**    The MOVE command is great, but it only lets you move directories at the same level. You can't, for example, use **move c:\docs c:\wp\docs** because that would put the DOCS directory one level deeper down in the hierarchy. You can move files to different levels, just not directories.

**Moving and renaming at the same time.**    You can use the MOVE command to move a file to a different location and give it a new name, all with the same command-line command. For example, to move a file named DOC.TXT to the WPDOCS directory and rename it as MYLETTER.TXT, just type

```
move doc.txt c:\wpdocs\myletter.txt
```

**You can overwrite existing files with MOVE.**    MOVE is like RENAME, except that it doesn't warn you about overwriting files that already exist with the same name. You can overwrite an existing file or directory that has the same name as the new name you're using. For example, if you use

```
move doc.txt c:\letters\letter.txt
```

and there's already a LETTER.TXT file in the LETTERS directory, it's history. If you look at what's in the file, it's what *was* in DOC.TXT.

**How to tell if your MOVE is successful.**    If your files have been moved successfully, you'll see "[ok]" on the screen after the command is completed. If you're going to use the MOVE command in a batch file, you can test for a code to see if the move was successful. IF ERRORLEVEL=0, the move was OK; IF ERRORLEVEL=1, it wasn't.

**Moving several files with MOVE.** Instead of moving one file at a time, you can move several files at once. The trick is to separate their names with commas, like this:

```
move doc1.txt,doc2.txt c:\wpdocs
```

If you're running DOS 6, ignore the next three tips. They're true only with earlier versions of DOS.

**Moving files at the command line.** For DOS 5 or earlier versions, to move a file from one directory to another at the command line, you have to COPY it to its new location and then DELete it from its original location. (But the Shell has a Move command that the command line doesn't have.)

For example, moving the file DOC.DOC from a directory named C:\WP51\DOCS to a directory named C:\WORD\TEXT takes two commands (assuming the current directory is C:\WP51\DOCS):

```
copy doc.doc c:\word\text
del doc.doc
```

**Copying and renaming files at the same time.** This job is *easier* at the command line! In fact, it can't be done by dragging files with the mouse at the Shell.

To rename a file as you copy it, be sure the new name is typed at the end of the path. To rename DOC.DOC to DOC.TXT, for example, type

```
copy doc.doc c:word\text\doc.txt
```

That will leave you with two files: DOC.DOC in your original C:\WP51\DOCS directory and DOC.TXT in your C:\WORD\TEXT directory.

## Chapter 4: Command-Line Tricks

**Moving directories at the command line.** DOS 5 and earlier versions won't let you rename a directory at the command line. So, if you want to move a complete directory from one location to another from the command line, you have to make a new directory (MD), COPY all the files into it, DEL all the files from the original directory, change out of it (CD) if you're in it (you *can't* delete the directory you're in), and then remove the original empty directory (RD).

If you're renaming directories and reorganizing your files in DOS 5, it's worth firing up the Shell just to get that directory-renaming feature.

**Rules for directory names apply to file names.** You can use the entire alphabet and all the numbers in directory names and file names, in addition to the following characters:

$ ~ # ! ' ( ) { } - _ ^

In addition, you can use extensions with directory names, although most folks don't. It gives you another way to categorize your files and get more control over your directory and subdirectory listings, however. For example, you might want to add an extension to a directory name—such as CLIENTS.WP or ACCOUNTS.123—to indicate what kind of documents are stored in it.

**Be careful with backslashes when creating directories.** If you specify a new subdirectory with a backslash, it's just under the root directory. If you don't use a backslash, the subdirectory will appear under the current directory. If you're in the C:\TEXT directory, for example, **md \docs** creates a subdirectory named C:\DOCS and **md docs** creates a subdirectory named C:\TEXT\DOCS.

**When you make a directory, you don't automatically change to it.** I forget this even after all these years. If you want to do anything in your new directory, you have either to change (CD) to it or specify its path. For example, if you're at the root directory and you make a directory (MD) named C:\TEXT and decide to copy all the files from a floppy disk in drive A into your new directory, you have first to change (CD) to it and then to enter either

```
copy a:*.* or copy a:*.* c:\text
```

**DOS 6 lets you delete directories full of files.** A new DELTREE command in DOS 6 lets you quickly clean off your disks by erasing entire directories and all the files and subdirectories in them, too. As you might expect, you should use this command with care. First, get a directory listing of what you're planning to delete to make sure nothing you want to keep is buried several levels deep.

Say, for example, that you want to delete your C:\WP51 directory and all its subdirectories—C:\WP51\DOCS, C:\WP51\MACROS, C:\WP51\VOODOO, C:\WP51\VOODOO\DOS, C:\WP51\VOODOO\MAC, and so forth. Just entering

```
deltree c:\wp51
```

will do it. You'll be prompted to confirm, but you can use the /Y switch with DELTREE to turn off the prompts for a really fast and risky way to delete directories. And yes, DELTREE removes hidden and system files as well as read-only files, too. It really cleans house.

**Get a directory listing before you use a wildcard with DELTREE.** Although you can use wildcards with DELTREE, it's really dangerous to do that *unless* you test what you're planning to delete by first getting a directory listing of it. Say that you want to delete several directories that are named C:\MAYDOCS, C:\FEBDOCS, and C:\JANDOCS. If you enter **deltree ???docs** and a wildcard happens to match a file name in the directory you're in, that file will be deleted as well as the directories you wanted to delete. To avoid having to use UNDELETE, especially since you probably won't be aware you deleted that file, do a **dir ???docs** first to see what's going to be de-leted before you use DELTREE with that same wildcard pattern.

## Chapter 4: Command-Line Tricks

**You can't remove a directory that's not empty unless you've got DOS 6, as you saw in the preceding tip.** A directory has to be empty of everything except the period (.) and dot dot (..) notations that appear at the beginning of every directory listing you get with the DIR command. These are abbreviations for the current directory and the parent directory, respectively. They're included in the total count of the files in the directory, but they're not really files.

To delete all the files in a directory, you can use the wildcard pattern (as in DEL *.*). DOS will ask you to verify whether you really want to do that.

If you've deleted all the files in a directory (and moved out of it, too, since you can't remove the current directory) and you still can't delete the directory, there may be hidden files in it. Do a **dir /a** to see if any hidden files are lurking there. Some programs create hidden files as part of their copy protection.

To get rid of the hidden or system files you can't see, clear their attributes like this:

```
attrib -h -r -s *.*
```

Then you can change out of that directory and delete it.

**A dangerous way to delete.** There's a speedy, little-known, and dangerous way to delete all the files in a directory: just give the directory's name. For example:

```
del c:\wp51\report
```

deletes all the files in the REPORT subdirectory of C:\WP51. You're asked to confirm that you want to delete all the files in the subdirectory, but it's easy to think you're deleting a document named RE-PORT when you're actually deleting all the files in the *directory* named REPORT.

**The Shell's All Files view doesn't show all files.** The Shell's All Files view doesn't normally show you hidden files, even though its name leads you to think so. To see all files, you have to choose File Display Options from the Options menu and check the Display Hidden/System Files box.

At the command line, **dir /a:h** lets you see the hidden files in the current directory; **dir /a** lets you see them all, too. Issuing **chkdsk/v | more** will show all the files on the disk, including hidden files.

**Get a directory listing of a directory before you delete it.** You may not remember everything that's in a directory, and something important may be lurking there. Before you erase all the files in it, get a directory listing and check to see what it contains. The DIR command with the O:/D switch will show you the oldest files first; those are the ones you may have forgotten about.

**Alphabetizing directory listings.** If you want to have your directories automatically alphabetized whenever you get a directory listing, put this line in your AUTOEXEC.BAT file:

```
set dircmd=/o:n /p
```

**Trickle-down switches.** Be careful: DOS wants its switches in trickle-down ordering, like some politicians. If you want a wide listing with alphabetized directories first, you might think you could enter

```
dir /w /o:g /o:n
```

But all this line gives you is an alphabetical listing. Instead, call for the wide listing first, then the alphabetic order, and then the grouping of directories before files, like this:

```
dir /w /o:n /o:/g
```

*Thanks to Colin "Slug" Creitz, of Lititz, PA.*

**Lost in your directories? Use TREE.** If you get lost in your directory structure, remember that you can always issue the TREE command at the command prompt to see where you are. Use TREE /F to see all the file names, too.

A word of warning: the TREE command only scrolls down. It's much easier to browse through your filing system with the Shell.

**You can get to the Editor from the command line.** You don't have to start the Shell to use the graphical Editor. Just enter **edit** at the command line, and the Editor will start (if there's enough room in RAM for it).

Starting it with **edit /h** will put as many lines of text on your screen as your monitor can display.

See Chapter 7, "Batch Files," for more tips on using the Editor.

## THE NEW, IMPROVED DIR COMMAND

You'll only use the DIR command at the command line, since you have a choice of so many different views in the Shell. You may not be aware that starting with DOS 5, there were significant improvements to the old DIR workhorse. Since it's strictly a command-line command, I'm putting these tips in this chapter instead of in Chapter 9, "Arcane Commands," where you'll find little-known facts about little-known commands.

**Sort your directory listings easily.** A new /O switch lets you specify the order in which you want the DIR command to sort your files. Now you can easily see your files sorted by date or by extension.

Here's how to use the new /O option. After an /O:, specify any combination of the following (you'll see some examples in the following tips):

- d    Sort by date and time (oldest first).
- e    Sort by extension.
- g    Sort with directories grouped, then files.
- n    Sort by name.
- s    Sort by size (smallest first).
- -    Prefix for above values sorts in reverse order.

The /O switch automatically alphabetizes your files if you don't specify any other values.

A new /A switch displays only-file names that have the attributes you specify. Issue **dir /a** to display *all* the files in a directory, even hidden files. Also, combine the /A switch with the following values (again, don't put spaces between the switch and the values):

- a    Display files that are ready for archiving (files that haven't been backed up).
- d    Display directories only.
- h    Display hidden files only.
- r    Display only read-only files.
- s    Display only system files.
- -    Prefix for above values means "not."

That's not all! There's a new /L switch that tells DOS to display names in lowercase; a /B switch that specifies a listing of files and directories only, with no other information; and an /S switch that lists file and directory names in all subdirectories.

And there are still the old standby switches: /W for a wide listing and /P to pause after each screen of text.

DOS 6 adds a new /C switch to DIR. When you use this switch, you'll see information about how much file compression you're getting if you've compressed your disk with DoubleSpace. Each file's compression ratio is listed, as well as the average compression ratio for the whole disk.

Here comes the voodoo.

**Want to see all the hard-disk files you haven't backed up yet?** Use this line:

    dir c:\ /a:a /o:-d /s /w

**Want to see a directory's file names in the order you've been working on them?** Use this line:

    dir /b /o:-d /p

**Want to get a printable list of file names in a directory?** If you don't care about dates and times but just want an alphabetical list of the files on the disk, this is useful for printing out a disk directory for a floppy disk in drive A:

```
dir a: /b /o
```

For a reverse alphabetical order list (Z to A), use

```
dir a: /o:-n
```

 **Want to see all the files on your hard disk?** Yes, you can do this at the command line, with

```
dir c:\ /s /a /w /p
```

Note that the /S (for subdirectories) has to come first. The /W and /P switches specify a wide listing and a pause after each screen of text. The /A switch tells DOS to show all the files, even hidden files. Files are shown directory by directory.

The command **chkdsk /v** will very rapidly show all the files on your hard disk.

Use **chkdsk /v | more** to see them one screen at a time.

 **Want to see all your hidden files?** To list all the hidden files on your disk, use this command:

```
dir \ /s /a:h
```

The \ says "start at the root," and the /S says "look in all subdirectories." The /a tells your computer to search file attributes and the :h specifies a search for the attribute "hidden."

**Want to see all the files in a directory in alphabetical order?** This combination works best for most folks:

```
dir /a /o:n /p
```

It displays all the files in a directory (including hidden and system files) in alphabetical order, and pauses after each screen of text.

**There are two ways to get alphabetical listings with DIR.** If you issue the DIR command as **dir /o:n**, you'll get a nice alphabetical listing—but your directories will be alphabetized with everything else, like this:

```
Volume in drive C has no label
Volume Serial Number is 171E-7B59
Directory of C:\WP51\DOCS
.            <DIR>           08-31-91      9:14a
..           <DIR>           08-31-91      9:14a
FIG4-2   TXT        443      09-01-91      8:14a
RPMSWAP  TMP    2162688      08-31-91      1:41p
VOODOO       <DIR>           08-31-91      9:14a
XENO         <DIR>           08-31-91      2:54p
         5 file(s)   2162688 bytes
                    29317120 bytes free
```

You won't be able to see all the subdirectories of a big directory on the screen at the same time. To see directories listed alphabetically first, before files, use DIR /O. It gives you a listing of all the directories together, as shown below:

```
Volume in drive C has no label
Volume Serial Number is 171E-7B59
Directory of C:\WP51\DOCS
.            <DIR>           08-31-91      9:14a
..           <DIR>           08-31-91      9:14a
VOODOO       <DIR>           08-31-91      9:14a
XENO         <DIR>           08-31-91      2:54p
FIG4-2   TXT        443      09-01-91      8:14a
RPMSWAP  TMP    2162688      08-31-91      1:41p
         6 file(s)   2163131 bytes
                    29315072 bytes free
```

**Use DIR to see if a file is in a directory.** If you're at the command line looking for a file, you know it can be pretty hard to find. If you've narrowed the search down to a directory or two, use **dir** *filename* to see if the file you're looking for is there. If it isn't, you'll get a "File not found" message.

**Find a file, any file, anywhere on your hard disk, in seconds, with one command.** You can use the /S switch with DIR to tell DOS to search the current directory and all its subdirectories. So,

## Chapter 4: Command-Line Tricks

to find any file whose name (or part of its name) you know, go to the root directory and use the DIR command with the /S switch. Say that you're looking for a file named AUG. At the command line, enter

```
dir aug /s
```

DOS will present a list of each occurrence of that file anywhere on your hard disk.

If you're not sure of the exact file name, use wildcards.
Entering

```
dir au* /s
```

will find all the files starting with AU followed by anything, such as AUGUST, AUGUST.TXT, AUG, AUTO, and so forth. This line will automatically find all the files with or without any extensions.

You can also use the ATTRIB command to find any file. To use it instead of DIR to find the files named AUG.TXT, enter the command this way:

```
attrib aug.txt /s
```

The difference between using ATTRIB and DIR is that with ATTRIB you get a compact listing of the path to each file that's been found, like this:

```
C:\WP51\AUG.TXT
C:\LOTUS\AUG.TXT
```

If you use the DIR command, DOS shows each listing separately, as though it were getting a directory listing of each directory. If a large number of files have the name you're looking for, use ATTRIB to get the more compact listing.

> ⚠ **The FIND command may not be what you think.** The FIND command lets you search through specified files to locate strings of text. Although it will locate file names, it's usually faster to use the Shell's Search feature because it lets you use wildcards.

For instance, if the file you're looking for has the phrase *Western Industrial* in it and is either in a file named OCT.RPT, NOV.RPT or DEC.RPT, use the FIND command:

```
find /i western industrial oct.rpt nov.rpt dec.rpt
```

(Since FIND is one of the very few commands in DOS where uppercase and lowercase count, the /I switch tells FIND to ignore case.)

FIND won't let you use wildcards, so you have to specify the files to search. You can also search a whole directory—but that can take a while.

**Finding files by date.** It's nice to use the FIND command, combined with the DIR command, to locate files that were created or modified on a certain date in the current directory. Issue it like this:

```
dir | find 2-16-93
```

**Combine sorting and finding.** You can use the DIR command (along with its switches) as well as the FIND command first to search for a certain category of files and then to locate files by date. Here's an example of how to search for all the files on your hard disk that have a .DOC extension and were created or modified on February 16, 1993:

```
dir c:\*.doc /s | find 2-16-93
```

## WILDCARD TIPS... & TRAPS

The wildcards * and ? are powerful shortcuts—but they can be misused. Wildcards aren't used exclusively at the command line; they also can be used in many dialog boxes in the Shell. Check out the following tricks and pitfalls.

**Use wildcards with DIR.** DIR is one of the commands that lets you use the wildcards * (for any number of characters or none at all) and ? (for any one character or, sometimes, none at all). For example, you can get a directory listing of all files ending in .DOC like this:

```
dir *.doc
```

You can see all the files that begin with REPORT, end with any other character and have the .DOC extension, like this:

```
dir report?.doc
```

You'd see this list if the files were in that directory:

```
report2.doc
report.doc
```

It's the "or none at all" part of the wildcard definition that can create confusion. For example, if you have files named TEST.TXT, TEST1.TXT and TEST2.TXT, enter either **dir test?.*** or **dir test*.*** to get the listing

```
test     .txt
test1    .txt
test2    .txt
```

Try it and see. But if you enter **????** (for what you *think* is four characters), you'll only get TEST.TEXT along with DOC.TXT, A.DOC, AB.TXT, ANY.TST and TEST (which are one, two, three and four characters, with and without extensions)!

Confused? Here's the way it works. If you put **?** at the beginning of or within a file name, it stands for just one character. But if you put it at the end of the file name (before the extension, if there is one), it acts like one character or no characters. Look at these examples:

**dir ????** produces

```
.           <DIR>
..          <DIR>
A           .TXT
AB          .TXT
ABC         .TXT
ABCD        .TXT
```

**dir ????.txt** produces

```
A           .TXT
AB          .TXT
ABC         .TXT
ABCD        .TXT
```

**dir ab??** produces

```
AB      .TXT
ABC     .TXT
ABCD    .TXT
```

So, as you can see, in some cases ? stands for no character at all.

**Use the wildcard ? with * to specify a pattern.** If you're copying a bunch of files in a directory that has files with names such as WK92.WK1, WK91.WK1, QT92.WK1 and QT89.WK1, and all you want to do is copy the ones that have "92" in their names, you'll find that **copy *92.*** gets you the same results as **copy *.*** Use **copy ??92.*** instead.

The command **copy ??92.*** will copy only files that have exactly four characters in their names—and "92" must be the last two characters. For example, it will copy TR92.DOC and XX92.TXT, but it won't copy OCT92.WK1 or 92Q1.TXT.

**With what commands can you use wildcards?** You can use wildcards with ATTRIB, BACKUP, COPY, CHKDSK, COMP, DEL, DELTREE, DIR, ERASE, PRINT, RECOVER (but don't!), REN, REPLACE, RESTORE and XCOPY.

**Understand the wildcard pattern before you use it.** Be sure to specify the whole wildcard pattern, including any extension. For example, *.* specifies an eight-character file name and a three-character extension. REPORT?.TXT specifies any file names up to seven characters long, beginning with REPORT and having a .TXT extension.

**Don't use wildcards to shorten names.** If you use wildcards to rename files, don't truncate the new names. In other words, keep the same number of characters in the name. Why? Consider this: you have files named TEXT.TXT, TEXT1.TXT and TEXT2.TXT. You issue

```
ren text?.* tex?.*
```

thinking you'll get TEX1.TXT, TEX2.TXT and so forth. But remember, wildcards can specify "no character at all." If you shorten names, you'll get a "Duplicate file name or file not found" message.

**Which is it, a duplicate file or a file not found?** It's one or the other. Either there's already a file with the new name in the directory or there's no file with the old name.

To find out which, do a DIR of the new name. If there's already a file by the new name, you'll see it.

**Be careful when copying with wildcards.** Say you want to copy all those TEXT*.* files to a directory named DOCS on a floppy disk in drive B. You issue this command:

```
copy text*.* b:docs
```

DOS lists all three of your TEXT*.* files; but if you look at the bottom of the listing, reports that it has copied only one file. This is what happened: no directory named DOCS existed on the disk in drive B, so each time a file was copied, it was given the name DOCS—and all you wound up with was the last file, TEXT2.TXT, as DOCS on drive B.

## SPECIAL SYMBOLS & COMMANDS

The "heavy" books call the special commands we're going to talk about here "redirection, pipes and filters." Knowing about these gives you DOS voodoo power.

**Use the Shell instead of MORE.** The commands MORE, SORT and FIND are all special commands, called *filters*, that let you process data. MORE lets you see text one screen at a time, but it's easier to do this in the Shell: simply press F9 and PgDn to see the contents of a file.

> **You can sort text files in DOS, but . . .** The SORT command will rearrange lines in a text file—alphabetically by the first character in each line, unless you specify otherwise. But it's awkward to use because you have to specify which column position to sort on. If you have a word processing or database program that will sort for you, try using that instead.
>
> Just for the record, though, here's an example of how to sort files in DOS. Suppose you have a simple client list called CLIENT.TXT, made up of your client's name, company and telephone number:
>
> | John    | Calhoun | Christie Sailboats  | (415)879-0111 |
> | Enrique | Lopez   | Fiesta Construction | (408)976-2201 |
> | Terry   | Berman  | Adtek, Inc.         | (415)493-5700 |
> | Matt    | Kim     | PageMaking          | (212)778-2387 |
>
> The SORT command **sort < client.txt** sorts this list alphabetically by the first letter in each line, like this:
>
> | Enrique | Lopez   | Fiesta Construction | (408)976-2201 |
> | John    | Calhoun | Christie Sailboats  | (415)879-0111 |
> | Matt    | Kim     | PageMaking          | (212)778-2387 |
> | Terry   | Berman  | Adtek, Inc.         | (415)493-5700 |
>
> You can also sort it by last name, company name or area code.
>
> To sort it by last name, count over to see which position the first letter of the last name is in. In this case, it's column 9. If you give the SORT command as **sort < client.txt /+9**, you'll get
>
> | Terry   | Berman  | Adtek, Inc.         | (415)493-5700 |
> | John    | Calhoun | Christie Sailboats  | (415)879-0111 |
> | Matt    | Kim     | PageMaking          | (212)778-2387 |
> | Enrique | Lopez   | Fiesta Construction | (408)976-2201 |
>
> It's still a pain, however, to figure out which column everything is in.

> **Redirection with < and > .** The > and < symbols redirect output from one place to another. Normally, what you type at the keyboard is displayed on the screen. However, you can also send the results of a command to your printer with the > symbol. For example, **dir > prn** sends a directory listing to your printer.

Another neat thing: redirection can send what you'd normally see on the screen to a file. The previous tip showed you how to sort an address list alphabetically. You can put the results of the sort—the alphabetic list—into another file in addition to just looking at it on the screen. DOS will create the file for you if it doesn't exist.

Say your address list is called CLIENT.DOC and you want to sort it and put the sorted list in a new file called LASTNAME.DOC. Do it this way:

```
sort < client.doc > lastname.doc
```

Notice that the first symbol is <. That means "take the input from." The > symbol means "put the output in." Your sorted file ends up as LASTNAME.DOC, and your original file, CLIENT.DOC, is still in its original order.

**Files zipping by? Pipe with |.** *Piping* is another way of directing data where you want it. The | command tells DOS to "take the output of this command and send it to one of the filter commands" (usually SORT or MORE).

You'll use piping with the MORE command most often. It causes the screen display to pause each time a screen full of text is presented (it sends the text to a temporary file, where it's filtered one screen at a time).

For example, suppose you want to read the contents of a pretty big README file. You'd normally use the TYPE command, but that makes the file zip by too fast to read. Use **type readme | more** instead, and you'll see it one screen at a time.

You can do the same thing with the DIR command. (This works just like the /P switch with DIR.) For example, if your directory listing is longer than one screen, you can see it one screen at a time with **dir | more**. Use MORE with TREE, too, to see your file structure one screen at a time.

## MOVING ON

With this command-line magic in your bag of tricks, it's time to move on to another basic area of DOS: working with disks and disk drives, something you do each day you turn on your computer.

# Chapter 5
# DISK & DRIVE MAGIC

Every time you turn on your computer, you work with disks and drives—you can't get away from it. Most programs you buy are supplied on floppy disks, unless you download them from an information service or electronic bulletin board. And floppy disks, like coat hangers and bunnies, are amazingly adept at arithmetic: they multiply like crazy.

Explore the magic you can work on your disks and drives.

## THE USUAL CAUTIONS & THEN SOME

You've probably read the usual floppy disk cautions many times before: don't spill coffee on them, keep them away from your three-year-old's sticky fingers and so forth. But some equipment generates hidden magnetic fields you may not be aware of. Do you store your floppy disks right next to your phone? When it rings, it generates a magnetic field. Do you have a modem? Its power converter generates a magnetic field, too. Do you have a stereo in your office with a speaker next to your disk storage box? That's another magnetic field. These magnetic fields can do much more harm to your disks than the X-rays at the airport (in fact, X-rays don't hurt your disks at all, but they will mess up the film in your camera).

Don't put paper clips on disks or write on them with ballpoint pens or rip old labels off them violently, either. But do move them away from the telephone.

## FORMATTING DISKS

Don't you hate to format disks? It's so mindless. You can buy preformatted disks, but they're expensive. I buy mine in bulk, unformatted, for about a quarter each (for the 360k 5.25-inch kind) and try to format as many of them as I can in one sitting, while I'm doing something else, like reading a book.

Here are some charms to help relieve the formatting tedium.

**Don't format regular-density disks in a high-density disk drive without special switches.** You can format a low- or regular-density (360k or 720k) disk in a high-density disk drive, but don't do it unless you use the parameters that tell DOS what kind of disk you're using (see the next tip). You'll have problems later, and you may lose what you store on that disk.

Don't try to format a high-density 1.2mb (5.25-inch) or 1.44mb (3.5-inch) disk as a lower density disk, either. It may look like everything's working fine, but you can have trouble later.

**How to format 360k and 720k disks in high-density drives.** If you have a high-density (1.44mb) 3.5-inch disk drive but find yourself often having to format regular-density (720k) disks, write a batch file that will specify the parameters. The batch file, which I always forget, is **format b:/f:720**. (Drive B is my 3.5-inch drive.) Name it something easy to remember, like F720.BAT.

You can do the same thing for your 5.25-inch disk drive and your low-density 360k floppies. That batch file is **format a:/f:360** if drive A is your 5.25-inch drive.

You can put these commands as program items in your Disk Utilities group in the Shell. See the section called "Using the Disk Utilities," later in this chapter.

**Checking a disk's capacity.** Boy, is this a common problem! You want to reformat a disk to use again, but the original label has been removed and now there's a handwritten label on it. *What capacity is it?* If it's a low-density 360k disk and you have a high-density 1.2mb disk drive, you'll need to use the special switches mentioned in the previous tip to format the disk in the right capacity. DOS will check the disk's capacity before it starts formatting, but it will only tell you the "Existing format differs from that specified"; then it will go ahead and try to format the 360k disk as a 1.2mb disk (or the 720k disk as a 1.44mb disk).

Here's how to determine a disk's capacity. Put the disk in drive A and click on the drive A icon (in the Shell), or do a **dir a:** from the command line. Anything with a total of 360,640 bytes on it (or thereabouts) is a low-density 360k disk; anything with 1,228,800 bytes is a high-density (1.2mb) disk.

If you're using 3.5-inch disks, there's no problem. The 1.44mb (high-density) disks have *two square holes*; the 720k (regular-density) disks have only one.

**How to tell regular-density and high-density 5.25-inch disks at a glance.** Regular-density 5.25-inch disks have a slightly raised plastic hub ring, sometimes colored, in the center; high-density 5.25-inch floppies don't.
*Thanks to Dennis McMahon, Boiling Springs, PA, for this tip!*

**DOS will format your disks in the highest capacity it can.** DOS automatically formats your floppy disks in the highest capacity your disk drive can handle, unless you provide parameters by using switches with the FORMAT command (see the previous trap).

If you're reformatting a disk, DOS will check the disk's format. You may *think* DOS will format it in the same capacity, but it won't: it will go right ahead and format it as a higher density disk if it can—and if you haven't specified those switches.

If you're not sure what capacity the drive is, just let the formatting begin. You'll see something like "Formatting 1.2mb" if it's formatting in a high-density 5.25-inch drive. Press Ctrl-C to cancel the formatting if you've just put a 360k disk in there, and format it with **format a:/f:360** (if you're using drive A).

**How can you tell when a disk needs to be formatted?** If you get a "General failure" message after DOS reads drive A or B, it means that the disk in the drive hasn't been formatted yet. That message always scares me. My immediate reaction is that something terrible is wrong with the disk drive. Wish Microsoft would change that.

**Label your formatted disks.** I often find as I'm formatting disks that there are two piles of disks on my desk: one pile to be formatted, and one pile that has been formatted. There's no way to tell the "done" disks from the undone disks.

Put a new paper label on disks you've formatted; or make a tiny check mark on the label if the disk already has one; or scratch out the writing on a handwritten label; or do something to indicate the disk is formatted and ready to use. Otherwise, you may wind up reformatting disks that don't need it.

**Do a Quick Format on used disks.** Starting with DOS 5, there's a command called Quick Format (in the Shell's Disk Utilities). Its equivalent at the command line is **format /q**. Use it on disks that have already been formatted. It's a lot faster than a regular format, and you can recycle used disks quickly.

**What quick formatting does.** If you're interested in how quick formatting works and how it can accomplish so much so quickly, here's the secret: it erases the disk's file allocation table (FAT) and its root directory. It leaves the formatted tracks and sectors alone.

**The absolutely fastest way to format.** For the fastest way to format used disks, start from the command line, not from the Shell (which will just take you out to the command line when you format, anyway). Then give the command as

```
format a: /q /u
```

This does an unconditional Quick Format on the disk in drive A, and boy, is it fast!

When you format with the /U switch, DOS does an unconditional format, which means that you can't unformat the disk with the UNFORMAT command. Normally, DOS 5 will save information about what's on the disk so that you can unformat it if you decide later that you formatted it by mistake. But brand-new disks don't have any information on them, so it's always safe to unconditionally format them.

One more fine point: if you specify a capacity for a disk (with one of those /f:*size* switches), the disk will be unconditionally formatted. You can recycle used disks very, very quickly this way, but you won't be able to unformat them later.

**Sneaky format trick.** If a child who can read has access to your computer, you may worry about the unauthorized formatting of disks you've stored valuable data on. A sneaky way to prevent this is to rename or password-protect the Format option in the Disk Utilities group (see Chapter 3, "Working With Programs," for details about how to do this).

This works for larger children, too, like those over 21.

**What use is an electronic label?** When you format a disk, DOS asks you if you want to add a label to it. You can use up to 11 characters, including spaces, so your disk names can be much more meaningful than your file names.

I've never found much use for labeling disks this way. It's much more important to put a paper label on the outside of the disk. But different people like different things.

If you don't label a disk when you format it and you decide later that it would be a good idea, just issue the LABEL command and the drive letter, like this:

```
label a:
```

You'll be prompted for a label.

**Making a system disk.** To format a disk that has the DOS system files on it as a startup disk, issue the FORMAT command (for a disk in drive A) as

```
format a: /s
```

Use the SYS command to do this on a disk (in drive B) that's already been formatted:

```
sys b:
```

Although you can start your computer with a disk that has only the bare-bones system files on it, put your AUTOEXEC.BAT and CONFIG.SYS files on it, too, to make sure your machine will start in the normal way.

You may also want to put CHKDSK.EXE and a few of the more essential DOS commands on it. That way, if it turns out there's something wrong with your hard disk, you can check it out. See the tip for doing a minimal DOS installation in Chapter 1, "Beyond Magic," for some suggestions about which DOS commands might be of use.

**What are unconditional formats?** If you initially format a disk with the /U switch, DOS does an unconditional format, which means the disk can't be unformatted with the UNFORMAT command. Normally, whether you're doing a quick format or a regular format, DOS will save information about what's on the disk so you can unformat it.

But brand-new disks don't have any information on them, so they're always unconditionally formatted.

Also, a disk is unconditionally formatted if you specify its capacity with the /F:*size* switch.

**If you want to unformat a disk, do it now.** Once you've written data onto a reformatted disk, you may not be able to get back all the files that were originally on it, because they'll have been written over. So if you think you've formatted a disk by mistake, unformat it *now*, before you use it.

**How to unformat a floppy disk.** The UNFORMAT command isn't in the Shell's Disk Utilities group (unless you added it, which might be a good idea if you use it often). Run it from the command line. If the disk you want to unformat is in drive A, enter

```
unformat a:
```

You may get some bewildering messages as you unformat. Here's a little background and explanation of what's on the screen.

The UNFORMAT utility was originally called REBUILD when it was part of PC Tools, so "rebuilding" is the same as "unformatting." You'll see both words used interchangeably. The utility looks for a mirror, or deletion-tracking, file that contains information about the files you've created. If you've never used the MIRROR command before, there won't be any mirror file, so you can save time by not letting the utility search your hard disk for one (which can take a while).

Even if you don't have a mirror file, in most cases the UNFORMAT utility will be able to rebuild the disk anyway, so don't worry. At least try it and see. You don't have much to lose if you've reformatted the disk by mistake and really need those files back.

There are two steps to the process: first, the utility searches for information about the files that were previously on the disk; then it writes those files back onto the disk (with your permission, of course).

DOS 6 doesn't use the MIRROR command, so it's a bit less confusing to do an UNFORMAT. In either case, you either will or won't be able to recover the files that were on the disk, and the sooner you unformat, the better. As you use the disk and add new files to it, the chances of recovering anything become fewer and fewer.

**Make a deletion-tracking file in case you need to unformat a disk.** Telling DOS 5 to automatically keep track of your file information so you can get those files back is very simple. Just put this line in your AUTOEXEC.BAT file:

```
mirror c: /ta /tc
```

This sets up a deletion-tracking file for drives A and C. If you have a drive B or a drive D and so on, add /TB or /TD switches to the line.

**You can usually restore lost partitions with UNFORMAT.** If you have divided your hard disk into partitions, such as drive D or drive E, you may someday see the dread message "Invalid drive specification." This means that DOS can't find your logical drive.

However, if you're running DOS 5 (DOS 6 doesn't contain MIRROR, which is too bad, because this is a neat trick) and you've had the foresight to copy your partitioning information onto a floppy disk, you can get your logical drive back. To do this, issue the command

```
mirror /partn
```

You'll be prompted for a floppy disk. Make it a system disk so you can use it as a bootable floppy disk if a catastrophe happens. Then copy UNFORMAT.EXE onto it. Label it and keep it safe somewhere away from your hard disk, on the chance that if disaster strikes your hard disk, it might also strike the box of floppies next to it.

Then, if you ever need it, use the command

```
unformat /partn
```

You'll need to insert the floppy disk with the partitioning information on it. After UNFORMAT is done, restart your computer and run UNFORMAT *again* to restore your files.

Sound complicated? It beats losing a drive and everything on it.

*Caution*: You won't be able to do this if your hard disk has been formatted with third-party partitioning software.

**See a list of files before you rebuild a disk.** You can use the UNFORMAT command with the /L switch to see a list of disk files. That way, you can decide whether you need them.

**UNFORMAT can save your hard disk, too.** Even if you haven't partitioned your hard disk into smaller logical drives, you can use the previous tip. Your entire hard disk (drive C) is really just one giant partition. Make yourself a mirror partition file on a floppy so you can rebuild your hard disk if you ever have to.

## TRICKS FOR UNDELETING FILES

Starting with DOS 5, you can undelete files you erased by mistake. The trick is to do it right away, before your deleted files get written over.

Here's how it works. When a file is deleted, it isn't really removed from a disk. DOS just changes the first character in its name and doesn't regard it as a file any more. It will write over the space the file occupies as soon as it gets a chance. So undelete as soon as you realize you want your file back.

The undelete methods for DOS 5 and 6 are a little different because DOS 6 added new, more reliable features. It kept the standard DOS 5 way of undeleting, but that's the least safe way to undelete in DOS 6. If you are running DOS 6, use the new features described in the following tricks. Starting with the trick "You don't have to know a file's name to undelete it," we'll be discussing the old way to undelete, which is called "standard" in DOS 6.

**Delete Sentry or Delete Tracker replace DOS 5's MIRROR command.** If you've got a MIRROR line that was left in your AUTOEXEC.BAT from DOS 5, you can take it out. With DOS 6's delete protection, that command is no longer used. If you set up deletion protection during setup, DOS will automatically put a REM at the beginning of that line to disable it. If you edit your AUTOEXEC.BAT later to set up delete protection, take the MIRROR line out yourself.

**Starting up deletion protection.** When you installed DOS 6, you decided whether to install Microsoft Undelete for DOS, Windows, or both. If you don't do anything else, DOS 6 uses "standard" deletion protection, which is the least safe of all. There are two higher levels of delete protection you can use—Delete Sentry (the safest) and Delete Tracker, which is safer than the "standard" method—but DOS won't use them unless you tell it to.

The safest thing to do is put this line in your AUTOEXEC.BAT file:

```
undelete /s
```

This sets up Delete Sentry protection that's on all the time.

The second safest thing to do is to use this line, for Delete Tracker, in your AUTOEXEC.BAT:

```
undelete /t
```

See the tip "What's the difference between Delete Sentry and Delete Tracker?" for details.

If you want to run Delete Sentry or Delete Tracker interactively from the command line so that it starts only when you tell it to, enter the command this way:

```
undelete /sc
```

or

```
undelete /tc
```

for Sentry or Tracker, respectively, on drive C.

**So what happened to just plain UNDELETE in DOS 6?** It's still there, too, but the Delete Sentry or Delete Tracker methods are safer. When you type **undelete** and press Enter, DOS 6 assumes you want to use Delete Sentry, if it's available, or Delete Tracker, if Delete Sentry isn't available. If you haven't set up either one of these, you can use the "MS-DOS directory" method of undeleting a file.

If delete Sentry or Delete Tracker are in effect, DOS prompts you, file by file, whether you want to undelete all the files that have been deleted from the current directory (unfortunately, you may still have to guess what the first letter of a file's name was; see the tip "You don't have to know a file's name to undelete it," elsewhere in this chapter). If you haven't set up Delete Tracker or Delete Sentry, DOS will report that it's using the "MS-DOS directory" method, and you may still be able to get a file back. Enter

```
undelete /dos
```

at the command line (just plain UNDELETE works too, but the safest route is to follow Microsoft protocol). Using UNDELETE this way works just like it always did, and the things it can't undelete are the same (see "UNDELETE can't undelete some things").

**6. Use the Windows Undelete utility if you have Windows on your computer.** When you install DOS 6, setup will detect whether your computer has Microsoft Windows. If it does, the setup program will fix you up with a Microsoft Tools group that includes an Undelete utility with a few more options than the DOS command-line version. If you've got that utility, try it first instead of the command-line version. The command-line version is a little more powerful, but the Windows version is easier to use.

Files that you undelete can be in either Perfect, Excellent, Good, Poor or Destroyed condition. If a file's reported as Destroyed or Poor, forget it. (You can't undelete Poor files with the Windows Undelete facility anyway; you'll have to use the DOS utility, but why bother. Destroyed files are history.)

If you need to undelete a file that's reported as in Good condition, part of the disk space it uses is being used by another file. If you have the Windows version of Undelete on your computer, use it to recover files in Good condition because you can undelete them to a different drive or directory by choosing Undelete To from the Microsoft Tools Undelete utility's File menu (see Figure 5-1 ).

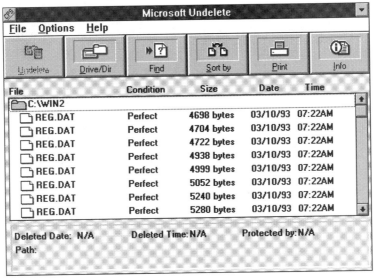

*Figure 5-1:* Using Windows' Undelete utility.

### What's the difference between Delete Sentry and Delete Tracker?

If you use the Delete Sentry method, you can be just about 100% secure that you can get back a deleted file. With Delete Tracker, only the names and cluster locations of files you delete are saved—and only a certain number of those are saved, depending on the size of the disk you're using. You can almost always get back a deleted file with Delete Tracker if you haven't saved any other files after you delete the file. So the trick to using Delete Tracker effectively is always to ask yourself immediately after you delete a file if you're sure you don't want that file.

Using Delete Sentry means that you have to devote part of your hard disk's space for holding the files you want to be able to undelete. (If you think you don't want to give up disk space, just remember all the hard disk space you'll reclaim with DOS 6's disk-compression utility.) Delete Sentry creates a hidden directory named C:\SENTRY that holds all the files you delete. When you delete a file, it's simply moved to the C:\SENTRY directory.

Delete Sentry will save not only the files you delete but also the files your programs delete, such as automatic .BAK files that programs like WordPerfect make and then delete and temporary files other programs make and then delete later.

About seven percent of your disk space will be devoted to the C:\SENTRY directory. When that directory fills up, Delete Sentry starts really deleting the oldest files.

When you set up DOS 6, you'll be asked whether you want either of these deletion-protection methods put in your AUTOEXEC.BAT so that it will always monitor deleted files. You can add these methods then or set up one of them later. See the tip "Starting up deletion protection" earlier in this chapter.

### Delete Sentry magic: You really can't see that hidden directory.

If you want to see how Sentry stores your deleted files, type **cd\sentry**, then enter **dir**. This will give you a listing of all the saved files Sentry is holding, but you won't recognize any of them, since their names are changed to Sentry's coded names.

**If you leave your computer on all the time, your SENTRY directory can fill up.** If you're the sort of person who leaves your computer running day and night, your SENTRY directory can fill up with deleted files. This happens because Delete Sentry checks the system date only when your computer starts. If there are no new dates, no purging takes place, and the directory fills up. To avoid this mess, turn off the computer every so often. Or purge your SENTRY directory manually; issue **help undelete** to see how.

**You don't have to know a file's name to undelete it.** If you want to undelete a file and haven't set up a deletion-tracking method, you'll need to supply the first letter in the file's name (sort of like "If you can guess it, you can have it"). If you don't recall the first character, type any character that will create a file with a name that doesn't already exist in the current direc-tory. For example, if you type $ and the name of the deleted file was TEXT, its restored name will be $EXT.

**Use the /DOS switch if you can't undelete.** Sometimes you may get a message saying that no files were found to undelete. If this happens, try using the command **undelete a: /dos** (to recover the files on a floppy disk in drive A). This tells DOS to ignore whatever is in the deletion-tracking file and to recover files it has listed as deleted.

**Get a list of deleted files first.** Instead of undeleting everything you deleted, get a list of what's been erased by using the following command:

    undelete a: /list

You can use **undelete /dt /list** to see what files are in the deletion-tracking file. The command **undelete /dos /list** will show you the files DOS lists as deleted.

**For best results, set up a deletion-tracking file.** DOS 5 uses the same deletion-tracking file you set up for unformatting disks to keep track of files you've deleted. This makes it an even better idea to put the **mirror c: /ta /tc** line in your AUTOEXEC.BAT file (see "Make a deletion-tracking file in case you need to unformat a disk," earlier in this chapter). With DOS 6, use Delete Sentry or Delete Tracker (see the tip "Starting up deletion protection" earlier in this chapter).

**You can use wildcards with UNDELETE.** If you want to undelete a group of files that have similar names but ignore the rest of the deleted files on the disk or in the directory, you can use the * and ? wildcards. For example,

    undelete b: *.DOC

will undelete all the files on the disk in drive B that have the .DOC extension.

**UNDELETE can't undelete some things.** The DOS UNDELETE command can't undelete a file if you've saved another file with the same name over it.

You can't undelete a directory you removed after deleting all the files in it; and you can't undelete any files in a deleted directory, either. And if you've formatted a disk, UNDELETE doesn't work unless you UNFORMAT first and then UNDELETE.

**If you need to undelete a directory, use Windows Undelete.** If you delete a directory and all the files in it by mistake (which can be easy to do with the new DELTREE command), you might be able to get it back with the Windows Undelete utility. If you've done anything that involves writing to disk, something else may be using that space, so the trick is to try to undelete the directory as soon as you discover you deleted it by mistake. You can't undelete a directory in DOS.

## MISCELLANEOUS DISK TRICKS

The following wizardry defies categorization. We'll take a look at some hot new DOS 6 tips first.

**You saw in Chapter 1 that a neat new disk-compression program comes with DOS 6.** If you didn't install them during setup, you can install them later. Just be sure to turn off any memory-resident programs (including Windows or the Shell) before running DoubleSpace. This rule is important! If you're running programs, they may conflict with the work of this utility, and you'll wind up with a mess of bits of files in places on your hard disk.

**Some third-party defragmentation programs aren't compatible with DoubleSpace, and some disk utilities aren't, either.** If you're having trouble because you've compressed your disk with a different compression program and you want to switch to Double-Space, read that README.TXT file that's in your DOS directory. It has instructions for getting around all kinds of problems that you may run into. It also tells you about ways to get out of trouble if you're using utilities such as Norton Utilities or PC Tools.

**Before you defragment or compress your disk, do a little house-cleaning first.** It's always a good idea to back up any files you haven't already backed up before you optimize (defragment) your disk or compress it. After you've backed up or copied essential files, delete all unnecessary files (see the tips about that later in this chapter). Then undelete any files you deleted by mistake! (After you defragment your disk, you won't be able to undelete.) Then defragment your hard disk with DEFRAG if you're not using DoubleSpace. If you're using DoubleSpace, use this command:

```
dblspace /defrag.
```

**You can defragment a compressed drive, too.** DoubleSpace has a Defragment command that you can use to defragment a drive that's been compressed. This approach works a little differently from defragmenting an uncompressed drive, which you do with the DEFRAG command. When you defragment a DoubleSpaced drive, all the data is put at the beginning of the volume and all the space is at the end, but files aren't reorganized so that they're next to each other. You won't gain any disk access speed, but you will gain disk space.

You can run DoubleSpace and Defragment at the command line this way:

```
dblspace /defrag
```

How often should you defragment a disk? Once every couple of months is enough, unless you're a really heavy user. In that case, do it monthly.

**An undocumented switch for defragmenting drives!** You can have DEFRAG defragment your compressed drive. It will automatically start DoubleSpace. To do this, use the (undocumented, as far as I can tell) /Q switch with DEFRAG.

First, do a CHKDSK with the /F switch. Then use this command:

```
DEFRAG /Q /H
```

The /H switch says "move hidden files." As to exactly what the /Q switch does, your guess is as good as mine, but it degragments your compressed drive.

**Compress your floppy disks, too.** DoubleSpace can compress floppy disks, which increases their capacity tremendously. Instead of running a compression program like PKZIP on each file that you want to compress, run DoubleSpace on your floppies. You can use them almost exactly as before, except that they'll hold much, much more. For example, I do a lot of TIFF (Tagged Image File Format) screen dumps, and those files are huge. Using compression on them really saves space because there are a lot of blank spaces in graphics files that can be represented much more compactly than in normal format.

Here's how to compress a floppy disk and use it after it's been compressed. You'll need formatted disks, and you can use disks that have data already on them. The disk may be compressed, not erased. But don't use a disk that's already completely full; it needs to have about .65mb of free space on it. So you can't compress 360k 5.25-inch disks because they're too small to start with.

With the formatted floppy on the drive, start DoubleSpace by typing **dblspace** at the DOS prompt. Choose Existing Drive from the

Compress menu, pick the drive the floppy's in and type **c** for Compress. Then wait while the file gets compressed.

A couple of things to note about the process: if DoubleSpace does not "see" your floppy drive, use the Tools menu and choose Options. Add another letter to the list of drives DoubleSpace knows about. After you do that, DoubleSpace will ask you if you want to restart your computer so the changes can take effect; let it restart.

Also, don't panic when you see the message that "drive" B (or A) will be compressed and that once a drive is compressed, it can't be uncompressed. All that's going to happen is that the disk in the drive will be compressed. You can keep on using regular floppy disks in that drive.

DoubleSpace will run CHKDSK on the disk and then report that it will take a relatively short time to compress the disk, about a minute. Don't believe it. Compression will take longer, so go get a cup of coffee or something.

After the disk has been compressed, it's *mounted* (see the next tip) and ready to use.

**To use a compressed floppy disk, you have to mount it first.**
Here's where using compressed floppies is a little different from using regular uncompressed floppies; you have to *mount* the disk first—in other words, use a command that lets DOS read what's on the disk. If a floppy disk hasn't been mounted and you do a DIR on it, all DOS will see is a file named READTHIS.TXT and another file, called DBLSPACE.BIN, that keeps track of where the compressed files are. (If you read the READTHIS.TXT file, it tells you that you need to mount the disk.)

To mount a floppy disk in drive A, type **a:** and press Enter to change to drive A. Then type **dblspace /mount** and press Enter. (You can also give the command in the form **dblspace /mount a:**.) You'll see a message when the disk is mounted, and you can use it just as you would a regular disk. The only difference is that if you restart your computer and put the same floppy disk back in the drive or, without restarting, put a different *compressed* disk in the same floppy drive, you'll have to mount that disk.

You can put a regular floppy disk in the drive, and DOS can read it without your doing anything extra.

**Put DBLSPACE /MOUNT B: in your AUTOEXEC.BAT.** If you usually leave a compressed data disk in drive B, put a **dblspace /mount b:** line in your AUTOEXEC.BAT file so that DOS will mount the disk each time you start your computer.

**You can't transfer files via compressed floppy disks to another computer unless it's running DoubleSpace, too.** If you're planning to exchange data with other people who may not have DOS 6 and DoubleSpace, don't compress your floppies.

**Removing DoubleSpace.** Here's one way—see the README.TXT file in your DOS directory for the other.

Back up all your files to an uncompressed drive. Be sure to back up your backup program, too. If you're backing up with MSBACKUP, those files are MSB*.* plus DEFAULT.SET.

At the command prompt, type **dblspace /list**. Your uncompressed drive's name is listed under CVF Filename. Copy COMMAND.COM from your compressed drive to it. Make sure your uncompressed drive is current (type **c:** in this example). Change to its root directory with **cd \**. To delete your compressed drive, type **deltree dblspace.000**. (Use the CVF name of your drive; to delete all of them, **deltree dblspace.***).

Restart your computer and restore your backed-up files. If you've backed up to floppy disks, copy your backup program files onto your hard disk and then run the backup from the hard disk.

**Virus ALERT!** If your computer suddenly slows down or you start seeing error messages that you've never seen before, you may have a virus. DOS 6 comes with an anti-virus program (VSAFE) that can constantly monitor your system for you, or you can choose to use a variation on that program (MSAV) that will only run when you tell it to. Use them.

**Keep a clean startup floppy on hand.** Just in case of virus damage, keep a floppy disk on hand that you can use to start your computer if everything locks up on you (but this shouldn't ever happen to you if you keep VSAFE running as a TSR). See the instructions in Chapter 10 for how to make a startup floppy. Also copy the

MSAV.EXE program from your hard disk onto this startup floppy (it takes up about 16k of space). To make sure that this emergency disk doesn't get infected, too, write-protect the disk after you've made it. (Open the hole of a 3.5-inch disk; cover the tab of a 5.25-inch disk.)

Now start your computer from the bootable floppy. Then run MSAV and scan your hard disk. But don't stop after your hard disk is working again. Scan all your floppies, starting with the ones you used most recently. They may have the virus on them. If you have a tape backup, be aware that it may be infected, too. Restore it onto your hard disk and scan those files, too, or reformat your backup tape so that you won't be tempted to restore from it.

**The best protection from a virus is to run VSAFE as a TSR from your AUTOEXEC.BAT.** VSAFE constantly scans for viruses if you put it in your AUTOEXEC.BAT, where it will run as a TSR that takes about 22k of memory. If you install programs frequently, download files from information utilities or accept floppy disks from other users, your best bet is to keep VSAFE on all the time by putting it in your AUTOEXEC.BAT. Put this command in your AUTOEXEC.BAT file:

```
vsafe
```

**As long as you're using VSAFE, tell it to do what you want it to.**
You can use several switches with VSAFE. By default, four of them are on:

1   Checks for viruses that can erase your hard disk
4   Checks executable files for viruses
5   Checks boot sectors of all disks for anything that tries to write to them
6   Checks for anything that tries to write to the boot sector of your hard disk

There are four more options you can use:

8   Checks for anything that tries to modify executable files
2   Checks for attempts to stay in memory
3   Checks for anything that tries to write to disk
7   Checks for anything that tries to write to a floppy's boot sector

To see which options are in effect, go to the command line and press Alt-V. Then turn on off any options that you want by typing the number next to them.

This procedure will run VSAFE with the options you've chosen *for the current session only*. If you want it to run in the background all the time, put VSAFE in your AUTOEXEC.BAT.

Use + or - to turn a switch on and off. For example, if you want VSAFE to check for changes made to executable files (a particularly nasty type of virus), you'd enter the line in your AUTOEXEC.BAT this way:

```
vsafe /+8
```

If you're running Windows, drag the Vsafe Manager icon to your StartUp Group to use it as a TSR. That way, you'll be sure to pick up any error messages VSAFE generates while you're running Windows.

**Turn off VSAFE before installing Windows.** If you have a VSAFE line in your AUTOEXEC.BAT, edit that line to begin with REM before you install Microsoft Windows; then save AUTOEXEC.BAT, restart your computer and install Windows. After you're done, go back and take the REM out and save your AUTOEXEC.BAT. Then edit WIN.INI (it should be in your C:\WINDOWS directory) to add this line:

```
load=mwavtsr.exe
```

If you don't, you may not be able to see virus warnings while you're running Windows.

**Hot key conflict? Reset VSAFE's hot key.** You can change VSAFE's default hot key, Alt-V, to Alt plus another letter or Ctrl plus another letter if you already have a TSR that uses Alt-V. (How will you know? When you press Alt-V, VSAFE won't start.) In your AUTOEXEC.BAT, locate the VSAFE line and add one of these switches to the end of it: **/ax** for an Alt key combination or **/cx** for a Ctrl key combination (where *x* is the letter of the key you want to use). For example, to change the hot key to Alt-Y, you'd enter **/ay**.

## Chapter 5: Disk & Drive Magic    131

**"Out of memory" messages? Take VSAFE out of memory.** If you're getting "Out of memory" messages, you can free up about 22k of RAM by removing VSAFE from memory. Type **vsafe /u** at the command line, or press Alt-U at the command line to use the default hot key. If you have VSAFE in your AUTOEXEC.BAT, it will come back on the next time you start your computer, or you can type **autoexec** at the command line to rerun your AUTOEXEC.BAT without turning off the computer, once you've finished with the program that needs so much memory.

**Running MSAV.** The difference between DOS 6's MSAV and VSAFE is that MSAV runs only on startup (if it's in your AUTOEXEC.BAT), but VSAFE runs all the time. To run MSAV "manually"—whenever you want to, enter **msav** at the command line. You'll see the screen shown in Figure 5-2.

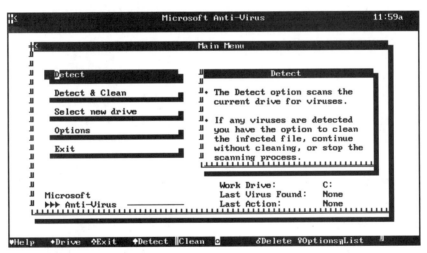

*Figure 5-2:* The MSAV main screen.

Choose Options from the MSAV main menu to set different options for MSAV (see Figure 5-3). The next few tricks explain how some of these options work.

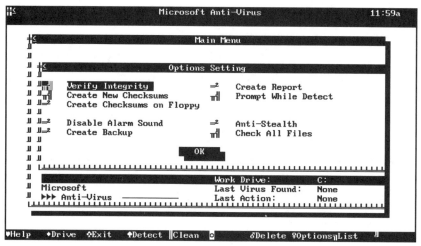

*Figure 5-3:* Setting MSAV's options.

**You can put MSAV in your AUTOEXEC.BAT, too.** MSAV will scan your memory and drives each time you start your computer if you add this line to your AUTOEXEC.BAT file:

    msav /n

If you're on a network, use this form of the command so that MSAV will scan only local drives, not your network drives:

    msav /n /l

**Stealth viruses are a horse of another color.** One particularly nasty type of virus is called a *stealth* virus—that's a generic term, not a specific virus name like Number of the Beast or Bad Boy. Stealth viruses infect files without seeming to change them, so they're harder to detect. To make sure you check for viruses of this type, use the Anti-Stealth option in MSAV. It makes the program run just a bit slower, so it's off by default. Run this option from time to time, just to make sure, especially if you've gotten a bunch of new files from a friend of a friend.

**Checking for unknown viruses.** Of course, no anti-virus program can be *completely* up-to-date, so Microsoft Anti-Virus provides a way to check for viruses it doesn't know about. This involves checking files on the basis of statistics it keeps about them and then checking to see if those statistics change. To keep this kind of protection going, keep the Verify Integrity and Checksum options in effect.

If the Verify Integrity and Checksum options are in effect, MSAV will stop if it detects a file that's been changed since the last time you checked for viruses. If you know the change is OK, (because you installed a new version of the program, for example), choose Update so you won't be bothered the next time you scan your hard disk. One way to tell is to look at the Checksum value, which shows what the checksum was before and what it's been changed to. If those two numbers don't match (they're in hexadecimal format, so don't worry if they look weird), you may have a virus. The safest thing to do is delete that file and reinstall it from the original program disk. Check that disk for viruses first!

**Keep your virus list up-to-date.** New viruses are being created all the time. Every couple of months or so (more frequently if you hear of a virus scare), call Central Point Software's hot line and get your virus list updated so that DOS's anti-virus programs can check for the latest viruses. That number is 503/690-2660 for a human being and 503/690-6650 for the electronic bulletin board, where you can download the latest files via modem.

To see the list of viruses that you're protected against, press F9 when you're at MSAV's main screen, then, to see details about what a particular virus you've selected does, including what its side effects are, click the info button. This may help you decide whether you have a virus or not, depending on the effects of that particular virus.

If you're running Microsoft Anti-Virus from Windows, choose Virus List from the Scan menu to see the viruses you're protected against.

**Get lots of "Help" on the anti-virus program.** Microsoft licensed MSAV and VSAFE from Central Point Software, and MSAV has its own Help system as well as the regular help you can get in DOS 6 by typing **help msav** or **fasthelp msav** at the command line. When you see the MSAV main screen, choose Help (F1). Press F8 for the next Help topic or F7 to see the previous one. Pressing F3 exits Help and takes you back to the main screen.

**Reboot after cleaning up viruses!** If you run MSAV to check for viruses and it caught any, restart your computer after it's done, to make sure any viruses it found are cleaned from memory.

**Running Windows? Check for viruses from there.** DOS 6 checks during setup to see whether you have Windows on your system and asks you whether you want to install the Windows versions of Microsoft Anti-Virus, Undelete and Backup if it detects Windows. (You can install both the Windows and DOS versions if you want to and if you have enough room on your hard disk.) The Windows version of Microsoft Anti-Virus has other capabilities than the DOS version, as you might expect, since Windows is a graphical interface. For example, it lets you drag and drop files in the File Manager to scan them before copying them to your hard disk, and the dialog boxes are more ex-planatory. If you have Windows, use its version of Microsoft Anti-Virus.

**Microsoft Anti-Virus may call new programs "viruses."** When you upgrade to a new version of a program, you obviously have to change executable files and sometimes the filing system on your hard disk. Upgrade installation programs may also try to change your AUTOEXEC.BAT, CONFIG.SYS and file system. It can be very annoying to get virus alerts when all you're trying to do is install a new program or a new version of an old program.

To avoid unwanted scares, scan floppy disks before you copy files from them or install programs from them—even programs that came in shrink wrap from the manufacturer! (I got a virus once on one of these; it can happen to you.)

After you've scanned the program's floppies, write-protect them. *Then* install or upgrade the program. Finally, scan your hard drive to update the checklist of files that the anti-virus program maintains.

**DOS 6 has new features that you can use with laptop computers.** Two hot new DOS 6 commands—INTERLNK and POWER—are designed for use with laptops. The INTERLNK program lets you control your desktop computer from your laptop so it's easy to transfer files from one to the other, and the POWER command conserves your laptop's battery power when it's idle.

You'll need a serial or parallel cable connected to the appropriate port on both computers before you can use INTERLNK.EXE. You'll also need to put a DEVICE=INTERLNK.EXE statement in your CONFIG.SYS (ditto for POWER.EXE, if you want to use that one, too), along with any options you may want to use. As there are many different types of laptops with all sorts of requirements out there, I'll leave it to you to get help on INTERLNK and POWER. Just type **help interlnk** or **help power** at the command line.

**Lock a disk and its contents can't be changed.** It's a very good idea to lock program disks, as well as disks that contain important information such as budgets or salary projections, to ensure they won't be erased or overwritten.

To write-protect a 5.25-inch disk, *cover* the write-protect notch on the side of the disk, so no light can shine through.

To write-protect a 3.5-inch disk, *open* the write-protect slot.

**Another way to hide a file.** You learned in Chapter 2, "Shell Secrets," how to hide a file so it doesn't appear in directory listings, and how to make a file read-only so it can't be changed. Here's a little spell to fix a file so nobody knows its name, even though information about it shows up in directory listings.

You type extended ASCII characters by holding down the Alt key and using the numeric keypad on your keyboard. The extended ASCII character 255 stands for a blank; if you name files with it, their size and date will show up, but their names will be invisible!

Here's an example. Say you have a file named DOC1. At the command line, issue the command **ren doc1 255**. (You get the 255 by holding down the Alt key, typing **255** on the numeric keypad and releasing the Alt key.) After you use this command, DOC1's name becomes invisible when you get a directory listing. (Try it and see.)

If you've used one blank for a file name, you can use two blanks (255 255), three blanks (255 255 255) and so forth for other files. You can also use ASCII 219, which makes a solid box, or ASCII 229, which is a s (lowercase sigma). Here are a few more.

| ASCII code | Symbol |
|---|---|
| 225 | ß (beta) |
| 234 | Ω (Omega) |
| 254 | ■ (square bullet) |

These symbols will show on your screen as the file name. To get a "standard" file name back, just rename the file again.

To hide a directory, do this: **attrib +h** *directory name*.

To unhide it, use **attrib -h** *directory name*. Hidden directories will show up in the Shell and the Windows File Manager, though.

**Rereading a disk.** If you're using the Shell and you exit temporarily to the command line to copy some files to a disk, or to erase some, the Shell screen won't reflect your changes when you return to it. Press F5 or choose Refresh from the View menu to force it to reread the disk (click the drive icon first if the drive the disk is on isn't current). Or you can just double-click on the disk-drive icon.

**Keeping your floppies fresh and speedy.** As DOS writes data on a disk, it uses whatever sectors it can find. When it starts with a freshly formatted disk, it can write files into sectors that are next to each other. As you work with a floppy disk over a long period of time, however, your files get fragmented: pieces of them are stored in different sectors all over the disk, depending on the space DOS finds available. The net result is that disk access time increases. Your disk slows down.

Copying files from your frequently used floppies onto fresh floppy disks guarantees they'll be written in sectors that are next to each other. If you then reformat the old disks, they'll be practically as good as new with clean, empty sectors all next to each other.

Doing a DISKCOPY doesn't unfragment files. It simply creates a snapshot of exactly what's on a disk. Compare (using DISKCOMP) a disk you made with COPY *.* to one you made with DISKCOPY. They won't match. COPY *.* rearranges the data to put related file information in contiguous clusters.

**Use CHKDSK *.* to see if you can speed up your hard disk.**
Use **chkdsk c:\ *.*** to get a report of how your files are being stored. You'll find out whether they're mostly contiguous (next to each other). If a large number of files aren't contiguous, you could probably speed up your hard disk by optimizing (or "defragmenting") it with a third-party utility program like the Norton Utilities. You can also back the whole thing up, reformat your hard disk and restore the backed-up files; that will defragment your disk, too, if you don't have a third-party utility program. (Any good disk-optimizing program will undoubtedly tell you to back up your hard disk before using it, anyway.)

**Delete files before running DEFRAG.** DOS 6 comes with a neat DEFRAG command that will clean up your hard disk so that it runs faster. If you want to clean up your hard disk by freeing disk space with DOS 6's new DEFRAG command, do a little disk housekeeping first and delete all the unnecessary files that are cluttering it up. They include outdated data files (you can put these on a floppy for long-term storage), old backup files (which usually have a .BAK extension), old README files that you no longer want, and anything that CHKDSK found (they end in .CHK; see Chapter 9 for how to run CHKDSK and why you can't use these files anyway).

To run DEFRAG, type **defrag** at the DOS prompt. *Warning*: it takes a while to optimize a big hard disk. It took almost two hours on mine (a 200mb hard disk). You'll see a screen indicating how the defragmentation is progressing as it moves bits of files around, showing used, bad, unused and unmovable clusters.

**Don't run DEFRAG if Windows is running.** Microsoft Windows plays games with memory and saves things in places all over your disk. So be sure to exit from Windows before you run DEFRAG (or any other defragmenting/optimizing program). Don't try to run it from the DOS prompt within Windows.

**Automate DEFRAG a bit.** DEFRAG takes a while to do its job, as you've seen in a previous trick. To have DEFRAG automatically restart your computer after it's done so that you'll be ready to work when you get back from that extended coffee break, enter the DEFRAG command like this:

```
defrag /b
```

Also, run DEFRAG with this /B switch if you're using FASTOPEN in your AUTOEXEC.BAT (which you shouldn't be doing with DOS 6; see Chapter 10).

**More tricks for speeding up your hard disk.** There are two other things you can do to speed up a hard disk. Check your path statement in the AUTOEXEC.BAT file. It shouldn't be too long (127 characters max), and the directories you use most often should be near the beginning.

You can also set up a disk cache. See Chapter 10, "Managing Memory," for tips about this topic.

**Damaged disk? Maybe you can save something.** If you get a message that a file or disk can't be read, try RECOVER (although RECOVER is usually not a lot of help). It reads a file one sector at a time and creates a file called FILE0001.REC. The part of the file or disk that couldn't be read will be missing from the file, however; so you can see that trying to recover it isn't much use if the file is a program file because it will probably need the missing part to run. And if it's a text file, you can look at it with the Editor or your word processing program to figure out (maybe) what's missing.

To use RECOVER (assuming the floppy disk is in drive A), enter

```
recover a:filename
```

Before you try to work with the recovered files, be sure to copy them onto another disk that doesn't have damaged sectors. And please get rid of each damaged disk before you use it again by mistake!

The Norton Utilities, PC Tools and other third-party utilities do a much better job than DOS at recovering damaged disks and files. DOS 6 doesn't even include RECOVER.

**Don't use RECOVER for recovering all the files on a hard disk.** Don't *ever* give the command RECOVER C:. It will destroy your Directory Tree structure. RECOVER recovers files only; it doesn't pay attention to directories. If you use RECOVER C:, you'll get a hard disk full of files named FILE000*n*.REC, all at the root directory level.

Recover files name by name unless you really don't care about the tree structure. For example, you can (try to) recover all the files on a floppy disk in drive A with **recover a:**.

**When to use UNDELETE versus RECOVER.** If you delete a file by mistake, use UNDELETE, not RECOVER. Use RECOVER only when a floppy disk can't be read.

## ORGANIZING YOUR DISK FILES

You may not have thought about it, but the basic strategy you use for storing files on floppy disks should be *different* from the filing system you use on your hard disk. Why? Because of the way you use them, as you'll see in the following tips.

**Directories on floppy disks.** Yes, you can have directories on floppy disks, too, just like on hard disks. Some folks aren't aware of this. It's a real help if you don't overuse it and make so many subdirectories you're always having to change, change, change to so you can find a file you work with every day.

You use the filing system on floppy disks for a completely different purpose than the system used on hard disks (and backup copies). Think about it. When you use a floppy disk, you mainly want to locate files quickly. But your hard disk needs to be organized in a logical way that keeps programs and their data related but separate.

Floppy disks are inexpensive, and if keeping files in one level of directories on a floppy disk helps you locate them quickly, do it. You shouldn't have to search through complex directory levels to find a file. And there's no point in insisting on filling up a floppy disk with files just because there's room for more. Keep related files on the same floppy and stop at a logical point, even if there's room for more. For example, I kept the chapters of this book on a backup floppy disk, but I put correspondence to Ventana Press on a different floppy disk. Keep floppies where you can find them.

An aside. Actually, I keep three sets of backup floppy disks: my hard disks and I survived the Loma Prieta quake, but I'm not sure what will happen if there's another big one. I keep two backup floppies at home and one in a different location, just in case.

**There's a maximum on the number of files a directory on a floppy can hold.** A directory on a double-density floppy disk can hold at most 112 files, even if there's extra unused space on the disk. A high-density floppy disk can hold 224 files per directory. To get around this limitation, create subdirectories on the floppy disk and store files in them because each directory can hold that maximum number of files.

*Thanks to Gus Hallgren, Green Valley, AZ, for this tip.*

**Your hard disk filing system should be different from your floppy disk filing system.** If you want to be able to do backups easily, organize your hard disk for it. For example, you probably make disk copies of program disks with DISKCOPY, so you only need to back up data files, not program files. Keep your program files and data files in separate branches of directories on your hard disk (such as C:\PROGS and C:\DATA for instance), and then you can do an **xcopy \data\*.* a: /s /m** or a **backup \data\*.* a:/s /m** without backing up your program files, too. (The /S switch tells

DOS to back up files in subdirectories, and the /M switch tells DOS to back up only the files not changed since the last backup.)

Normally, the Backup Fixed Disk command in the Shell is set to back up *everything* on your hard disk. Do you really want to do that? No, probably not. See Chapter 6, "A Miscellany of Alchemy," for some more strategies for making backups easier.

**Keep your root directory clean.** The only *files* that need to be in your root directory are your AUTOEXEC.BAT file, your CONFIG.SYS file and a few more, like COMMAND.COM, that DOS put there when you installed it. There can be a lot of directories, though.

You may want to clean out your root directory from time to time, to get rid of the clutter that really belongs in another directory. Batch files, for example, have a habit of winding up in the root directory; but, to run batch files from any directory, put them in a directory called BATCH and put it in your path.

**Don't use more than three levels of subdirectories.** A good general rule to follow is not to have more than three levels of subdirectories. If you have more levels than that, consider using SUBST to substitute logical drive letters for complex paths (see the "Logical Drives" section later in this chapter).

## COPYING TRICKS

Copying files from disk to disk—and copying disks themselves—are a couple of things you can't get away from in DOS. Here's some voodoo to make copying easier.

**Before copying, check a disk's free space.** There's no point in copying a bunch of files onto a floppy disk only to get that "Insufficient disk space" message before you're done and not know which files have been copied and which haven't. (There are tricks for getting around this; see Chapter 1, "Beyond Magic," and the Windows tips in Chapter 6.) Issue the DIR command to make sure there's enough space left on the disk. Or, if you're in the Shell, click the floppy drive icon (with the floppy disk in, of course) and choose Show Information from the Options menu. Next to "Avail" will be the number of bytes available.

**Make disk copies with unformatted disks to save time.** You don't have to use a formatted disk to DISKCOPY; DOS will format the disk as it makes the copy. This saves time and allows you to put your attention elsewhere.

**Be careful with the source and the target in a DISKCOPY.** Unless you specify two disk drives, DOS will consider the current drive to be the target drive. If you mistakenly issue the command **diskcopy b:** while drive A is current, you'll copy the disk in drive B onto the disk in drive A.

**You *can* DISKCOPY with only one drive.** This has to be one of the most frequently raised issues of all time. Yes, if you have only one floppy disk drive, you can specify it as both the source and the target, and DOS will figure it out. Just issue **diskcopy a:** or **diskcopy b:**, depending on what you have. You'll be prompted to switch disks.

But if you have two floppy disk drives of different capacity, see the next trap.

**You can't make disk copies of different-sized disks.** You can't DISKCOPY a 5.25-inch disk onto a 3.5-inch disk, and vice versa. The capacities of both disks have to be the same. (For your information, 5.25-inch disks are either 360k or 1.2mb; 3.5-inch disks are either 720k or 1.44mb.) You can't have a 5.25-inch disk in drive A and a 3.5-inch disk in drive B and do a DISKCOPY. But, as usual, there are ways around that.

If you want all the files on one disk to be put on the other, just do a **copy \*.\*** or, if there are subdirectories, do an **xcopy \*.\* /s**. You won't get an exact copy of the disk, but you will get copies of the files that are on it.

## Chapter 5: Disk & Drive Magic 143

If there are more files on your source disk than will fit on the destination disk (if you're trying to copy from a 1.44mb disk to a 1.2mb disk, for example), you can make a temporary directory on your hard disk, copy the files into it and then XCOPY them to two other disks with ATTRIB and XCOPY, as shown in Chapter 1.

 **You can't DISKCOPY hard disks.** DISKCOPY works only with floppy disks.

**Copying and preserving the directory structure.** If you're copying files in directories and subdirectories onto a floppy disk and want to preserve the directory structure, use XCOPY instead of COPY. Issue it like this:

```
xcopy c:\wp51 a: /s /e
```

This command copies all the files in the WP51 directory as well as any subdirectories under it (indicated by the /S switch) and any empty subdirectories (indicated by the /E switch).

This is a quick way to move files onto a laptop or electronic checkbook and keep them in the same corresponding directories as on your hard disk.

**Replacing changed files.** If you used the previous trick to copy files onto your portable computer and then changed a bunch of files while you were traveling, here's the spell that will update them from your laptop back to your hard disk:

```
replace a:*.* c:\ /s /u
```

This says, in effect, "Look in all the subdirectories on your hard disk and update any that have the same names as the more recent ones on drive A." The /S switch matches file names; the /U switch prevents unchanged files on drive A from being written back onto your hard disk.

Because you can't combine the /S and /A switches, you'll have to reissue REPLACE to catch any brand-new files on your floppy. Do it this way:

```
replace a:*.* c: /a
```

This will pick up any new files you created. You'll need to move them into the directories they belong to; they'll appear in your root directory on drive C if you don't. Or, you can change to the directory they belong in and then issue the command.

You can use this same trick of specifying the hard disk as the source and the floppy as the target to take more recent files from your hard disk and put them on a floppy disk, instead of using XCOPY, as in the previous tip.

**If you suspect a disk is bad...** If you think for any reason that a disk might be bad, use the /V (VERIFY) switch with COPY and XCOPY. It's a little slower, but it checks the copy of each file and verifies that it's good.

When in doubt, throw the disk out.

## LOGICAL DRIVES

A logical drive (sometimes also called a *virtual drive*) is not really there, although DOS behaves as if it were. A logical drive can be a shorthand notation for another disk drive, or it can be another partition on your hard disk, or it can even be a subdirectory.

The most famous of all logical drives is a RAM drive. Accessing RAM is tremendously faster than accessing a real, physical hard disk, so it speeds up disk access time. Using a RAM disk is part of setting up your system to use DOS 5's and 6's memory-management techniques, so you'll find RAM disk voodoo in Chapter 10, "Managing Memory."

**Use SUBST to create a logical drive for shorthand.** If you find that you often have to use long directory names, use SUBST to set up a shorthand notation that uses a nonexistent drive as your long directory name. For example, the chapters of this book are in a directory called C:\WP51\DOCS\VOODOO. I set up a substitution like this at the DOS prompt:

```
subst e: c:\wp51\docs\voodoo
```

## Chapter 5: Disk & Drive Magic    145

Once you've done that, you can just type **e:** to change to that directory, or use E: anywhere you'd use C:\WP51\DOCS\VOODOO. For instance, you'd type **copy e:*.* a:** to copy all its files to a floppy disk in drive A.

When you change to drive E, the prompt will just show E:\>, but if you get a directory listing, you'll see that you're in the directory you specified.

If you work with lots of small directories, you might want to SUBST them like this:

```
subst e: c:\wp51\docs\voodoo\ch1
subst f: c:\wp51\docs\voodoo\ch2
subst g: c:\wp51\docs\voodoo\ch3
```

But be sure to put a LASTDRIVE command in your CONFIG.SYS file if you use drive letters beyond drive E (see the LASTDRIVE tip below).

**Keep your favorite substitutions.**   You can put your favorite SUBST commands in your AUTOEXEC.BAT file if you always want them to be in effect when you start, or you can put them in a batch file and run it whenever you like.

**Use LASTDRIVE if you use logical drives after drive E.**   Use LASTDRIVE (put it in your CONFIG.SYS file) if you want to set up a lot of substitutions for drives F through Z. DOS normally recognizes only drives A through E. In your CONFIG.SYS file, use **lastdrive=***highest letter you want to use.* (You don't have to do this if you're using DOS 6's new DoubleSpace program to create a compressed drive—DoubleSpace takes care of it for you.)

See Chapter 9, "Arcane Commands," for more on the LASTDRIVE command.

**Checking your substitutions.**   To see what your substitutions are, you can use the undocumented TRUENAME command (see Chapter 9). Or you can just type **subst** all by itself at the command line; it does the same thing. But why not use magic?

To cancel your substitution for drive E, enter **subst e: /d**.

⚡ **Don't set your last drive as drive Z.** You may think that by setting LASTDRIVE=Z you're covering all bases so that you can create RAM drives of any letter whenever you want, but what you're really doing is wasting RAM. DOS has to keep track of those potential drives whether you're using them or not, which eats up about 80 bytes of RAM per drive letter. So set a realistic LASTDRIVE—say, E or F or G, depending on how many physical hard drives you have and how many RAM disks you plan to use.

⚡ **Some commands don't work right with SUBST.** When you have a substitution in effect, don't use commands like BACKUP and RESTORE, which require DOS to know what's really in what directory. You may get what is euphemistically called "unexpected results."

Don't use those kinds of commands with ASSIGN and JOIN, either; they fool DOS into thinking one thing is another.

## USING THE DISK UTILITIES

The Shell has a built-in Disk Utilities group that contains several frequently used utility commands, such as those for formatting disks, backing up hard disks and so forth. All these commands can be used at the command line as well as in the Shell.

You've seen tricks for a lot of these procedures, such as formatting disks. But there are a few peculiarities about Shell utilities that you ought to be aware of.

⚡ **Don't back up with what is shown in the Shell's dialog box.** When you choose Backup Fixed Disk, the dialog box that appears is filled with **c:\*.\*  a: /s**. That means "Back up *everything* on your hard disk to floppies in drive A." Well, if you have a 20mb hard disk, you better get out about 60 360k floppies, because that's how many it's going to take.

By the way, the Shell's Search dialog box does this, too: it comes up with *.* in it, meaning "Search for everything."

You probably *don't* want to back up *everything* on drive C, do you? See Chapter 6, "A Miscellany of Alchemy," for some better backup strategies.

At least the Shell's Restore dialog box doesn't make the mistake of assuming you want to back up your whole hard disk. It's left blank; you can enter the switches you want to use and the directories you want to restore.

**If you format disks in different capacities, add these commands to the Disk Utilities group.** Do you recall from an earlier trick that there are (hard-to-remember) switches you can use to format a lower capacity floppy disk in a higher capacity drive? If you find you're doing this a lot through the Shell, add a couple of items to your Disk Utilities group: one for formatting 360k floppies in your 1.2mb 5.25-inch drive and one for formatting 720k floppies in your 1.44mb 3.5-inch drive.

For 360k disks, the command should be:

```
format a: /f:360
```

For 720k disks, it should be:

```
format b: /f:720
```

Call them something clever, like 360k Format and 720k Format. See Chapter 3, "Working With Programs," for how to add these items to the Disk Utilities group. You'll find this trick mentioned there, too. And in Chapter 6, you'll see a really radical solution to the problem—using Windows.

**Turn off those pesky FORMAT prompts.** There's a secret, undocumented switch for the FORMAT command that you can use to avoid being asked to insert disks, enter a volume label and, of course, whether you want to format another disk. Here's how to use it.

Put a disk in drive A and enter

```
format a: /autotest
```

DOS will read the disk in drive A, format it (showing you messages about its percent of progress) and return you to the DOS prompt with no further prompting. To format another disk, take the newly formatted disk out of the drive, put a fresh one in and press F3.

> **Don't use CHKDSK from the DOS Shell.** Don't use CHKDSK on the current disk when any files are open, such as when you're in the Shell and exit temporarily to DOS. Your computer may hang up and you'll have to restart it.

## WORKING WITH YOUR HARD DISK

Let's hope you never have to repartition or reformat your hard disk. But it's more scary than it is complicated. The sleight of hand in this section may get you through it without having to blow the dust off one of those doorstop-sized books.

The following skills are not so much tricks as they are procedures, and once you start either of these processes you have to see them through to the end. They are serious procedures, and you could wind up losing valuable data if you don't back up what you don't want to lose.

First, a little background. If your hard disk is brand new, right out of the box, it may not have been partitioned and formatted yet. These processes prepare the hard disk for use with DOS. Most dealers do it for you as a matter of course nowadays (and install DOS for you, too). But if you buy a mail-order disk, you may need to do these things yourself.

Partitioning a hard disk allows you to divide it into smaller "logical" drives (so called because they're not physically separate), like drive C, drive D, drive E and so forth. (If you have only one partition, it's called drive C—if drives A and B are your floppy drives.) Partitioning a large hard disk into smaller drives is usually a good idea, because your computer won't have to search the whole huge hard drive each time you ask it to do something. If your hard disk is relatively small, say 40mb, there's not much point in partitioning it, however.

One of these drives will be the primary DOS partition, where your DOS files will be stored. This is usually drive C, your first hard drive.

Your new hard disk comes with documentation that tells you how to partition it (or it may have been partitioned for you). You can also partition it with FDISK, a menu-driven utility that comes with DOS. This is one case in which you'll probably want to get out the manual.

**Partitioning erases all the data on a disk.** If you decide to repartition a disk, you'll need to back up everything you want to keep before you begin. Partitioning destroys everything on a disk.

You can't edit the size of your partitions; you have to repartition them to make them larger or smaller. For example, you can't change your drive D from 40mb to 60mb without erasing everything on it.

**Don't format your hard disk unless you have to.** After you partition a hard disk, you have to format it. Formatting erases everything on a disk, too. You don't want to do it to your hard disk very often. Formatting the hard disk is a serious procedure, but there are times when you may have to do it.

When should you format your hard disk? If you've been using it for a long time and there are many fragmented files on it, you may want to consider reformatting it to speed up disk access. Also, if you get one of those dreaded messages that your hard disk can't be read or that your file allocation table is bad, it may be necessary to reformat.

Having a disk utility program like PC Tools or the Norton Utilities can save you, in many cases, from having to reformat your hard disk. At the very least, these utilities can often tell you what's wrong with a sick disk.

**Do you need to format a brand-new hard disk?** Usually any hard disk you buy has some version of DOS on it because it was tested at some point before it was sold to you. So the answer is usually that you don't need to format a new hard disk. If you're getting the DOS prompt, you're in business.

If you've partitioned your hard disk into smaller logical drives, you will need to format each one of them. Run the CHKDSK command to see if you need to format any of your logical drives. If CHKDSK reports that the drive is not a DOS disk, it probably needs to be formatted. (That is, unless you've put a different operating system on it, like UNIX or OS/2.)

**Start from a floppy disk.** If you're going to format your hard disk, start from a floppy disk that has the DOS system files and the FORMAT.EXE command on it. Then, to format drive C, enter

```
format c: /s
```

The /S switch makes the disk a bootable system disk. Don't forget to use it!

Don't use the /S switch when you format your other logical drives, however; just use **format d:** and **format e:** and so forth. You don't need the system files on anything except your startup disk.

**Arcane SYS command failure.** Have you ever tried to put a system on a disk only to find that COMMAND.COM didn't get copied? This problem can occur if there's a path in your environment that's longer than 256 characters. Here's what happens: you're tying to put a system on a floppy so you can use it as a boot disk, so you enter

```
sys a:
```

to put the system files on the floppy disk in drive A. There's disk activity on A, and you see the message "System transferred," but then everything hangs up.

Check your AUTOEXEC.BAT to see if you've got a path in your environment that's longer than 256 characters. If so, shorten it or REM it out temporarily, and you should be able to transfer the system to the floppy disk.

**Remember to install DOS, too.** Don't forget to install DOS 5 on your newly formatted disk. Use the Setup program; you can't **copy \*.\*** with DOS 5 and 6 because the files are compressed. Recall (from Chapter 1) that you need a different set of disks, labeled "OEM version," if you're installing DOS on a disk that doesn't already have a version of DOS on it.

## MOVING ON

Chapter 6 contains a wealth of wizardry that defies classification, such as tips for copying files, making backups, restoring files and getting printouts of the screen. If you haven't found what you're looking for yet, chances are it'll be in Chapter 6.

# Chapter 6

# A MISCELLANY OF ALCHEMY

The conjury in this chapter, frankly, wouldn't quite fit anywhere else. But that doesn't mean it isn't magic! In fact, some of my favorite strategies are here. You may find exactly what you've been looking for.

Need some skills for deleting files, streamlining the path in your AUTOEXEC.BAT file, making backups, finding files, copying and printing? Here are the tricks you'll need to do all that and more.

## TIPS FOR DELETING FILES

Even with the UNDELETE command, it's better to avoid erasing files you really would rather keep. Following are a few tips to prevent deleting files by mistake.

 **Get a preview of the files you're deleting.** If you're deleting a bunch of files with wildcards in their names in a big directory, do a DIR with the pattern you're using (such as DIR ??93.*) to see which files will be affected. (In the Shell, run the DIR command.)

If you need more help on using wildcard patterns, look back in Chapter 4 for the section "Wildcard Tips . . . and Traps."

**Be careful when using wildcards to delete files.** When you use wildcards, it's easy to delete files that you didn't mean to delete. Here's an example. Say that you wanted to delete all the files beginning with CH and ending in 1—CH1.TXT, CH11.TXT, CH21.TXT and so on. You may think that entering

    del *1.txt

would delete the files you intended, but that's not the case. DOS ignores everything after the * (asterisk) up to the . (period) in a file name. So entering **del *1.txt** is the same as entering

    del *.txt

which wipes out CH2.TXT, CH3.TXT, CH4.TXT and so on.

**Use the /P switch to be prompted.** Use the /P switch if you're deleting files at the command line. DOS will prompt you with each file name before deleting it.

**A DEL *.* shortcut.** Just when you thought that "*.*" was a shortcut, here's a new one. Entering **del .** is the same as entering **del *.***, and it's a bit faster.
*Thanks to Jim Stewart, Glasgow, Scotland!*

**Suppressing the "Are you sure?" prompt.** Here's another advanced trick you can use with the DEL command, but be warned that it's dangerous. You can suppress the "All files in directory will be deleted! Are you sure? Y/N" prompt that appears whenever you try to delete all the files in a directory using DEL *.*. This trick is handy if you're creating batch files that clean off hard disks in a hurry so that you don't have to respond to the prompt—but be careful with it; otherwise, you can lose files that you didn't really intend to delete.

The trick is to store the Y response and its carriage return to the prompt in a file by itself and direct the input to the DEL prompt to that file. First, at the root directory, where it will always get read, create the file that contains the Y response (I'll just call it Y):

```
c:\>copy con y
y
^Z
```

Now you can direct the input requested by DEL to the Y file:

```
DEL *.* < c:\y
```

**You can't delete read-only files at the command line.**  DELete or ERASE won't delete read-only files—or system or hidden files, either. So protect your important files by making them read-only (see Chapter 2, "Shell Secrets").

The Shell, however, *will* let you delete read-only files if you choose Yes after reading the message, "Warning! File is read-only!"

**Protect DOS itself.**  DOS needs the file COMMAND.COM in the root directory so that it can operate. COMMAND.COM has to be in the root directory, not the DOS directory, so that it can be read on startup. If you're doing some cleanup housekeeping to keep files from proliferating at the root, you could possibly delete COMMAND.COM and be left wondering why your machine won't start next time. To prevent this problem from happening, protect COMMAND.COM by making it a read-only file, as follows:

```
attrib +r command.com
```

**Copies of read-only files *are not* read-only.**  If you think you've protected a file by making it read-only, be aware that copies of it are not read-only.

**Avoid *.* pitfalls.**  It's possible to delete application program files if you delete with the wildcard for everything (*.*) in a directory that contains your program files. You won't be happy if you have to reinstall the program. Protect program files (or any other file you don't want to delete by mistake) by giving them the read-only attribute (+r). At the command line, use **attrib +r *.*** to protect all the files in a program directory. In the Shell, choose Change Attributes from the File menu.

> ⚡ **Protect yourself against overwrites.** You'll destroy a file if you write over it. Then even UNDELETE won't get it back for you.

If you use the COPY command at the command line, DOS doesn't give you any warning about overwriting an existing file with the same name; it just goes ahead and makes the copy. The Shell, however, will warn you if there's already a file with the same name (unless you've used the Options menu and turned off that Confirmation dialog box).

If you're not using the Shell, you can quickly do a DIR of the directory to which you're copying the file to see if there's already a file there by that name. Remember, UNDELETE won't get a file back if it has been overwritten.

## AUTOEXEC.BAT ARTS

You can protect the integrity of your AUTOEXEC.BAT file in a couple of ways. And, as long as you're messing with your AUTOEXEC.BAT, I'll show you some other skills you can use to speed up your computer by streamlining your path.

> ⚡ **Some programs will modify your AUTOEXEC.BAT file.** Most programs today come with their own installation programs that go in and add a new directory to the path statement in your AUTOEXEC.BAT file. Although your path can be 127 characters long, in practice it's best kept to a length of just a few directories, say three or four.

If you let the path get too long, you'll slow yourself down; DOS checks each and every directory specified in your path when you issue a command, until it finds the command. And some memory-resident programs don't like paths that are longer than one line. I had that problem with HiJaak, a screen graphics program, for example. It wouldn't install until I shortened my path.

There's a way to stop these programs from modifying your AUTOEXEC.BAT file. Once you have your AUTOEXEC.BAT file running as you like it, rename it something like BOOT.BAT. Then create a new AUTOEXEC.BAT file of only two lines:

```
@echo off
call boot.bat
```

Now, the programs designed to alter your AUTOEXEC.BAT file will still do exactly that, but they'll modify the new AUTOEXEC.BAT, not the BOOT.BAT—so it will be easy to check for any changes. Anything in the new AUTOEXEC.BAT other than the two lines given above will be a change put in by the program you installed; so you can decide whether you want to keep or delete those changes (put them in your BOOT.BAT file if you want them). Not every program you own has to be in your path, as you'll see in the next trick.

**See what's in your path.** You can type **path** at the prompt to see what your current path is, without having to look in your AUTOEXEC.BAT file.

If a program doesn't run, check the path to make sure the directory to its program files is specified correctly.

**Shortening your path.** Keep in your path only directories you access most frequently. For the others, make a neat batch file that just changes to the program directory and starts the program when you type the program's name at the command prompt (in the Shell, choose Run). That way, you don't have to remember the exact command used to start the program, and you don't slow your computer down with a long path. Say you use a spreadsheet program called CRUNCH only from time to time, and the command used to start it is CRYPTIC.EXE. Instead of putting its directory in your path, make the following batch file and name it CRUNCH.BAT:

```
cd c:\crunch
cryptic
```

Keep the batch file in your handy BATCH directory, which of course should be in your path so you can run all your batch files from any directory.

Now, you can just type **crunch** as the command to start the program, and you'll automatically switch to its directory. You don't have to remember that the "real" command is—cryptic, crunch or whatever.

Remember, you don't need to include directories in your path that store data; DOS searches only for program (executable) files when it uses a path statement.

**Put the directories you use most often at the beginning of your path.** If the directories read most often are at the beginning of your path, you'll cut down on the amount of disk-reading DOS has to do when you issue commands. If you just can't bear to shorten your path as suggested above, at least edit it so frequently used directories are near the beginning.

There's an example in Chapter 7, "Batch Files," of how to use the Editor to edit a path.

**Don't use spaces in the path.** DOS stops reading a path when it comes to a space, so don't use a space between directories in your path. You can use a space after the word PATH, though.

**You can change directories and change the path, too.** The PATH command doesn't change the current directory; it just tells DOS where to look for program files. You can be working in one directory (saving files, for instance) and ask DOS to look in a completely different directory for the program files you need.

Say you want to work on files stored in a directory named DOCS\REPORTS, but your word processing program files are in a directory named \WORD. Enter the following lines:

```
cd docs\reports
path \word
```

This temporarily sets your path to the \WORD directory, where DOS will look for executable files, but leaves DOCS\REPORTS as your current directory, where the files you save will be stored if you don't specify a different directory.

## Chapter 6: A Miscellany of Alchemy

**You can temporarily suspend your path.**   If you enter **path ;** at the DOS prompt, you'll temporarily cancel your path (DOS will search only the current directory). Then you can do things like manually install TSRs (terminate-and-stay resident programs, also called memory-resident programs) that don't like your path statement.

**Use the PATH command before you start the Shell.**   If you know you're going to change the path temporarily as you work from the Shell (to run a memory-resident screen-dump program, for example), change the path from the command line *before* you start the Shell. Otherwise, the Shell will use the path it started with in your AUTOEXEC.BAT file.

**You can have a fancy AUTOEXEC.BAT file, too.**   If, back in Chapter 1, you saw some of the neat new things you can do with your CONFIG.SYS in DOS 6, you'll be glad to know that you can set up your AUTOEXEC.BAT for different configurations, too.

When you use a startup menu in your CONFIG.SYS file, DOS defines an environmental variable named CONFIG and sets it to the configuration you choose (in our example, either "RAY" or "KAY"). So in the AUTOEXEC.BAT you have DOS branch to either of those setups and execute any commands you want, such as starting a special program, logging on to a network or loading a mouse driver. You'll be editing your AUTOEXEC.BAT file, so to be safe, make a backup copy and put it somewhere safe (another directory, under another name, on a floppy, etc.). That way, you can get the original back if anything goes wrong.

Let's assume that KAY always wants to start WordPerfect and RAY wants to start a TOPS network (FLASHDRV is a batch file that starts the network). A sample AUTOEXEC.BAT file would look like the following:

```
C:\DOS\SMARTDRV.EXE
C:\DOS\MSAV
CALL C:\DOS\mouse
GOTO "%config%"
:KAY
PATH=C:\DOS; C:\wp51
wp
goto end
:RAY
PATH=C:\DOS; C:\TOPS
flashdrv
:end
```

When you start your computer, the AUTOEXEC.BAT file starts SmartDrive and the DOS 6 Anti-Virus program. It then looks to see which CONFIG (KAY or RAY) has been chosen from the startup screen branches to that section and carries out the commands there.

After you've edited your AUTOEXEC.BAT to make it do this kind of magic, save it under a different name, such as AUTOEXEC.TST. (Don't save it as AUTOEXEC.BAT; otherwise, you'll overwrite the AUTOEXEC.BAT that started your computer successfully.) Then rename AUTOEXEC.BAT as AUTOEXEC.OLD; finally, rename AUTOEXEC.TST as AUTOEXEC.BAT and restart your computer.

You may have to experiment to get your setup just as you want it, so be sure to keep a copy of your untouched AUTOEXEC.BAT and CONFIG.SYS files safely on a floppy disk so that you can get them back if something goes awry.

Read on for some more tricks for your AUTOEXEC.BAT.

**Adding a line to your AUTOEXEC.BAT file without an editor (without retyping, too).** Have you ever needed to add just one or two lines to the end of your AUTOEXEC.BAT or CONFIG.SYS files, and there's no editor handy? You can use a combination of COPY and COPY CON commands to combine the existing AUTOEXEC.BAT file with the lines you want to add to the end of the AUTOEXEC.BAT file and still avoid retyping the whole thing. Here's how to do it.

```
C:\>COPY C:\AUTOEXEC.BAT + CON {Enter}
C:\AUTOEXEC.BAT
CON
{type the line or lines to add and press Enter after
each one}
{press F6 and Enter}
```

To use the same technique with CONFIG.SYS, follow this pattern:

```
C:\>COPY C:\CONFIG.SYS + CON {Enter}
C:\CONFIG.SYS
CON
{type the line or lines to add and press Enter after
each one}
{press F6 and Enter}
```

*Thanks to Gus Hallgren, Green Valley, AZ.*

For another twist on the same trick, you can add lines to the *beginning* of a file. Use this command, substituting the name of the file you want to add the lines to in place of *FILE*:

```
COPY CON+FILE1 FILE2
```

Then type the lines you want to put at the beginning of *FILE1*. Press F6 to end the file. A new file, *FILE2*, is created and those lines are put into it and combined with what's in *FILE1*. Just be careful that no file already exists that has the same name you give *FILE2*, or you'll overwrite it.

You can use this trick to put comments at the beginning of your CONFIG.SYS file, for example. Here's how. Go to your root directory and issue this command:

```
copy con+config.sys temp
```

(Here, CONFIG.SYS is *FILE1* and TEMP is *FILE2*). Now type your comments, pressing Enter after each line. Press F6 at the very end, when you're done. Press Enter again to get back the DOS prompt.

Now look at TEMP (you can **TYPE TEMP**). You'll see the comments you added at the beginning of the contents of your CONFIG.SYS file. If all is well, rename TEMP as CONFIG.SYS and reboot.

*Thanks to Homer B. Tilton, Tucson, AZ, for this tip.*

## BACKUP TRICKS

DOS has three commands for making backups, or duplicate copies, of files and disks: BACKUP (Backup Fixed Disk in the Shell), XCOPY and COPY. In addition, DISKCOPY makes duplicates of floppy disks, such as disks of programs you buy.

Here are some ideas for making backups. In Chapter 7, you'll find batch files you can use to automate backups. RESTORE tips are in Chapter 9 ("Arcane Commands"), but let's hope you'll never have to RESTORE—if you do, you've had a disk crash.

DOS 6 adds a neat, easy-to-use Microsoft Backup utility that can greatly simplify the backup chore. So if you have DOS 6, skip all the tricks in this section that use the BACKUP command except the ones for Version 6, which use the MSBACKUP command.

**.BAK files aren't really backups.** Files automatically created by some programs and stored on the hard disk are called "backup" files but aren't really backups. They're just extra copies, usually of the next most-recent version. If your hard disk fails, they'll go right along with it. A real backup is on a different disk kept somewhere apart from your computer.

I usually keep at least two backups of anything important, just in case something goes wrong with one of them and my hard disk, too. Because I live in earthquake country, I sometimes keep three backup disks and store one away from home.

**You don't have to use the BACKUP command to make backups.** I choose not to use the BACKUP command because it has limitations. You have to use RESTORE on all your backed-up files; or, if you've lost a file or two, you have to figure out which backup disk the files you want to restore are on; or you have to feed backup disks until RESTORE finds the file it's looking for. (And RESTORE has some quirks of its own; see Chapter 9.)

Instead of using BACKUP, you can use DISKCOPY, as you work, to make copies of program disks, and COPY or XCOPY to make copies of important files.

XCOPY is my favorite for making backups because it has several options that let me specify which files I want to copy, such as files made after a certain date or files not previously copied. Since XCOPY also has a neat /S switch that lets it copy files in subdirectories, you can use this line to back up files in a selected directory and in all its subdirectories:

```
xcopy \directory name \*.* a: /s /m
```

The /M switch tells DOS to back up only the files changed since the last XCOPY or BACKUP. It looks at the file's archive attribute, since DOS turns on a file's archive attribute any time a file is created or written to.

When each floppy disk gets full, XCOPY will stop. Put in a fresh disk and issue the XCOPY command again, just as you did the first time. The /M switch ensures that all the copied files now have their archive attributes turned off, signifying that archiving or copying is no longer needed.

**Backing up from a certain date.** To make copies only of files created on or after a certain date, use the XCOPY command like this:

```
xcopy c:\ a: /s /d:02-16-93
```

The /S switch backs up all files in the current directory (which in this case is the root, C:\) and in all subdirectories; the /D switch backs up only those files changed or created on or after February 16, 1993.

This handy shortcut can save you from having to do a major backup of everything put on your hard disk since the day you installed it.

**Use CHKDSK to calculate how many disks you'll need.** Here's some wizardry to help you figure out how many floppy disks you need for a backup, whether you're using BACKUP or XCOPY.

If you're backing up the whole hard disk, run CHKDSK to see how many bytes of total disk space and how many bytes available are reported. Subtract the number of bytes available from the total disk space, and that's the number of bytes you'll have to back up. Divide that number by the capacity of the floppy disks you use (360,000 for 360k 5.25-inch floppies, and 1,200,000 for 1.2mb 3.5-inch floppies). That will tell you approximately how many floppies you'll need.

If you're not backing up your whole hard disk, there's an easy way to choose the files you want to back up with XCOPY and to see how many total bytes they are. Use the Shell. Turn on Select Across Directories and select the files you want to back up. You can sort them by name or by date, for example (use File Display Options). When you've selected the files you want to back up, choose Show Information from the Options menu. Under "Selected" will be the number of files selected and their total size. Divide that size by the capacity of your floppy disks, and you have the magic number!

**Delete unnecessary files before doing a backup.** Before you do a backup, take a minute and delete any files you really don't need any more, which are probably your oldest files. Sort them by date in the Shell (with File Display Options), or use **dir o/:d** at the command line, to see the oldest first.

**Those .BAK and .BK! files can be deleted.** The .BAK and .BK! files created by some word processing programs are good candidates for deletion. Search for all files ending in .BAK on your hard disk and see if you can delete all or most of them. It's easiest to find them in the Shell, using the Search feature.

**Archive the files you don't want to restore.** Make copies of files going to long-term storage; don't bother to back them up and restore them if you don't have a current use for them on your hard disk.

**Don't make backups from Windows.** DOS needs to read exactly what's on your disk, and Windows may try to access files while you're doing the backup. As a result, the file allocation table (FAT) will change, and you won't be able to restore your files.

**One-liners for BACKUP.** To save you the research, here's a list of favorite ways to do a backup. The line

    backup c:\*.* a: /s

backs up everything on your hard disk. (You've been warned about that one.) The line

    backup c:\*.* a: /s /m

backs up all the files on your hard disk that have been changed or created since the last backup. The line

    backup c:\reports /s d:2-16-93

backs up all the files in the REPORTS directory, and in any of its subdirectories, that have been changed or created on or since February 16, 1993. The line

    backup c:\reports\oct a: /a

backs up the OCT file onto a disk in drive A that already has files on it (the /A switch tells DOS to add the file(s) to the disk). If you don't specify /A, BACKUP overwrites anything already on the disk.

**Backing up and formatting disks at the same time.** The BACKUP command, with the /F switch, will format unformatted disks as it backs up your files. This saves you a great deal of tedium, since you won't have to sit there and format a stack of disks before you do a backup.

**BACKUP will format your disks in the capacity of your drive.** Be sure to specify what capacity you want BACKUP to use. For instance, if you have a high-density disk drive and regular-density disks, BACKUP will try to format them as high-density disks and your entire backup may be useless.

To simultaneously back up files in a directory and format a 360k disk in a high-density disk drive, give the command as

    backup c:\directory\*.* a:/f:360

**Backing up to another hard disk.** If you have a second hard disk, back up to it instead of floppies. It's much more convenient. In fact, if your work has to be completely backed up often, you might want to purchase a second hard disk just as a backup disk.

**BACKUP doesn't back up system files.** The BACKUP command ignores system files, so if you want to make a duplicate of a system disk (one you can use to start your computer), use DISKCOPY instead.

**Backing up without the /A switch will overwrite files.** If there are already files on the disk you're backing up to and you want to keep them, use the /A switch with the BACKUP command. Otherwise, BACKUP will overwrite everything on the disk. If you're making an incremental backup to a disk that already has yesterday's work on it, you'll lose that work if you leave out the /A switch.

**Different kinds of backups.** You'll find all sorts of uses for DOS 6's Microsoft Backup utility now that you've got it. (One use that isn't immediately obvious is transferring files from your main desktop PC to a laptop and back again.) In the process of discovering what backups can do, you may see the terms *incremental backup* and *differential backup*. These are two different types of backups.

An incremental backup backs up the files that have changed since the last backup, but a differential backup is a little more subtle. It backs up all the files that have changed since the last full backup (which backs up everything). Here are examples. Say that you do a full backup on Friday; then on Monday, you do an incremental backup, backing up all the documents you worked with on Monday. On Tuesday, you do another incremental backup, backing up just the files that were changed on Tuesday. You continue backing up incrementally each day until Friday, when you do a full backup again. That's how to use an incremental backup.

For a differential backup, you do the Friday full backup. Then on Monday you back up all files that were changed on Monday. On Tuesday, you back up all files that were changed since Monday. On

Wednesday you back up all files that were changed since Monday. Each day during the week, you back up all the files changed since the last full backup. When Friday rolls around, you do a full backup again. That's how a differential backup works.

Which to choose? Well, differential backups may take a little longer than an incremental backup if you've done a high volume of work. However, you'll wind up having to keep track of fewer floppy disks because each differential backup contains all the files that were backed up after the last full backup. Choose differential backups if you find that you're using roughly the same set of files every day. Choose the incremental method if you work with different files every day.

You can back up to floppies, to a tape drive or to a removable cartridge. In the tips that follow, I'll use floppies as the example, but if you have a tape drive with software to support it, you'll probably find that it's even more convenient than using DOS for backups. DOS 6 doesn't support tape drives directly, but you can still use them with the software they come with.

**If you choose the differential backup method, alternate sets of floppy disks.** It's tempting to use the same floppy over and over again for differential backups, but take some good advice and alternate disks. Use one disk for Tuesday's differential backup and another for Wednesday's. That way, even if a disk is bad and you aren't aware of it, if a file on your backup disk becomes corrupted or if a backup fails for any reason, you'll still have the files from the last full backup, missing only one day's worth of work.

**Stick to one backup scheme or the other until your next full backup.** No matter which scheme you decide to use—differential or incremental—between full backups, stick to it until the next full backup. Otherwise, you (and the backup program) may get confused if you need to restore files.

**Use the incremental method if you need to preserve earlier versions of files.** The incremental backup method adds data to your backup disk and doesn't overwrite it, as the differential method does. In a differential backup, existing versions of files on the backup disk are replaced with their newer versions from the hard disk. So if you need access to earlier versions of files, choose Incremental.

When you restore files, use the Version button and pick the version you want to restore. You'll be prompted to insert the correct disk. *This is another good reason to clearly label all your backup disks.*

**Microsoft Backup compresses files.** Don't bother running CHKDSK and figuring out how many bytes you're going to back up and then dividing that number by the capacity of the floppy disks you're going to use. DOS 6's Microsoft Backup utility compresses the files. It also tells you politely how many floppy disks you'll need to have on hand.

**You only have to configure your system once for backups.** The first time you run Microsoft Backup, it will identify the drives on your computer, check your processor speed, video display, and so forth. This process takes a few minutes. First, remove any floppy disks from your drives. Second, locate two floppy disks that you can use for the compatibility test. They don't have to be formatted, but the test will go much faster if they're already formatted.

Of course, if you add a new hard disk to your system, you'll need to configure it, too.

**If you have Windows, you may need to increase the "DMA buffer size."** Without getting into the details of what the DMA buffer is and why it needs to be bigger, just let me say that if you get a message that the DMA buffer size needs to be increased when you run Microsoft Backup, here's how to do it. (It happened to me, so it can happen to you.)

1. In the Windows Program Manager, choose Run from the File menu and type **sysedit** in the box. You'll see all your windows .INI files as well as your AUTOEXEC.BAT and CONFIG.SYS.

2. Make sure your CONFIG.SYS has these lines:

```
FILES=30
BUFFERS=30
STACKS=9,256
```

3. In your SYSTEM.INI file, find the [386enh] section and add this line to it:

   ```
   DMABufferSize=32
   ```

   Then be sure to run Backup with the Full Screen and Exclusive options turned on when you run SYSTEM.INI from Windows. Use the Settings command on the window's Control menu. If you're wondering what that is or how to display it, let me sell you a neat book called *Voodoo Windows*....

**Make several setup files.** You can create setup files for Microsoft Backup and save them so that you don't have to go through the whole process of specifying what kind of backup you want to do each time you back up. After you make your choices and set all the options for the backup, choose Save Setup As from the File menu (see Figure 6-1). Enter a name for the setup file you're saving and a short description of what it's for. For example, you might want to call your full backup setup FULL_C to indicate that you're backing up all of drive C. Save your incremental backup setup as INC_C and your differential setup as DIFF_C, and you'll save time.

*Figure 6-1:* Saving a setup file.

You can even create setup files for backing up specific directories. For example, I keep letters in a C:\CORRES directory, so I created a setup file named ICORRES (for incremental backup for the CORRES directory) that I specified to do an incremental backup to drive B.

To use your saved setup file, choose Setup from the File menu and pick the setup you want to use. This naming tip can really save you a lot of time if you usually back up only one or two specific directories because you don't have to think very much about what you're doing.

Speed setups: You can also specify a setup file at the command prompt when you start the backup program. Enter the command as **msbackup** *setupfile*, where *setupfile* is the name of the setup file you want to use. Include the path in the command if the setup file is not in the current directory or a directory that's in the PATH statement in your AUTOEXEC.BAT. If there's no setup file by that name, you'll be taken to Microsoft Backup, where you can create one.

**Got a laptop? Make your backup screen easier to read.** If you have a laptop computer, you'll probably use DOS 6's new Backup utility to transfer files between your desktop PC and your laptop. If your laptop has a liquid crystal display (LCD), enter the Backup utility command as **msbackup /lcd**. You'll get a special, easier-to-read screen.

**If you create special setup files, be sure to specify a directory to back up.** If you create setup files for different backup situations, always be sure that you're backing up an entire directory when you set up an incremental or differential backup. If you've selected only specific files to back up, only those files will get backed up, not any new files you've created. So be sure to specify a particular directory when you make those setup files.

**Fastest backups.** For fastest—although not safest—backups, use the Compress option. Turn off the Verify Backup Data option. And use high-density disks so you don't have to sit there and feed the computer more disks quite so often.

### Keep the Use Error Correction on Diskettes option turned on.

It's all too easy to spend the time backing up to a set of floppy disks, only to find later that sectors on one or more disks were bad. For peace of mind, keep the Use Error Correction on Diskettes option (see Figure 6-2) turned on so that if the program tries to write to a bad spot on a floppy disk, it will either repair that spot or move to another location. To get to the Disk Backup Options screen, click Backup at the main screen; then choose Options.

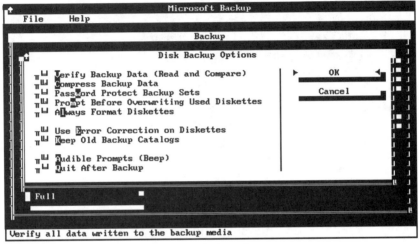

*Figure 6-2:* Options you can set for backups.

### How often should you run the Compare function?

Short answer: about once a month. More often if you're a heavy user. The Compare feature compares the backed-up files to their originals, and it can take a while. Run Compare from time to time to make sure everything's working OK, but don't do it every time you back up. And don't do it on a full backup! Also, don't bother leaving Data Verification on if you're planning to compare files after a backup. It will just slow down the backup.

If any errors are reported after you do a backup, run the Compare function to find out which files have been affected.

**Want to back up files by date?** The Backup by date option is kind of hidden, but it's there. Choose Backup from the main screen; then choose Select Files, and you'll see a Special button (see Figure 6-3). Choose it, and you'll be able to specify a date range.

*Figure 6-3:* Choose Special to specify a date range.

*Warning:* specifying a range doesn't automatically back up files that have been changed after a certain date and before another date. The range just excludes any files that lie outside the date range you specify. You need to select the specific files you want to back up.

**Restoring backed-up files.** Here's hoping that you'll never have to restore files, because if you do, it means that something disastrous has happened to your hard disk or to the files that are on it. But if you do, some of the information in this tip may help.

- Information about your backups is always kept on the *last* disk of a backup set as well as on your hard disk. If the information on your hard disk becomes inaccessible (in other words, if your hard disk gets fried), you can retrieve the backup information from the last floppy disk in the backup set. This information is kept in a special catalog file ending in .CAT. Each setup file that you create maintains a corresponding master catalog file that's monitored until the next time you do a full backup.

When you finish the next full backup, that .CAT file is erased. (By checking the Keep Old Catalogs option in the Options screen, you can maintain older catalogs if you think you might ever need to get one back.)

- Here's how to read a catalog's file name. Consider this one: CD30216A.INC. The C is the first drive backed up (drive C), and the D is the last drive backed up on February 16, 1993. The 3 represents the last digit of the year; the 02 is the month; and the 16 is the day. The A indicates that this backup was the first of the day, and the .INC indicates an incremental backup. A full backup ends in .FUL, and a differential backup ends in .DIF.

- When you restore files, you'll be asked to specify which backup catalog to use. To select a catalog that's different from the one the screen is displaying when you choose Restore, type **k** or click under Backup Set Catalog (see Figure 6-4).

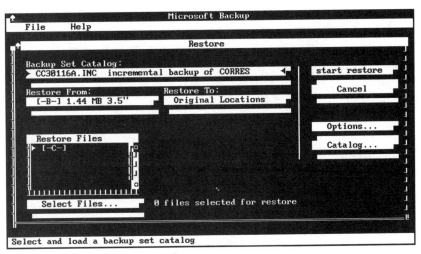

*Figure 6-4:* Picking a backup catalog.

- Microsoft Backup can rebuild catalog files even from damaged disks. But for belt-and-suspenders security, keep a copy of all your catalog files (*.CAT) on a floppy disk so that if your hard disk ever dies completely, Microsoft Backup will have a record of where all your backed-up files are.

- Unlike DOS's RESTORE command, Microsoft Backup will let you restore files to a different location from the one where they were originally, so you can easily transfer files between one computer and another—say, between your desktop PC and a laptop. (For the trick to outwitting the RESTORE command and restoring to a different location, see Chapter 9, "Arcane Commands.")

## COPYING TRICKS

You copy files practically every day. If you think about it, you'll realize that, without COPY or its more powerful variation XCOPY, you can't do much with your files—like move them from floppy disks onto hard disks and vice versa. So, of course, there are lots of tricks for copying. In addition to the other copying tricks scattered throughout this book, here's some more copy conjury.

**XCOPY is faster than COPY.** If you're copying large numbers of files, use XCOPY instead of COPY. The XCOPY command works faster because it reads as many files as it can and copies them as a group.

**You can't rename and move files at the same time.** You can't specify a different drive or directory for a file when you rename it; it has to stay in the same directory. For example, the command

    ren c:\doc.txt a:doc.bak

results in an "Invalid parameter" message.

You can COPY the file to a different location and rename it at the same time, however, this way:

    copy c:\doc.txt a:doc.bak

The file DOC.TXT stays on drive C unchanged, and a new copy named DOC.BAK is made on drive A.

**Use XCOPY to copy files by date.** If you know you want copies of files you've modified on or after a certain date, it's fastest to get them with XCOPY, like this:

```
xcopy *.* a: /d:02-16-93 /s
```

If you're in the root directory of your hard disk, this command will pick up all files modified on or after February 16, 1993, including any in any subdirectories (indicated by the /S switch).

However, because this command picks up all temporary files created by your word processing program, as well as any changes written to the DOSSHELL.INI file as you worked with the Shell, and all sorts of other housekeeping files DOS creates in your root directory and its subdirectories, you probably don't want to use it. It's a much better strategy to change to the directories you worked in and do XCOPY from there. That way, you can copy only the files you worked on today and keep your backups up-to-date without picking up all those temporary files.

**Get XCOPY to prompt you.** Give the XCOPY command as **xcopy /m /p** and it will prompt you for each file to copy. This is another spell for XCOPYing more than one disk full of files. Just don't copy any you've already copied.

**Don't use a file name as an XCOPY destination.** If you specify a file name as the XCOPY target, XCOPY will copy each source file, one by one, to the target file. Each subsequent copy will overwrite the previous copy, and you'll wind up with only the last file as the copy.

Suppose you issue this command to copy all the files and subdirectories in a directory named DOCS into a new directory named NEWDOCS:

```
xcopy c:\docs a:\newdocs /s
```

When you issue this command, XCOPY will ask you whether NEWDOCS specifies a file or a destination. Be sure to type **d** for destination! If you type **f** for file, you'll get the result described above: only the last file will be copied as that file name.

**Use COPY to combine files.** Use the plus symbol (+) to tell DOS to combine (or "concatenate") files. Suppose you've been working on Chapter 1 in three parts and you want to combine CH1A, CH1B and CH1C into a file named CH1FINAL in the same directory. Use this command:

```
copy ch1a + ch1b + ch1c ch1final
```

Some word processing programs have an Append command that does the same thing (appends the contents of one file to the end of another), but this is how DOS does it.

**You can create a virtual disk and copy files to it.** If you create a RAM disk, you can COPY or XCOPY the program and data files you're working with into that part of memory and use it just like a real disk drive. You have to use COPY or XCOPY to copy your files back to a real disk drive when you're done, though, because a RAM disk is just RAM, after all, and disappears when you turn off your computer. See Chapter 10, "Managing Memory," for an example of how to set up a RAM disk.

**You can use COPY both to create and to print files.** Create short files at the DOS prompt by entering the COPY command as **copy con** and specifying the name of the file you want to create. Whatever you type after that becomes a file when you press Ctrl-Z (or F6) and Enter (to indicate the end of a file). The drawback to this feature is that if you realize you made a mistake after you've exited from the file, you can't edit the file at the command line (you can, however, edit it in the Editor or in your word processing program). To correct one of these files, you have to enter it all over again and hope you don't make another mistake. For an example of how to use COPY CON to create batch files, see Chapter 7, "Batch Files."

You can also use the COPY command to copy text files to your printer instead of PRINTing them. These two commands do the same thing:

```
copy filenames prn:
print filenames
```

The difference between COPY and PRINT is that COPY doesn't give you control of your system until all the printing is done. PRINT lets you work while your documents are printing.

You may also need to send a form feed to your printer if you use COPY. For details, see the "Tricks for Printing From DOS" section later in this chapter.

**Windows does some things better than DOS does.** Bet you thought you wouldn't see this in a DOS book! You've probably got Windows 3.1 somewhere on your hard disk, although you may never use it. Believe it or not, there are some things Windows does better than DOS. Windows isn't really an operating system itself: strictly speaking, it's a DOS enhancer. As a consequence, it has a few features that can, under certain circumstances, work smoother than the DOS command-line techniques.

- **Quicker disk copying.** If you have 2mb of RAM (and you can't run windows 3.1 unless you do), Windows will read all of a floppy disk into memory and then do the disk copy, so there's no endless chain of back-and-forth disk swapping when you have only one floppy disk drive of the right capacity and you'd normally have to DISKCOPY A: A: or DISKCOPY B: B:. If you're copying even one or two disks with one floppy drive, I know from experience that it's worth firing up Windows for this feature alone.

    All you need to do, once Windows is started and you're in the File Manager, is put the disk you want to copy (the source disk) in the floppy drive; then choose Copy Disk from the Disk menu. Select the source and destination drives—the same one in both cases, if you have only one disk drive.

    When Windows is through reading the source disk, it will tell you that the copy is 50% completed. The 50% means that the File Manager is through reading the source disk and is ready to copy what it read onto the target disk, not that it's only read half the disk.

Put the destination disk in the drive and click OK. That's it: no more disk swapping. You can use an unformatted disk as the destination disk, and Windows will format it as it goes along.

- **Avoiding that "Disk Full" message.** If you've ever tried to copy large numbers of files from your hard disk to floppies, you've probably experienced that maddening situation that occurs when DOS has copied all the files that the floppy disk can hold and then stops when the disk is full, leaving you wondering which file it stopped at and which files remain to be copied. You can use the trick of turning the archive attribute on before you begin the copy (*if* you remember to do it and if you can remember which switches are involved) and then use XCOPY with the /M switch to copy the files, but Windows makes this much, much easier. Just select all the files you want to copy (pressing Ctrl-/ will select all the files in a directory), press F8 to start the copying, and respond to the confirmation prompts. The File Manager will stop when the first disk is full of copied files, and you'll be asked whether you want to retry or cancel. Just take out the disk that's full, put a blank, formatted disk in the drive, and click Retry. Windows will keep on copying until that disk is full, too, and you'll get the same message. Put a fresh disk in the drive and click Retry.

## TRICKS FOR FINDING THINGS

One of the most maddening things about working with computers is that so often you can't remember which subdirectory you put a file in. DOS 5 and 6 have features that make it much easier to locate lost files. Take advantage of them: they can save you a lot of time and frustration.

**Really misplaced a file? Search your whole hard disk.** If you have no idea where you stored a file, you can search your whole hard disk for it. It's easiest to do this in the Shell, and there are two different ways to do it. They differ only in how they display the results of what they find.

- Select the All Files view; then choose File Display Options from the Options menu and enter the file name or pattern you're searching for. The results will be displayed in a box on the right of the screen (see Figure 6-5), and you can click on each file to see more information about it in the box on the left.
- Choose Search from the File menu. Make sure the Search Entire Disk box is checked, and enter the file name or pattern of what you're searching for. Figure 6-6 shows the results of a search like this. Notice that the located files are preceded by the path name to where they're stored.

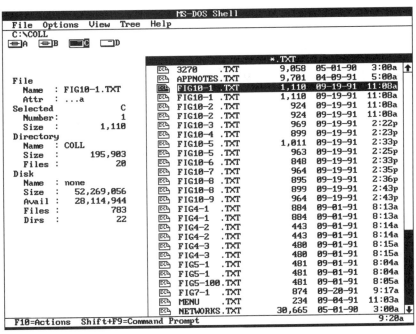

*Figure 6-5:* You can search your hard disk with the All Files view.

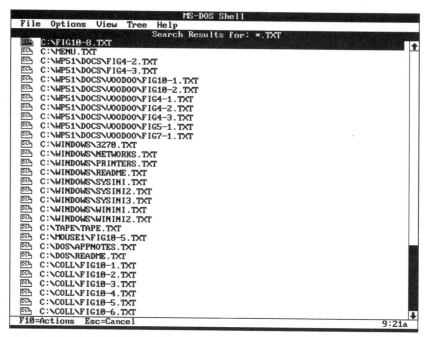

*Figure 6-6:* The Shell's Search feature gets the same results, displayed differently.

**Quick file locating.** If you're looking for a specific file in a directory and its subdirectories, try **attrib filename /s**. The file name can use any of the wildcard characters. You'll get a listing of the path and file names of all matching files in the current directory and its subdirectories.

For example, if you're looking for a file called "chap7," enter **attrib chap7 /s** at the DOS prompt in your root directory. You'll get a list of all the files named chap7 in any of your subdirectories, like C:\WP51\DOCS\CHAP7 and C:\WP51\DOCS\VOODOO\CHAP7.

## TRICKS FOR PRINTING FROM DOS

Most of the time you'll print files from your application programs because they can handle formatted text and DOS can't. But sometimes it's nice to print directly from DOS, maybe to address an envelope quickly or print a directory listing to use as a disk label. Here are some printing spells.

**Don't print anything but text-only files with DOS.** Don't print files that contain special formatting, such as documents created with your word processing, spreadsheet or database programs, with DOS's PRINT command. If you do, your printer may give you what is euphemistically called "unexpected results," like spitting out a page when it shouldn't.

Just print text-only files with DOS. These are files created with the DOS Editor or with a special command or key sequence in your program. In DOS WordPerfect 5.1, for example, it's Text In/Out.

**How to tell if a file is text-only.** In the Shell, press F9 when a file is highlighted to see if there are any formatting codes in it. If you can read it and there isn't any garbage in it, it's probably a text-only file and will print just fine. Check the whole file to be sure (click on PgDn to scroll through it).

**Printing files from the Shell.** To print files from the Shell, you have to use the PRINT command before you choose Print from the File menu. Exit to the command line and type **print** at the DOS prompt, or Run the PRINT command.

If you want to print files from the Shell without having to remember to issue the PRINT command first, put the PRINT command in your AUTOEXEC.BAT file.

If you want to cancel print jobs or check the print queue's status (see the tips below), you'll need to use the Run command or press Shift-F9 to temporarily exit to the DOS prompt.

**Print a quick directory listing for your disks.** If you need to label your floppy disks with a directory listing, try this to get a printout of what's on the floppy disk in drive A:

```
tree a: > prn
```

You can also use **dir > prn** to print a regular directory listing. And you can **chkdsk > prn** to get a printed status check of your disk. The /V switch, used with CHKDSK, will list every single file on your hard disk.

You can also do a screen dump of a directory listing by pressing the Shift-Print Screen key combination. On some keyboards, all you have to do is press the Print Screen key.

*Hint:* Do a **dir /w** to get a wide listing to tape to a floppy disk's paper sleeve.

With certain printers, you have to eject the page to see the printed screen dump. There's usually a button on the printer, probably labeled "Form Feed," that will do this. You can also eject a page by typing **echo ^L > prn** at the DOS prompt.

**Printing graphics.** If you have a printer that prints graphics, you can use DOS to print screen dumps of graphics screens (the Shell in graphics mode is a graphics screen, for example). The secret is to enter the GRAPHICS command at the command line (just type **graphics**) before you try to use Shift-Print Screen.

There are a lot of switches you can use with the GRAPHICS command, depending on what kind of printer you have. Check out both your printer's manual and the DOS manual if you're interested.

**Addressing envelopes.** Some printers will echo what you type at the keyboard. This is handy for addressing envelopes, if your printer accepts envelopes. (Some accept pin-feed paper only.)

With the envelope positioned in the printer and the printer online, type **copy con prn**. Then type the return address and the address for the envelope. Insert blank lines with the Enter key and indent text by pressing the Tab key or the space bar. You may have to experiment a bit to get the address positioned properly. (Try six tabs over for the address block on a business envelope.)

To finish, press F6 or Ctrl-Z and Enter. The printer should print the address on the envelope. To eject the envelope, you may need to press the printer's form-feed button.

**Checking the print queue.** You can work on something else while DOS prints your text-only files. To see which files are in line to be printed, use the PRINT command with no switches.

**You can increase the size of the print queue.** Normally, DOS keeps track of 10 files in the print queue. If you want to send more than 10 files to your printer at once, use the command **print** *file names* /q: *number,* where *number* can be any number up to 32.

If you're printing from the Shell and you exceed the number that DOS has been told to keep track of, you'll get a "Print queue is full" dialog box.

**If you increase the size of the print queue, you may have to reboot.** If you change the number of files DOS can handle in the print queue and then want to change that number again, you'll have to restart your computer and reissue the PRINT command with the new switch. If you're going to print a lot of files and want to avoid all that, just specify 32 (the maximum) the first time you use PRINT.

**Speed up printing with the /B switch.** You can use a little-known switch with the PRINT command to speed up your printing jobs. The /B switch lets you increase the print buffer from its default size of 512 bytes.

Here's how to print DOC1, DOC2 and DOC3 with a larger print buffer and more time for the printer to be in control:

```
print /b:8192 doc1 doc2 doc3
```

You can increase the print buffer size from 512 bytes all the way up to 16,384 bytes.

Since accessing what's in the print buffer in RAM is faster than accessing your hard disk, the former can speed up your printing jobs.

**Stopping printing.** If the paper in your printer jams and your printer's printing garbage, here's how to stop all printing, short of turning off the printer:

```
print /t
```

Remember it as T for Terminate.

To cancel printing of just one file, use the PRINT command like this:

```
print filename /c
```

## MOVING ON

This chapter should make life with DOS a little easier. But there are still secrets waiting to be discovered. The next chapter, "Batch Files," explores how DOS can do your bidding using more than one command at a time, to work some batch-file magic.

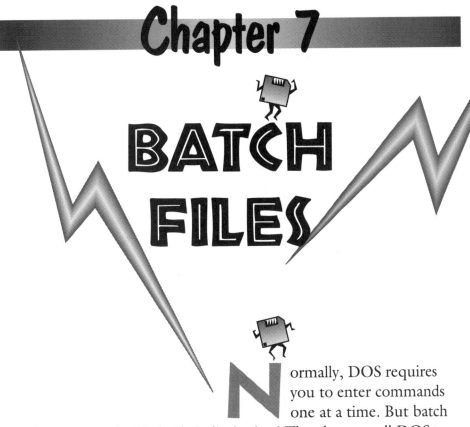

# Chapter 7
# BATCH FILES

Normally, DOS requires you to enter commands one at a time. But batch files let you outwit this built-in limitation! They let you tell DOS to carry out several commands, one right after the other. You can create menus with batch files, use them to automate your daily backup procedure, switch to different directories and start programs with them—you'll be amazed at what they can do.

DOS 5 and 6 come with their own full-screen text editor that makes it easy to create these magic batch files. (EDLIN, that notorious line editor that comes with all versions of DOS, is still in DOS 5, for those who like it, but it's not included in DOS 6.)

In this chapter, we'll first explore how to use the Editor and then learn some batch file spells. We'll reveal some sample batch files to give you ideas for creating your own.

## TIPS FOR USING THE EDITOR

The DOS Editor comes with mouse and cut-and-paste abilities as well as a full range of keyboard shortcuts. Of course, you can always use your favorite word processing program to create and edit batch files, but if you stick with the DOS Editor, you can avoid a fundamental trap: it automatically saves files in ASCII format, so you don't run the chance of inadvertently saving a file with invisible word processing format codes in it, as it's so easy to do in your word processing program.

**Use a mouse with the Editor.** The Editor is somewhat awkward to use without a mouse, so the real secret to getting the most from the Editor is to have a mouse. You can cut and paste text more easily.

You might not find the Editor awkward, however, if you're used to WordStar or Microsoft Word; most of the keyboard shortcuts are the same.

**Keyboard shortcuts in the Editor.** There are all kinds of keyboard shortcuts in the Editor. As you're typing, you may not want to reach for the mouse to select a word or a single line. Here are several of the most useful keyboard shortcuts:

- Press Home or End to move to the beginning or end of a line.
- Press Ctrl-Left Arrow and Ctrl-Right Arrow to move one word left or right.
- Press Ctrl-T to delete the word at the cursor (cursor must be on the first character of the word).
- Press Shift-Down Arrow to select the current line as well as the line below.
- Press Shift-Up Arrow to select the current line and the line above.
- Press Shift-Ctrl-Right Arrow or Left Arrow to select one word right or left at a time. Hold down Shift and Ctrl and keep pressing the arrow keys to select several words.
- Press Ctrl-Y to cut the current line.
- Press Ctrl-Q and type **y** to cut to the end of the line.
- Press Ctrl-Ins to copy what you've selected.

- Press Shift-Del to cut what you've selected.
- Press Shift-Ins to paste what you've cut or copied.
- An easy way to remember these last two cut-and-paste shortcuts is that when you cut and paste, you're shifting text from one location to another, in and out of a buffer.

**Clearing text.** If you want to get rid of text forever—without putting it in the buffer, where you can get it back again, select the text (drag the mouse over it) and press Del, or choose Clear from the Edit menu.

**Using the Editor to change your AUTOEXEC.BAT file.** One of the most common uses for the Editor is to modify your AUTOEXEC.BAT file. Here's an example of how to change your PATH command. (If you're unsure about what you're doing, make a copy of your AUTOEXEC.BAT file with the following line and practice on the copy instead of the real thing:

```
copy c:\autoexec.bat autoexec.sam
```

- Start the Editor with **edit c:\autoexec.bat** or, in the Shell, click on Editor and give **c:\autoexec.bat** as the file to edit.
- Move the cursor to the line beginning with PATH, SET PATH= or PATH=. If there isn't a line like any of these, create your own, putting it near the beginning of the file. Press End and Enter to insert a blank line; then type the path command. At the very minimum, it should include **path c:\;c:\dos**, which tells DOS to search your root directory and your DOS directory for executable files.
- Use the editing keys to change the path to whatever you'd like it to be, using some of the tips from Chapter 6, "A Miscellany of Alchemy," to keep your path short, meaningful and powerful.
- When you're done, press Alt-F, type **x** and then press Enter. The Editor saves all files as text-only files, so you don't have to use a special SAVE command for ASCII files, like you do in

word processing programs. Just choosing Yes will save the file in text-only format.

- At the command line, issue the command **autoexec** or restart your computer with Ctrl-Alt-Del; your edited AUTOEXEC.BAT file will be in effect.

**Why is everything indented in the Editor?** Whenever you press Enter to move to a new line in the Editor, the new line will be indented just like the line above. This feature is designed for programmers who indent lines of code. To remove the indent, press Backspace.

Once a line is indented, pressing Home takes you to the beginning of the text on that line. To go to the very beginning of the line (the left edge of the Editor), press Ctrl-Q and type **s**.

**Other Editor quirks.** Although the Editor's keyboard shortcuts may seem familiar if you've used Microsoft Word and WordStar, you may notice that there's a basic way in which the Editor does not behave like either of these word processing programs: there's no word wrap. When you type to the end of a line, the text doesn't wrap to the next line. Instead, the display shifts right.

If you're editing text-only files created in a word processing program, you may find this feature annoying because some of the lines will be so long. You may find that pressing Ctrl-PgUp and Ctrl-PgDn to scroll the screen right and left will help you find your place. Once you've found your place, you can use the Editor's built-in bookmarks to find it again (see "Use a bookmark in the Editor," below). Pressing Enter to break a line for easier reading inserts a hard return into your text file at that point, which you may not want.

The Editor is not a substitute for a word processing program. It's useful mainly for creating and editing batch files and writing programs.

**Tricks for searching in the Editor.** The Editor has a useful Search feature that also lets you search and replace. Here's a good thing to know: select the text you want to search for *before* you choose Find, or press Ctrl-Q and type **f** (a shortcut for using the Find feature). The selected text will already be in the Find What box.

If you want to find every occurrence of something, no matter how it's capitalized, don't check the Match Uppercase/Lowercase box.

If you want to find *exactly* what you've entered, check Whole Word and Match Uppercase/Lowercase. If Whole Word isn't checked and you're searching for *ion*, for example, Find will bring up words like redemption, circulation, addition and so forth.

To search for the next occurrence of a word, press F3.

**Use a bookmark in the Editor.** The Editor has four built-in bookmarks for finding your place in a long file. These are handy for quickly getting back to where you were, or where you want to add text later.

To insert a bookmark, press Ctrl-K and type a number from 0 to 3. To find that place again, press Ctrl-Q and type the number you chose. You can think of Ctrl-Q as Quest; while you're at it, think of Ctrl-K as Keep (the medieval castle kind).

*Thanks to Matthew Porter, Crofton, MD, for this mnemonic tip!*

Once you exit the Editor, the bookmarks will be gone, even if you save the file. They're good for the current session only, so don't try to use them a few days later.

**Dialog box tricks.** Sometimes when you're in a dialog box in the Editor, you don't want to take your hands off the keyboard to use the mouse.

You can move from area to area in a dialog box by pressing Tab. Press Shift-Tab to move backward.

Also, to select a function without using the mouse, you can press Alt and the first letter of a button. For example, press Alt-N for No, Alt-C for Cancel, and so forth.

Typing **n** for No is the quickest way to exit that "Do you want to save this file?" dialog box.

**Maximize the Editor's display.** Start the Editor with **edit** *filename* **/h** or **edit /h** (or just enter **/h** as the file to edit, if you've double-clicked on Edit in the Shell) to get your monitor's maximum number of lines on the screen.

**Change the Editor's window size.** Once you've opened a Help window (press F1), you can change the size of the window you're in by holding down the Alt key and pressing plus (+) or minus (-). This makes it convenient to have a small Help window open to refer to while you're getting used to the Editor.

**Don't use the Editor on your formatted documents.** If you're in the Editor and you open a document created in your word processing program and save it, you'll lose its formatting. Word processing programs put in invisible formatting characters that the Editor ignores.

You can open text files like AUTOEXEC.BAT and CONFIG.SYS in the Editor, though. And it's great for creating batch files, as you'll see later in this chapter.

**Customizing the Editor.** You can change the screen colors in the Editor (if you have a color monitor, of course), hide the scroll bars, and reset the tabs with the Options menu Display command.

If you're not using a mouse, you may want to get rid of the scroll bars. They just take up room on the screen.

Tabs are preset for eight spaces, which is normal for files that some programmers use. If you're not using the Editor for writing programs, however, you can change tabs to five spaces, which is more standard for many word processing programs.

**Don't delete QBasic.** The Editor runs under the QBasic interpreter. So if it can't find the QBASIC.EXE file (which should either be in the same directory as EDIT.COM or in your search path), the Editor won't work. If you want to save some disk space by deleting QBasic and you're not a programmer, think again.

## BATCH FILE TIPS

Using batch files can save a lot of time. Most often, batch files are described as ways to automate complicated sets of instructions. (In fact, many installation programs are simply batch files.) But batch files are also good for doing simple things you're in danger of forgetting, like making backup copies of your daily work.

**You can put batch files in your AUTOEXEC.BAT file.** Batch files in your AUTOEXEC.BAT file are executed when your computer starts, so you can use them to start a favorite program automatically each time you start your computer. They can also turn off that pesky Num Lock key.

**Batch files aren't word processing files.** Batch files are just text files with a .BAT extension. You don't create them with your word processing program, however. Word processing programs put in all sorts of formatting information, and DOS can't handle that. It wants plain vanilla text. (Text files are also called text-only files, ASCII files, or DOS Text files.)

Most word processing programs let you create text-only files, but not in the "normal" way you create documents with DOS. In DOS WordPerfect 5.1, for example, you use Text In/Out commands, not RETRIEVE and SAVE, as in DOS.

Batch files also have to follow DOS's file-naming conventions. They use only eight characters with a three-character extension, and don't use these characters:

| | | | |
|---|---|---|---|
| <> | angle brackets | [ ] | square brackets |
| \ / | slashes | \| | bar |
| : | colon | , | comma |
| = | equals | + | plus |
| " | quotation mark | ; | semicolon |

**Use the keyboard to create short batch files.**   You can create a short text file in DOS: at the command prompt, type the **copy con** *filename* command. See Chapter 4, "Command-Line Tricks," for examples.

**Create batch files in your root directory.**   It's a good idea to store batch files in your root directory so you can execute them from any directory. An even better idea, which keeps your root directory from getting cluttered, is to create a new directory for them and put it in your path. For instance, if you create a directory named BATCH and store your batch files in it, you'll want to add the path to the BATCH directory in your path statement, as follows:

```
path = c:\dos;c:\batch
```

**Put your favorite batch files in the Shell.**   Put batch files you use a lot in the Shell, either in a program group of their own or as program items within a group. Just give the batch file's name as the command in the Add Program dialog box, which you get after you choose New Program Item.

The title you give the batch file doesn't have to be its real name. You can use anything you like, perhaps something more descriptive than that eight-character name. Just be sure to give the batch file's name (without the .BAT) as the command in the Add Programs dialog box.

You can assign a shortcut key to a batch file, too, as with any other program item.

**Running a batch file.**   To execute your batch file, just use its name. Don't type .BAT.

**Stopping a batch file.**   To stop a batch file, press Ctrl-Break or Ctrl-C.

**Using replaceable parameters in batch files.**   What if you want to have a batch file that operates only on the files you specify? DOS lets you use the percent symbol (%) and a number as replaceable parameters; that is, they stand for file names or other replaceable parameters in a batch file. You can have up to 10 of these dummy placeholders (%0 through %9) in a batch file.

First, set up the batch file. Say you want to copy a file into another directory and delete it from the current directory at the same time. In other words, you want to move it from one directory to another. To do this, you could write a batch file, named MOVEIT.BAT, like this:

```
copy %1 %2
del %1
```

When you run the file, give the name of the file to be copied in place of the %1 and the name of the directory it's to be copied into as the %2. For example, if you want to copy OCT.RPT (which is in the current directory) to a directory named C:\LOTUS\REPORTS, type

```
moveit oct.rpt c:\lotus\reports
```

The file name OCT.RPT is used in place of the %1, and the directory name C:\LOTUS\REPORTS is used in place of the %2. It looks like it doesn't save time, but it sure beats typing both lines out fully. A listing of your current directory will show you that OCT.RPT is gone, and a listing of the REPORTS directory will show you that it's there.

Once you create MOVEIT.BAT, you can move all the files in the current directory to another directory by typing

```
moveit *.* newdirectory
```

**Other replaceable parameters.** Here are some examples of how to get results with those replaceable parameters (the % symbol and a number):

- COPY %1 %2. Copies the file you name first to the location you name second.
- TYPE %1. Displays the contents of a specified file all at once.
- TYPE %1 %2 %3. Displays the contents of three specified files.
- MORE < %1. Displays, screen by screen, the contents of a specified file.

- MORE < %1 %2 %3. Displays the contents of three specified files, screen by screen.
- SORT < %1. Alphabetically sorts a specified file.
- CD %1. Changes to a specified directory.
- DIR %1. Gives you a directory listing of the directory of a specified file.
- Your batch files can use another type of variable, called an *environmental variable*, but you may have to set it up with the SET command. (See the "SET yourself a variable" tip in Chapter 9, "Arcane Commands.") You'll also see an example of it in use in a batch file later in this chapter.

**Watch the spacing around variables.** Be sure to leave a space before and after replaceable parameters or environmental variables, or your batch file won't work. This is one instance in DOS in which spacing *is* important. It's not usually important with switches because they're preceded with a slash (/), which says to DOS, "Hey, a switch is coming next." But if you don't leave a space before and after a variable, DOS reads the variable as part of the command that precedes it or follows it. So **cd%1** would be interpreted as **cdword**, for example, if you typed **word** as the name of the variable for the directory to change to.

**Avoid double DOS prompts.** If you get a double DOS prompt after you run a batch file, you or your word processing program (some do this automatically) ended the batch file with a hard return; and every time DOS sees a carriage return, it displays the system prompt. Go back and edit the file so that Ctrl-Z is the last character in the last command. Use the Editor instead of the word processing program that may be causing the problem. To create a Ctrl-Z in the Editor, press Ctrl-P and then press Ctrl-Z.

By the way, if you ever need to create an Esc character in the Editor (to simulate pressing the Esc key in a batch file), press Ctrl-P and then press Esc.

*Thanks to Matthew Porter, again!*

**Putting a pause in a batch file.** In a batch file, the PAUSE command stops the batch file until you press any key. It's useful for prompting you to put a disk in drive A, for example.

You could add a message reminding yourself to put a backup disk in drive A with this line:

```
ECHO Press Control + Break to cancel
PAUSE
```

or

```
ECHO Control+Break to cancel, or any other key to →
continue
PAUSE > NUL
```

*Thanks to Jim Dettwiler, Vancouver, WA, for this tip.*

**Turning off the screen display with ECHO.** ECHO OFF lets you turn off the screen as DOS executes each command, so the batch file executes invisibly. ECHO is always on; you'll see the screen action unless you turn it off. ECHO OFF is usually entered as the first line in a batch file if screen action isn't desired.

**Turning off the screen display of a line with @.** The @ symbol, placed at the beginning of a line in a batch file, turns off the display of that line only. You can <u>also stop DOS from displaying any command in a batch file by starting it with @.</u> For example, suppose you want to present the message "Today is Tuesday" when a batch file is executed. If you enter **echo Today is Tuesday**, you get

```
echo Today is Tuesday
Today is Tuesday
```

To prevent this, begin the echo line with @. You'll get one "Today is Tuesday" message.

**You can make batch files execute invisibly.** <u>@ECHO OFF turns off the display of the line it begins *and* all the lines that follow; start your batch files with @ECHO OFF if you don't want to see anything on the screen.</u> (This works in DOS 3.3 and later; however, only the @ symbol is necessary.)

**Giving yourself messages.** You can use ECHO to give yourself messages that indicate what the batch file is doing, even though it's executing invisibly. Say you turned ECHO off at the beginning of a batch file that moved files to another directory by copying them and then deleting the originals. You want a message to show that DOS has copied and deleted each file. Add the following line to the end of the file:

```
echo   File %1 has been moved
```

**Tips for using REM (REMARK).** REM, a batch command, can display messages and help you remember what each part of a batch file is supposed to do (when, three months later, you've forgotten what you wrote it for). You can use REM as the first line in a batch file to explain what's happening on the screen, or before a particularly cryptic line in a batch file to remind yourself of what's going on.

For example, if ECHO is on, insert a line like

```
rem Backup procedure beginning
```

to display "Backup procedure beginning" on your screen when DOS comes to that line in the file.

If you want to be able to see the remark in your batch file when you display it with the TYPE command, but *not* on the screen when the file runs, precede the remark with a colon (:), as in

```
:rem This is a remark.
```

The colon creates a label visible only when you display the file on the screen (and you really don't need to use REM).

A trickier use for REM is to tell DOS *not* to execute part of a batch file. Programmers call this "commenting out" or "remarking out" a part of the program. DOS doesn't execute anything on the line after REM, so you can disable part of your batch file with it. Suppose you have a line in your AUTOEXEC.BAT file that automatically sets up a mouse to be used with special "fine-tuning" options. Put REM at the beginning of that line and those options won't be used until you remove the REM.

**Don't use too many REMs.** Too many lines beginning with REM can slow down the operation of your batch file. If you're sure you'll never need those lines again, delete them. If you're not completely sure, make a copy of the batch file (call it .OLD instead of .BAT) so you don't lose those remarked-out lines.

**Don't use REM with redirection symbols.** If you use REM with a line that contains a redirection symbol (<, >, or |, explained in Chapter 4, "Command-Line Tricks"), DOS won't do what you expect! Instead of ignoring everything on that line, it will carry out the redirection. DOS first checks for redirection, starts to carry it out and *then* notices that the line is a remark. So you think you've disabled some lines and DOS thinks you haven't, and your batch file is giving you "unexpected results." This little quirk can drive you crazy if you're not aware of it!

**Creating blank lines in a message file.** You can put blank lines in message files to make them easier to read on the screen. Turn ECHO off and then begin each line with **echo.** (the word *echo* and a period). Don't forget the period. Like this:

```
@echo off
cls
echo.
echo.
echo Insert a disk in drive A
pause
```

When this message displays on your screen, there will be two blank lines before the "Insert a disk in drive A" line.

**Tips for using CALL.** The CALL command can start a second batch file from within the first, returning upon completion. This is called *nesting*. When the first batch file gets to the CALL line, the second batch file runs; when the second batch file finishes, control returns to the first batch file. (Without the CALL command, the second batch file starts but *never* returns to the first; this is called *chaining*.) For example, I have in my AUTOEXEC.BAT file a batch file called NUMOFF that magically turns off that pesky Num Lock key ("pesky" because I rarely use the numeric keypad for data entry). Then it continues executing the AUTOEXEC.BAT file's next line.

Also use a CALL command in a Shell program group to start a batch file before a program starts (see Chapter 3, "Working With Programs").

 **Use batch files to make decisions.** You can use a batch file to see if a certain condition is true and, if it is, to execute a different set of instructions.

The simplest way to set up a batch file with decision-making ability is to use a statement such as

```
if not exist %1 goto label
```

Here's an example:

```
@echo off
if not exist %1 goto message
type %1 | more
goto end
:message
echo There is no file by that name. Try again.
:end
```

Now when you type the name of a batch file, its contents are displayed on the screen. If no file by that name exists, the "There is no file by that name" message is displayed.

 **Use two equal signs to test for equality.** If you need to test whether the user has input exactly what you want, use *two* equal signs in an IF statement. One doesn't work.

 **Avoid error messages.** If you make a typing mistake or leave out a parameter in a batch file, DOS gives a "syntax error" message. Here's how to avoid it.

Put a character before the % in the variable; then something will always be there and the batch file will execute properly even if you forget to type something. Here's an example:

## Chapter 7: Batch Files

```
if .%1 == .%2 goto end
.
.
.
:end
```

Look closely and you'll see a period before each replaceable parameter; because the condition . == . will always be equal, the batch file will go to the end even if both parameters are left out.

**Avoid endless GOTO loops.** Be sure to use IF, IF EXIST or IF NOT EXIST in any batch file that has a GOTO, or you could set up an endless loop like this one:

```
:display
dir /o:n /s
goto display
```

To break out of an endless loop without having to turn off your computer, press Ctrl-C or Ctrl-Break.

**You can put a beep in a batch file.** The secret to getting your computer to beep at a certain point in a batch file is to hold down the Alt key and type **007** on the keypad (think of James Bond). A bullet will appear on the screen, and a beep will sound at that point when the batch file executes.

This is an artful way to get the user to read a message on the screen:

```
echo All data on your disk will be destroyed!
```

**The batch file commands.** Now you know some batch file basics, and you can get further into batch files with a textbook. Meanwhile, here's a summary of batch file commands:

- ECHO. ECHO OFF suppresses the display of commands on the screen; ECHO ON displays messages on the screen.
- REM. Annotates the lines in your batch file, disables commands temporarily, or shows annotations when ECHO is on.

- PAUSE. Inserts a pause in a batch file; when the file executes, it stops where a pause has been inserted and starts again when you press any key.
- CALL. Starts one batch file from within another (actually lets you set up programming subroutines).
- IF, IF EXIST, IF NOT EXIST. Does logical testing, or tests to see whether a condition is true so you can write batch files that branch to other sets of instructions.
- GOTO. Instructs DOS to continue executing the batch file at a different line.
- FOR, IN, DO. Sets up repetitions of commands, or loops, in a batch file.
- @. Suppresses the display of the command that follows it.
- SHIFT. Enables the use of more than 10 parameters (%0 %9) in a batch file.
- CHOICE. New with DOS 6, it lets you get input from the user.

## WHAT A BATCH FILE CAN DO

Adapt the following charms for your own uses to create batch files that work like waving a wand. A lot of them are fun, too.

**Use batch files to create your own menus.** Create menus for yourself or for others less experienced than you with batch files. Here's a simple example; make yours as complex as you like.

First, create the menu you want the user to see (see Figure 7-1 for an example). You can use the Editor or your word processing program (if it will save text-only files), but don't use any fancy formatting other than tabs, spaces and blank lines. Save it as MENU.TXT. (Store all these batch files in a directory in your path so you can execute them from any directory.)

Then create a batch file containing the command used to start the program for *each* of the items in your menu. Save each one as the letter or number of the item. For example, referring to Figure 7-1, the batch file used to start WordPerfect would be named 1.BAT and would consist of these lines:

```
cd \wp51
wp
```

The batch file that starts WordStar would be 2.BAT.

Then create a batch file named MENU.BAT to manage the menu. It should consist of these lines:

```
@echo off
cls
type menu.txt
```

This juggling saves you from having to begin each line in your menu with ECHO. See the next trick for a fuller explanation.

Now the menu you created appears whenever you type **menu** at the DOS prompt, and you can type the number of your choice to start that program running.

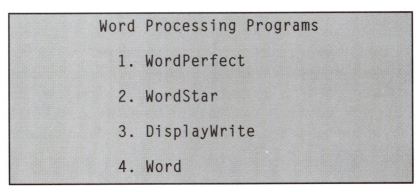

*Figure 7-1:* You can create simple or complex menu systems with batch files.

**Message trick: avoiding those ECHOs.** If you write batch files that display messages on the screen, you saw earlier in this chapter that you have to begin each line of the message with ECHO. This shows the line on the screen, while the rest of the file won't be displayed. Here's an example of a typical batch file using ECHO:

```
@echo off
cls
echo This is the message to your user.
echo This is the rest of the message.
pause. Press any key to begin.
[rest of batch file follows]
```

It's quicker, however, to create the message in a text file called MESSAGE.TXT and type it from your batch file:

```
@echo off
cls
type message.txt
pause
```

If your message is quite long, use

```
type message.txt | more
```

Then the user simply presses any key to see the next message screen.

If you're putting the batch file in the Shell as a program item, you can create a custom dialog box for it that serves the same purpose. See Chapter 3, "Working With Programs," for instructions on doing this.

**Blank lines in a batch file can cause problems.** If you leave a blank line at the end of a batch file—which is easy to do with the DOS Editor—DOS interprets it as an <Enter> keystroke. To prevent this error, be sure to put a ^Z (Ctrl-Z) character as the last line in the file, indicating the end of the file so that DOS doesn't save any stray hard returns.

However, if the last line in your batch file is a label, and you put the ^Z right after it, like this:

```
@Echo off
rem testloop.bat
:loop
[do whatever]
If [condition] goto end
goto loop
:end^Z
```

When the batch file hits that condition, it zaps the display. You don't see a prompt—nothing. The trick is to put the ^Z on the next line, as in the following:

```
:End
^Z
```

*Thanks to Don Rice, Los Angeles, CA, for this tip.*

**A new batch file command: CHOICE.** DOS 6 adds the CHOICE command to your repertoire of batch file commands. You use CHOICE to get input from the user without your having to create text files for a menu and batch files for the commands that the menu lists, as in the preceding example. Your batch file, for example, presents the choices 1, 2 or 3, or Y/N for Yes or No, and the user can type the number or letter of the response. Here's an example:

```
@echo off
cls
echo.
    echo 1   Run WordPerfect
    echo 2   Run Windows
    echo 3   Run Edit
echo.
    choice /c:123 Type number of program you want to run
    if errorlevel 3 goto Edit
    if errorlevel 2 goto Windows
    if errorlevel 1 goto WordPerfect
    :Edit
    edit
    goto End
    :Windows
    win
    goto End
    :WordPerfect
    cd c:\wp51
    wp.exe
    goto End
    :End
```

Note that the errorlevel statements are listed in descending order. When the batch file executes, the user can type 1, 2 or 3 to start WordPerfect, Microsoft Windows or the DOS Editor, respectively.

A couple of points about CHOICE: If you don't specify any text to go with the choices, the user sees just a [Y,N] message for Yes or No. For example, if your CHOICE line is **choice c:/yn**, your user will see

```
[Y,N]?
```

on the screen when that part of the batch file executes. If the user presses any other key, a beep will sound. (This is true whether you provide explanatory text with your choices or not.)

A neat trick you can do with CHOICE is specify which choice should be made after a certain amount of time has elapsed if the user hasn't pressed any key at all. Use this switch in the CHOICE line:

```
Tc, nn
```

The *c* should be the character that stands for the item you want to execute after *nn* seconds. For example, to have the batch file described above start WordPerfect if there's no response from the user after ten seconds, use this line:

```
choice /c:123 Type number of program you want to run T1,10
```

**You can create custom Help screens for other users.** It's very simple to create custom Help screens. Just create them as text-only files and then write a simple batch file called, in this example, ASSIST.BAT so it won't conflict with the HELP.EXE command:

```
@echo off
type %1.txt | more
pause
```

The user simply types **assist** *topic*, and whatever you've stored as a text file named TOPIC.TXT appears on the screen. Here are a few ideas for text files you could have on various topics: company policies, employees' working schedules, lunchroom menus, work assignments and complex procedures.

**Your AUTOEXEC.BAT file can be changed without your knowledge.** Most program installation procedures (those Setup or Install programs you run when you buy a new application program) go in and change your AUTOEXEC.BAT and CONFIG.SYS files. Some of them are polite and ask your permission; a few even tell you what they've changed. Others just do it and don't tell you.

At any rate, you can wind up with some unknown and unwanted things in your AUTOEXEC.BAT file. There's an easy way around this. Rename your AUTOEXEC.BAT file BOOT.BAT, for instance. Then create another AUTOEXEC.BAT file with these two lines:

```
@echo off
call boot.bat
```

Now installation programs can't make changes you're not aware of. After you've installed a program, take a look at your AUTOEXEC.BAT. The changes will be obvious; they're anything beyond the two simple lines. You can then edit your BOOT.BAT file to include those changes, if you want them.

Be careful, though: usually the changes an installation program makes are required for smooth operation.

**Make yourself a TYPE batch file.** If you often have to **type filename | more** to read lengthy README.TXT files (which lets you read a file one screen at a time) you can create a little batch file to save typing time:

```
@echo off
type %1 | more
```

Name the file something you can remember easily, like SEEIT.BAT. Then you can type **seeit** *filename* and press Enter to read those long READMEs; just press Enter again to read each screen.

**If you give a batch file the same name as a command, you may get "unexpected results."** You need to understand the order in which DOS goes through executable files. First, it looks in the current directory for a file that has the name of the command you entered plus a .COM extension; then it looks for one with an .EXE extension; then it looks for one with a .BAT extension. Then it looks in this same order (.COM, .EXE and .BAT) in each directory in your path. So, depending on what directory you're in, the batch file with the same name as the DOS command may not execute, because DOS will run its own .COM or .EXE command instead.

 **Here's a daily backup batch file.** Here's a batch file (UP-DATE) that updates your daily work:

```
@echo off
cls
echo Insert floppy disk in drive A
pause
xcopy %1 a: /s /m
```

To use this UPDATE batch file, first copy every file in the directory and its subdirectories onto a floppy disk, like this:

```
xcopy c:\docs a: /s
```

The XCOPY command with the /S switch searches through all the subdirectories of DOCS and copies all the files that have been changed or any new files not backed up yet.

Then you can make backup copies daily just by giving the UPDATE command plus the name of the directory you're working in. For example, if you've been working in a directory named DOCS, you'd type **update c:\docs**.

 **Here's another daily backup file.** Here's a neat batch file that fetches the current day's date and automatically backs up any files you've created or changed that day. It's a little more complicated than the batch file in the preceding tip. You create four batch files: one called CURRENT.BAT, which sets the string *today* as an environmental variable (that can be accessed by your batch files); one called TODAY.BAT, which gets the current date; one that's called UPDATE.BAT, which fetches the date and carries out the backup; and another called DAILY.BAT, which carries out the actual copying and specifies the directory you usually work with.

Working backward, here's the DAILY.BAT batch file to back up my C:\WP51\DOCS\VOODOO directory:

```
xcopy c:\wp51\docs\voodoo\*.* a: /d:%today% /s
```

The /S switch tells XCOPY to search all subdirectories for any new or changed files. Note that *today* is enclosed in percent signs, which tells DOS to look in the environment for where this variable is set (see "SET yourself a variable" in Chapter 9, "Arcane Commands," for details).

If you also regularly work in another directory, just add another line to the DAILY.BAT file. For example, if you work in Microsoft Word, too, add this line to DAILY.BAT:

```
xcopy c:\word\*.* a:\word /d:%today%
```

Notice that it's going to copy the files into a subdirectory called WORD on drive A, so you won't mix up your WordPerfect and Word documents.

Now you need to create the UPDATE.BAT file:

```
@echo off
cls
echo Insert floppy disk in drive A
pause
echo | more | date > today.bat
call today.bat
call daily.bat
```

This batch file reminds you to put a disk in drive A. After you press any key to continue, it puts the current date in a file named TODAY.BAT. The ECHO | MORE trick furnishes the carriage return needed to get the date into the file. (*Thank you very much, James Forney.*[1])

CURRENT.BAT is simply **set today=%4.**

It works because the date is the fourth string after the word *current* in "Current date is Sat 09-04-1993."

To use your new daily backup system, type UPDATE at the command line. You'll be prompted to put a fresh disk in drive A and press any key to begin. As the batch files execute, they'll copy your daily work onto that disk.

---

[1]James S. Forney, *DOS 5 Demystified* (Blue Ridge Summit, PA: TAB Books, 1991).

**Use different colors for different drives.** If you have a color monitor and more than one hard drive, such as a logical drive D, why not make that change-the-color-of-the-prompt trick you mastered back in Chapter 1 into a batch file that sets a different foreground and background color for each one of your drives? When you execute the batch file, it changes you to the drive you specify and changes the screen colors for you.

Here's an example of a batch file (D.BAT) that switches you to drive D and changes the screen color to red with black text:

```
@echo off
cls
d:
prompt $e[41m $e[30m$p$g
^Z
```

To execute it, just type **d** at the prompt instead of the usual **d:** that changes you to drive D.

If you want a different color on drive C, create and execute a file called C.BAT.

To switch back to the standard prompt, type

```
prompt $e[0m$p$g
```

This saves you from looking it up. You'll need to use this line if you lose your prompt because you've set the background and foreground to the same color.

## MOVING ON

Chapter 8, "Doskey Revealed," in a sense continues the topic of batch files—the macros you create with DOS 5 and 6's macro utility can easily be converted to batch files.

Entire books have been written on the subject of batch files. Without getting too complicated or too sophisticated, the tricks in this chapter should have given you a taste of what you can do with batch files and some tools for writing your own.

# Chapter 8

# DOSKEY REVEALED

If you like playing with batch files, you'll love the Doskey feature that's in DOS 5 and 6. It's a TSR (terminate-and-stay resident) program that remains in memory after it's started to let you create macros. Macros are just batch files by another name except they're much faster. But they're lost when the lights go out, or when you turn off your computer. Later in this chapter, however, you'll find a way around that.

You can do more than create macros with Doskey, however. In fact, a lot of folks (those who don't like batch files) never want to get into Doskey macros. There's an even simpler way to use Doskey: it remembers what commands you used so you can use them again without having to enter them again. You may prize Doskey most for this. In addition, it lets you issue several commands on a single line instead of the standard "one line, one command." Now that's magic (at least, for DOS).

You can use Doskey in several distinct ways:

- To give several commands at once, all on the same line.
- To repeat previously issued commands.
- To edit previous commands and use them again in a slightly different form.

- To create macros in DOS.
- To create batch files from your macros.

This chapter initiates you into voodoo Doskey.

## GIVING SEVERAL COMMANDS AT THE SAME TIME

It's certainly faster to type everything you want DOS to do and press Enter than to type a command, press Enter, wait, type the next command and so on. But if you're comfortable with the command sequence you're entering, why not use Doskey and enter them all at once?

**Load Doskey to begin.** Doskey isn't normally present when you start your computer. To put it in memory, type **doskey** at the command line.

If you hardly every use the Shell (see the trap below), why not put the DOSKEY command in your AUTOEXEC.BAT file? That way, a history of the commands you execute in any one session is always available. It's sure a lot easier to press the Up Arrow key to recall your previous command (and edit it, if you like) than to type it over again. Doskey takes up about 4k of RAM, though, so don't put it in your AUTOEXEC.BAT file if memory is at a premium.

**Don't try Doskey in the Shell.** Doskey only works at the command line, not in the Shell. If you don't put it in your AUTOEXEC.BAT file, load it from the command line.

**Issue several commands on a single line.** After Doskey is loaded, you can type several commands at once, separating each with a Ctrl-T. Pressing Ctrl-T puts a paragraph mark (¶) on your screen. Press Enter to end all the commands.

For example, wihtou DOS 6's move command, to move a directory from one place to another from the command line, you have to copy all the files in it to another directory (assuming it already exists), erase the files in the original directory and delete the original directory. (Remember, though, that the Shell lets you rename directories.) To move a directory named C:\FILES to C:\REPORTS\SEPT with Doskey, simply do this:

1. Load Doskey.
2. Enter **copy \*.\* c:\reports\sept** while you're in the FILES directory; then press Ctrl-T.
3. Enter **del \*.\*** and press Ctrl-T.
4. Enter **cd ..** and press Ctrl-T.
5. Enter **rd files** and press Enter.

You'll be asked to confirm that you really want to delete all the files; then DOS will go ahead and move the directory (copy, delete and remove it).

**What if you make a mistake?** If you're typing a long sequence of commands and you realize, before you press Enter, that you made a mistake, you usually backspace over the offending characters and retype the line. But with Doskey you can use the arrow keys to move to the mistake and correct it, which is a lot faster than backspacing and retyping.

If you've already used the command and you're recalling it from Doskey's history buffer (see below), there are several ways to edit it.

## RECALLING PREVIOUS COMMANDS

Even if you don't want to use Doskey to put more than one command on a line, you probably will want to use it to recall commands you used previously. This feature can really save you time, since a lot of your work at the DOS prompt—like copying bunches of files onto floppy disks, or getting a listing of different directories—consists of doing pretty much the same thing again and again.

After you load Doskey, it automatically keeps track of each command you issue. You can recall any of these commands and use them again, or recall and edit them to use for your current task.

> **Just press the Up Arrow key to repeat a command.** When Doskey is installed, pressing the Up Arrow key repeats the last command you gave. Press the Up Arrow key again to get the command before that, and so on.

Although F3 in DOS brings the previous command back, there's a difference: Doskey keeps a history of *all* the commands you've used, to a certain point (limited by the buffer size). Press PgUp to see the oldest command in the history list; press PgDn to see the latest.

> **Erasing the current command.** To get rid of the command currently displayed, press Esc, or press PgDn and the Down Arrow key.

> **Viewing the history list.** To see the whole history list, press F7. You can then choose which command you want to use again from this list, either by highlighting it with the Up and Down Arrow keys and pressing Enter, or by pressing F9, typing the number of the command and pressing Enter twice.

If you had entered the example described above in the "Issue several commands on a single line" tip, you'd press F7 to see the following commands, numbered in the order you entered them.

```
c:\>
1: copy *.* c:\reports\sept
2: del *.*
3: cd ..
4: rd test
c:\>
```

You may see different commands, depending on what you've done since loading Doskey.

> **Speed selecting.** There's an even faster way to use a command from the list Doskey displays: press Esc, then type the first few letters of the command, and then press F8. You can cycle through the commands with the same beginning letters by pressing F8 again.

**Recalling the next command in the list.** Assuming you've moved back somewhere in the Doskey list to use a previous command, you can press the Down Arrow key to display the next command in the list.

**Clearing the history list.** To clear the buffer of all previous commands and start a new list, press Alt-F7.

**Avoid deleting unwanted files with Doskey.** Use this neat tip along with Doskey so that you don't inadvertently delete files. At the DOS prompt, type **dir** *filename* (where *filename* is the file or file pattern name you want to delete, such as P*.DOC). After you see that those are indeed the files you want to delete, press F3 or the Up Arrow to have Doskey re-enter the command. Press Home to go to the beginning of the line. Then type **del** in place of **dir** and press Enter. Neat.

**How many commands does Doskey hold?** The default buffer size is 512 bytes. If you think of a byte as a character, that's a lot of commands. To change the buffer size so it will remember more commands, start Doskey with the **/bufsize=** switch and specify a new size greater than 512.

## EDITING DOSKEY COMMANDS

You probably don't want to reissue the same command over and over. Doskey has all sorts of rather arcane editing tricks to modify previous commands for future use. Because these shortcuts are easier to use than to read about, you might want to start Doskey, issue a few commands and practice along with these tips.

**Edit a command to use it again.** Once you've displayed a Doskey command, you can edit it. You might want to specify a different file name or wildcard pattern, or you might want to move files to a different directory. Use the arrow keys to move to a character; use the Backspace key or the Delete key to delete characters. For example, it's easier to change **copy *.txt a:** to **copy *.doc b:** by changing the **.txt** and the **a:** instead of retyping the whole command.

**Speed editing.** There are lots of neat shortcuts for editing a Doskey command. For example, if you press F2 and type a character, the previous command will be inserted, up to the character you just typed in. When you press F3, the rest of the previous command will be inserted. If the previous command was

```
dir *.bat /s /o:d
```

you could press F2 and type **.** to get **dir***. Then type **com** to change **bat** to **com**. Press F3 to get the rest of the previous command.

Here's the greatest trick of all, in my opinion: just press the Right Arrow key (or F1) to insert the characters from the previous command one at a time, or press Ctrl-R and the arrow key to recall one word at a time. The F2 and F3 tricks require a little thought on your part, but this one doesn't! The previous command just appears, character by character. When you get to the part you want to change, press Ins and type it; you can then recall more characters from the previous command with the Right Arrow key or F1.

**Editing word by word.** If a command is full of switches (like XCOPY C:\REPORTS A: /S /M /P), the quickest way to move between them is to press Ctrl-Right Arrow or Ctrl-Left Arrow. To DOS, anything separated by a space is a word.

**Editing a command doesn't change commands in the buffer.** Editing a command only changes the new command you're entering, not the commands already in the buffer. So feel free to edit away.

**Get help on Doskey.** Don't try to memorize everything about Doskey and its special symbols. You're already at the command line, and you can get a quick reminder of Doskey features by typing **help doskey** or **doskey /?**. Use it.

## USING DOSKEY FOR MACROS

Doskey also lets you define, or create, macros. A *macro* is simply a set of instructions you give to DOS. Defining a macro is just slightly different from using Doskey to issue several commands on one line. You type **doskey**, the name you want your macro to have, an equal sign (=), and then the commands you want the macro to perform. But instead of separating commands with Ctrl-T (as you do to put several commands on one line), use a dollar sign with t ($t); either a capital T or a lowercase t will work.

Suppose you want to see your most recent files first, followed by your document files (those with a .TXT extension) and your spreadsheet files (those with a .WKS extension). Set up a macro called DOIT that sorts a directory listing by date, like this:

```
doskey doit = dir *.txt /o:d $t dir *.wks /o:d
```

**Running your macros.** To run a macro you've created, type its name at the command prompt and press Enter, just like any DOS command.

**Stopping a macro.** Ctrl-C or Ctrl-Break stops the current macro command from executing. You may have to press it more than once to cancel the whole macro.

**Customize DOS commands to work *your way* by defining them as macros.** If you give a macro the same name as a DOS command (like COPY or ERASE), DOS will execute the macro instead of the command. Doskey first looks for and expands macros before passing the expanded command line to DOS.

Want to customize DOS commands to do what you want them to? Suppose you always want your directory listings sorted by date. Define a macro (name it DIR) as **dir /o:d**, which sorts the listing by date, and every time you issue the DIR command, your directory listing will be sorted by date.

If there are DOS commands you always use with the same switches like **xcopy /s /e b:** (which copies everything in the current directory, along with all the related subdirectories and even any empty subdirectories, to drive B) you can create a macro with the same name as the command (XCOPY, in this case). Then you won't have to remember the switches.

If you have a Doskey macro that has the same name as a regular DOS command (such as COPY, for example), DOS will run your macro instead of its own command. To avoid this and have DOS run the "real" command, type a space before typing the command's name at the DOS prompt.

**If you use MEM a lot, use this trick, too.** If you find that you're using the MEM command a lot, put these two lines in your AUTOEXEC.BAT file so that MEM will automatically pause after each screen of information, and so you won't have to watch screens full of figures zipping by:

```
c:\dos\doskey
doskey mem=mem.exe $* /p
```

**Use macros as shorthand.** You can set up a macro as a shorthand notation for a longer command. Suppose you're like me and tend to type "dossshell" with too many s's! Enter **doskey sh = dosshell** to abbreviate DOSSHELL to SH. Then you only have to type **sh** at the command line to enter the Shell.

This is good for any command that's tedious to type or hard to remember. To make your shorthand notation permanent, see the tips about turning your macros into batch files, later in this chapter.

## MACROS VERSUS BATCH FILES

Doskey macros are similar to batch files, but there are some pretty important differences. For one thing, macros exist only in RAM and, because RAM disks are faster than real disks, they carry out your commands faster than batch files. The most important difference, though, is that, like everything in RAM, macros disappear when you power down.

Keep these considerations in mind when you choose between making a procedure into a macro or a batch file.

**Macros are limited in size.** You can use only 127 characters in any one macro. Still, that's a pretty big macro! Batch files, on the other hand, can be as long as you like.

**You can't use GOTO in macros.** You can't use the GOTO command in macros. If you want to branch to different sets of commands, use batch files instead.

**Macros use different symbols as replaceable parameters.** Batch files use the symbols %0 through %9 as replaceable parameters; macros use $0 through $9.

**Macros can start batch files.** A macro can't start another macro, but it *can* start a batch file. A batch file, however, can load your saved macros into memory so you can use them on more than one occasion.

**Macros are faster than batch files.** Since macros exist only in RAM, they're faster than batch files, which are stored on disk. If you use a routine often (and it doesn't mind the limitations described above), make it a macro instead of a batch file. Read the next tip to learn how to save your macros.

## SAVING MACROS

Macros exist only in RAM, so they disappear when the power fails or when you turn off your computer. You can save your macros, however, as you'll see in the following tricks.

> **Turning macros into batch files.** If you turn a macro into a batch file, you can use it any time. To do this, direct your macro to a text file and then edit it to make just the lines you want to use into individual batch files.
>
> For example, store a bunch of macros you've just created in a file named MACROS.DOC:
>
>     doskey /h > macros.doc
>
> If you enter **type macros.doc** to see what's in the file, you'll see that it contains all the commands you've used, including the commands that defined the macros. Think of the /H switch as "history."
>
> You can then use a text editor to turn the macro commands in MACROS.DOC into batch files: edit the MACROS.DOC file to delete any lines you don't want and save (as a batch file with a .BAT extension) each group of commands you do want (see the next tip).

> **Use the /H switch if you're planning to change macros to batch files to reload macros with.** When you redirect macros to a file with the /H switch, each line will already begin with **doskey**, so you won't need to change that to make macros into batch files. For example, a line might appear this way:
>
>     doskey doit=dir *.txt /o:d $t dir *.wks /o:d
>
> Since this is a perfectly good DOS command, all you need to do is save it in a batch file.
>
> But look closely to see if there's any more editing to be done. Batch files have to follow the rules described in Chapter 7. Each command must begin on a separate line, for example, and the commands must have a syntax DOS can understand. There may be lines you don't want to include in your batch file, such as the **doskey /h** line that sent the macros to the file in the first place.
>
> Say you want to save the following macro, which displays your word processing documents and spreadsheets by date:
>
>     doskey doit=dir *.txt /o:d $t dir *.wks /o:d
>
> Let's assume you haven't turned off your computer, so it's still in memory. You want to save it as a batch file named DISPLAY.BAT.

Run

```
doskey /h > display.bat
```

Then edit the resulting DISPLAY.BAT file (use the Editor or your favorite word processing program) to get rid of everything except

```
doskey doit=dir *.txt /o:d $t dir *.wks /o:d
```

Save it as DISPLAY.BAT (remember to use text-only format). Now it will load the macro so you can use it any time you like!

**Keep a collection of your favorite macros.** Instead of sending your macros to a text file, extracting the lines you want and saving them as separate batch files, you can direct *all* the macros you've just created to a batch file. Here, the batch file is called MACROS.BAT (you can name it whatever you like):

```
doskey /h > macros.bat
```

Each time you create a few more macros you like, direct them to your MACROS.BAT file with the /H switch, like this:

```
doskey /h >> macros.bat
```

Notice that you use >> rather than > to append them to the MACROS.BAT file, which already contains macros.

Then edit MACROS.BAT to delete the lines you don't want and keep the lines you do want. All lines should begin with **doskey** (so they'll all be macros).

*Then*—this is the voodoo—call MACROS.BAT from your AUTOEXEC.BAT file so your favorite Doskey macros are in memory each time you start your computer. Assuming you've stored MACROS.BAT in your batch file directory, where you store all your other batch files (and put that in your path, of course), use these lines in your AUTOEXEC.BAT file:

```
doskey
call macros
```

Then, whenever you start up, your macros are automatically loaded in memory, along with Doskey.

If you don't want to call MACROS.BAT from your AUTOEXEC.BAT file but still want to have your favorite macros available at any time, just store MACROS.BAT in your MACROS directory (or wherever you keep macros in your path) and type **macros** at any time to get all your favorite macros in memory.

**Another way to turn macros into batch files.** You can also use Doskey's /M (/MACROS) switch to save the macros themselves, but each line won't begin with **doskey** because it's the command you *create* the macro with—it's not part of the macro itself. Enter the command this way:

```
doskey /m > macros.doc
```

(Of course, specify whatever file name you want to use in place of MACROS.DOC.)

**If you use the /M switch, you'll need to do additional editing before you can make batch files out of your macros.** To use macros made into batch files with the /M switch, you have to edit the file and add **doskey** (followed by a space) to the beginning of each line you want to be a command. And, of course, you have to save the batch file with a .BAT extension.

Here's an example of how a macro you saw earlier would appear in MACROS.DOC if you used the /M switch:

```
doit=dir *.txt /o:d $t dir *.wks /o:d
```

(Of course, if you had defined any other macros, they would be there, too.) However, by itself, DOIT makes no sense to DOS, so you need to add **doskey** (followed by a space) to the beginning of the line if you want to use it as a line in a batch file.

**You may also need to edit special symbols.** You may need to do even more editing if you're converting macros to batch file commands with the /M switch. For example, $g in Doskey is equivalent to the DOS redirection symbol > , and Doskey's $l is equivalent to DOS's <.

**Use Doskey to develop your batch files.** Use Doskey as you're developing batch files to test how they'll run. Test each command with Doskey on; then direct the commands to a file and turn it into a batch file. This method lets you see which line a problem is on as soon as it becomes a problem; then you don't have to guess how to debug a batch file several lines long.

**Deleting macros.** To delete a macro, do this:

```
doskey macroname =
```

No, there's nothing left off there. Just enter **doskey**, the macro's name, an equal sign (=) and Enter.

To delete *all* your macros, just press Alt-F10.


## MOVING ON

This discussion just scratches the surface of what you can do with macros. If you're interested in some of the more sophisticated hoops you can make DOS jump through (macros with replaceable parameters, for example, and piping and redirection), better get out one of those doorstopper books.

Chapter 9, "Arcane Commands," discusses some off-the-beaten-path shortcuts you can use with DOS commands that aren't always in your daily repertoire.

# Chapter 9
# ARCANE COMMANDS

This chapter introduces you to some obscure DOS commands and switches and some well-known DOS commands and switches, too. It's not intended to be a complete command reference showing the syntax and all the switches to use with each command. If you're doing something really complicated (like setting up your system to use with Icelandic), you can get online help or even read one of those computer tomes. This chapter initiates you, however, into several esoteric areas you otherwise might overlook.

**What's APPEND good for?**  APPEND was designed to get around the limitations of some older programs (like early WordStar versions) that didn't let you keep data files in one directory and program files in another. It's also useful for situations in which programs can't find special files called overlay files, which they need in order to run, and you're getting messages like "Can't find overlay *filename*." Programmers have some uses for it, too.

Think of APPEND as being like PATH, except that it lets you specify directories that hold data files; it can't be used with executable programs. For example, if you have a program that needs it, put it in your AUTOEXEC.BAT file. APPEND lets you work on one drive with directories from another drive. With the following line in your AUTOEXEC.BAT file, you can use the files in a directory named REPORTS on drive B, even though you're working in drive A:

```
append b:\reports
```

**You can't get a directory listing of an appended directory.** When you give the DIR command, DOS doesn't show files in the appended directory if they're not in the current directory. You have to use the appended directory's name to see files in an appended directory. So be warned.

You can reverse APPEND's effects by entering **append ;** at the command prompt.

**Don't use APPEND if you're running Windows.** Windows likes to be in control and doesn't run well (sometimes not at all) if you use APPEND. You shouldn't use FASTOPEN or SUBST when you're running Windows, either. And if you're running DOS 6, don't use these commands after Windows has started:

```
DEFRAG
MEMMAKER
VSAFE
```

**Don't use APPEND if you're running DOS 6, either.** Check your CONFIG.SYS file if you're using DOS 6 and take out any APPEND lines.

**Use SUBST instead of ASSIGN.** As you saw in Chapter 5, "Disk & Drive Magic," you can set up a shorthand notation for long path names in which you replace them with a drive letter. You then use either SUBST or ASSIGN to redirect disk operations from one drive to another. The following two lines do the same thing, but Microsoft recommends you use SUBST instead of ASSIGN (in fact, Microsoft removed ASSIGN from DOS 6):

```
assign a=b
subst a: b:
```

To cancel all assignments, just enter **assign** by itself, without any switches. To cancel substitutions, enter **subst** *drive* **1: /d**.

**Don't use ASSIGN on drive C.** Because DOS is stored on drive C (your hard disk, the one you boot from), you can get into trouble if you reassign drive C. So don't **assign c=d**. It's OK to **assign a=c** and **assign b=c**, though, to redirect floppy drive operations to drive C.

**Don't use some commands while others are in effect.** ASSIGN, JOIN and SUBST tell DOS to substitute other drive letters for the real thing, so don't use those commands with BACKUP, DISKCOPY, DISKCOMP, FORMAT, LABEL or RESTORE. BACKUP and the other commands need to know which physical drive is being referred to.

It's also a good idea to remove all your assignments, joins and substitutions if you're doing disk housekeeping, just so you (and DOS) both know exactly where you're moving files.

In fact, ASSIGN and JOIN are missing from DOS 6 because Microsoft relegated them to the scrap heap. If you can't live without them, you can order the Supplemental Disk; see Chapter 1 for how.

**The hidden hidden file.** If you run CHKDSK, you'll see that it reports three hidden files. You may know that two of them are the required system files IO.SYS and MSDOS.SYS (which were called IBMBIO.COM and IBMDOS.COM, respectively, before DOS 5), but what's the third one? It's your volume label.

**Delete the numbered files that CHKDSK finds.** When you run **chkdsk /f** to fix a disk, you'll be asked if you want any lost clusters (bits of files somehow separated from the files they belong to) to be converted to files. If you tell it Yes, CHKDSK will convert the lost clusters to numbered files in your root directory ending in .CHK. Just delete them; they're unusable and take up space on your disk. Looking at each one and trying to figure out which file it belongs to is like trying to put Humpty Dumpty together again.

> **Bad sectors don't mean you have a bad disk.** If **chkdsk /f** reports a few bad sectors, don't worry. They're parts of the disk that couldn't be read and were skipped over when the disk was formatted.

> **Use MEM instead of CHKDSK; it's faster.** Try using MEM instead of CHKDSK to see how much memory is available. MEM is faster because it doesn't read the disk.
>
> If you upgraded from DOS 3.3 to DOS 5, you may have missed this one. MEM was new in Version 4. CHKDSK is one of those "favorite" commands you're probably used to if you've used DOS 3.3 for very long. (Chapter 4, "Command-Line Tricks," has a few more CHKDSK tips.)

> **The Shell is also faster than CHKDSK.** You can quickly see file, directory and disk information in the Shell by choosing Show Information from the Options menu instead of running CHKDSK, which is pretty slow if you have a big hard disk.

> **Don't try running CHKDSK on a network.** You can't run CHKDSK on a network drive, or when any of those "Let's fool DOS" commands (ASSIGN, JOIN and SUBST) are in effect. Log off your net before you use CHKDSK to check your local disks.

> **Specify file names with CHKDSK to see which files may be bad or fragmented.** If you supply a file name or a wildcard pattern with the CHKDSK command (such as **chkdsk a:*.txt**), it will report logical errors in the specified files and list which of those files are fragmented (stored in noncontiguous blocks).
>
> If you've used the /F switch with CHKDSK and file names, and if there are logical errors in the files, DOS will ask you if you want the lost segments converted to chains. If you say Yes, they'll be named FILE0000.CHK, and so forth. It probably won't be of any use to try to look at these with the Editor, your word processing program, or the F9 key in the Shell. You might as well delete **\*.chk** to get rid of all of them. At least you'll know which files were bad.

**You *can* compare disks with one floppy drive.** If you only have one floppy drive, you can still use commands like DISKCOPY (which makes a duplicate copy of a disk) and DISKCOMP (which compares two disks). Give the command as **diskcomp a:** (or **diskcopy a:**) to compare or copy two disks in drive A. You'll be prompted to insert disks as needed.

But don't try to compare a 5.25-inch disk in drive A with a 3.5-inch disk in drive B: you have to compare disks of the same size and capacity.

**Synonyms for DOS commands.** You can abbreviate or use synonyms for a few DOS commands. Some are logical; some aren't.

- DELETE is the same as ERASE, but you can't abbreviate ERASE to ERA like you can abbreviate DELETE to DEL. And, although there's an UNDELETE command, there's no UNERASE command!

- RENAME can be abbreviated to REN.

- CHDIR can be abbreviated to CD.

- RMDIR can be abbreviated to RD.

- MKDIR can be abbreviated to MD.

- LOADHIGH can be abbreviated to LH.

- If you try to abbreviate any other commands, you'll get a "Bad command" message.

**Don't try to compare backed-up files.** BACKUP files on a floppy disk don't exactly compare with their corresponding versions on the hard disk or on another floppy disk. The backup procedure puts extra information in the backup copies that tells DOS where the backup files came from.

**If two files are different sizes, they're not the same.** If the COMP command reports that "Files are different sizes," it means that the files aren't the same (because they're different lengths). This command is useful if you're comparing two files just to see if they're the same, not to see *how* they're different.

**Don't look for COMP in DOS 6. It's not there.** Use the FC command instead of COMP.

The COMP command compares two files, very enigmatically reports that they're different sizes and tells you at which offset the compare errors are. That's not much help, but at least you'll know the files are not the same. To see where the differences are, use FC. It shows you where the differences are and gives a little bit of the context around them. To ignore uppercase and lowercase, use FC with the /C switch; to see the line numbers where the differences are, use the /N switch.

For example, to compare a file named DOC.TXT on drive A with a file named DOC.TXT on drive B, ignoring case differences, enter

```
fc a:doc.txt b:doc.txt /c
```

You may want to use | MORE at the end of this line if there are a lot of differences in the files, so you can display one screen at a time.

**Forget all those international commands!** If you're using a computer you bought in the United States and you're using it in English, there are a whole bunch of DOS commands you'll probably never need: CHCP, COUNTRY.SYS, DISPLAY.SYS, NLSFUNC, KEYB, KEYBOARD.SYS, PRINTER.SYS and a few others. Don't worry about them unless you're switching your system to a completely different language. Then, worry.

**Remember all those memory commands!** DOS also has a bunch of memory-management commands: DEVICEHIGH, LOADHIGH, EMM386.EXE, SMARTDRV.SYS, RAMDRIVE.SYS, DOS=HIGH and DOS=UMB. They're discussed in Chapter 10, "Managing Memory."

## Chapter 9: Arcane Commands 229

**Use DATE to check the day of the week.** If you're writing a novel or setting up an example that uses a hypothetical date, use the DATE command to see what day of the week a particular date really was, or will be.

Enter **date**, followed by the date you want to check. Enter **date** again to see what day of the week that is. Then be sure to reset your computer to the current day's date.

**An obscure switch to use with DIR.** **Dir /l** displays a directory listing in lowercase. Now *that's* arcane!

**A new DOS DIRCMD.**  A new DOS 5 (and 6) environmental variable, DIRCMD, lets you specify how you want directory listings to appear. Back in Chapter 4, you learned how to use the following command in your AUTOEXEC.BAT file to alphabetize directory listings and to pause after each screen of text:

```
set dircmd=/o:n /p
```

You can also use any of the DIR command's switches with it to customize your directory listings. To go back to the default, just type

```
set dircmd=.
```

**Loading the Shell with arcane switches.** You can start the DOS Shell with some fairly obscure switches that set its text or graphics screen quality. For example, **dosshell /t:l** loads the Shell in text mode with low resolution. The command **dosshell /g:l** loads it in graphics mode with low resolution. You can also use, with either the /T (text) or /G (graphics) switches: **m** for medium, **h** for high, **v** for very high, **s** for superhigh and **u** for ultrahigh resolution. The results will depend on what kind of monitor you have.

If you have a color monitor, use **dosshell /b** to start the Shell in black-and-white.

**Don't use EXPAND to expand files other than DOS 5 and 6 files.** Although DOS 5 and 6 come with an EXPAND command that can uncompress DOS files on the distribution disks, it's no substitute for file-compression/decompression programs like ZIP and

UNZIP. It's only good for DOS 5's and 6's files. (See "You can expand those compressed files individually," in Chapter 1, for an example of how to use it.)

**Use LASTDRIVE if you have more than five drives.** DOS assumes that the maximum number of drives you have is five—A through E. If you're using a few RAM drives, if you're part of a network, or if you're using the SUBST command to substitute drive letters for long path names, you may have more drives than that.

Put **lastdrive=[*f*]** in your CONFIG.SYS file (put in the letter of *your* last drive, whether it's real or virtual). It doesn't really matter where in the CONFIG.SYS file you put it, unlike some CONFIG.SYS commands.

Some third-party programs that create RAM disks don't require you to use LASTDRIVE. And some even go into your CONFIG.SYS file and put it there for you!

**Reboot if you're going to use your new drive.** Since LASTDRIVE can be specified only in the CONFIG.SYS file, and since you have to restart your computer for changes in CONFIG.SYS to take effect, you'll need to reboot to make DOS recognize your new last drive.

**An arcane DOS 5 MIRROR switch.** Normally, when you run MIRROR, your previous MIRROR.FIL (which keeps track of where everything is) is renamed MIRROR.BAK and a new MIRROR.FIL replaces it. You can specify the /1 (one) switch to save only one MIRROR file. This frees up a bit of space on your disk.

**An undocumented command: MSHERC.** A MSHERC command that's not in the manual (and no help is available for it, either) lets you work with programs that require the Hercules graphics card. If you regularly work with these kinds of programs, put the following line in your AUTOEXEC.BAT file so those programs can work:

    msherc.com

If you have a color monitor, put this line in your AUTOEXEC.BAT file:

```
msherc.com /half
```

If you hardly ever use a program that needs the Hercules adapter, leave the line out of your AUTOEXEC.BAT file and just enter **msherc** or **msherc /half** at the command line whenever you need it.

**Direct your printing to a serial printer with MODE.** Use the MODE command to redirect printing from a parallel port (LPT1) to a serial port (COM1) your printing will automatically go to your serial printer (which is like a laser printer). Put it in your AUTOEXEC.BAT file this way:

```
mode lpt1=com1
```

Then, all the printing requests that call for LPT1 will automatically go to COM1.

**The quirks of RESTORE.** DOS always expects you to restore backed-up files to the same directory from which they were backed up. If it can't find that directory, it tells you it can't find any files to restore. To outwit this, always give the RESTORE command not as **restore a:*.* c:** but as

```
restore a: c:directory\*.*
```

You can add the /S switch if you're also restoring subdirectories.

You can restore files to a different hard disk or drive, but be sure to use the same directory name you used when you backed up the files.

**Restoring by date.** Use the /A or the /B switch with RESTORE to restore only the files changed *before* or *after* a certain date. This is a neat trick. Entering the line:

```
restore a: c:\docs /a:10-28-92
```

restores files dated on or after October 28, 1992. To restore files with dates earlier than that, use

```
restore d: c:\docs /b:10-28-92.
```

**Using date and time switches with RESTORE.** RESTORE also has earlier and later time switches (/E and /L) that let you specify whether to restore files created before or after a certain time. But be careful! Don't use a time switch without a date switch or you'll get all sorts of files you may not want. Think about it!

**Restore disks in numerical order.** When you restore backed-up files with the RESTORE command, you'll be asked to insert them in the floppy drive beginning with disk 01. You have to restore files in the same order in which they were backed up, or the procedure won't work. That's another reason I prefer to use XCOPY instead of BACKUP and RESTORE. If something happens to one of those disks, you won't be able to restore the rest of them without a great deal of effort, such as restoring them file by file.

**Be prompted for the files you want to restore.** If it has been a while since you did a backup, chances are you have more-recent versions of some files on your hard disk than on backup disks. If you add the /P switch to RESTORE, you'll be prompted if there's a more recent version of a file on your hard disk.

**Don't RESTORE unless you have to.** There's really no reason to restore everything unless you have a dreaded hard disk crash. Restore only the files you need as you need them and see the next tip.

**Get a list of the files you've backed up.** If you use the /L switch with BACKUP, you'll get a list of the files you've backed up and the backup disk they're on. This is useful for restoring files whose names you've forgotten.

This list is really handy if you have a huge stack of backup disks and you're not sure what's on them. You might want to print the list and tape it to the paper sleeve of disk 1. (See Chapter 6, "A Miscellany of Alchemy," for quick screen-printing tricks.)

**SET yourself a variable.** The SET command lets you define an environmental variable that can be accessed by your batch files or by DOS commands. Your path is an environmental variable; so is the pattern you're using for your prompt. TEMP is another environmental variable frequently used for setting up a directory in which your programs store temporary files (see "Make yourself a RAM disk," in Chapter 10).

You can use SET to define other variables, such as today's date (**set today=2-16-93**), or a password (**set password=gobbledygook**), or whatever you type in a batch file (**set input=%1%**). Your batch files can access those variables as long as you remember to enclose them in percent symbols. For example, with

```
set text=c:\wordpro\reports\months
```

you can use **cd %text%** in a batch file to change to the directory named C:\WORDPRO\REPORTS\MONTHS.

To see which variables have been defined, type **set** at the DOS prompt.

**Sending a notice to other users.** Here's a neat trick. Say several people share a computer and want a list of expert DOS users and their extension numbers to appear whenever they type **expert** at the DOS prompt; then anyone who needs help can call someone on the list. But, because the experts who are available vary from week to week, everybody needs a weekly list.

To set up a weekly list, first create separate text files containing the experts' names and extension numbers for each week. For example, one file might contain three names: Ken Periat, ext. 3449; Carla Louis, ext. 7711; Jorge Olivera, ext. 6193. Then, if your files are for each week in August 1993, you'd save them as 8_2.TXT, 8_9.TXT, 8_16.TXT, 8_23.TXT and 8_30.TXT (the Mondays in August 1993).

Be sure to put a carriage return at the end of each file so the prompt will be displayed on a separate line when the file appears on the screen.

Then create the following batch file, called EXPERT.BAT, that displays the text file on the screen:

```
@echo off type %expert%
```

Now, at the beginning of the week of August 2, simply type **set expert=8_2.TXT** at the DOS prompt to get that week's list.

 **Arcane TREE switches.** Tired of the same old TREEs? Try **tree /a** for a different look.

To see all the files in your directories, use **tree /f**. Whoops, better use **tree /f | more** or everything will zip past too quickly to read.

**Don't use TREE for finding files.** If you're looking for a particular file, the TREE command is not the most efficient way to find it. The Shell's search feature finds it much quicker, as does the DOS command **dir\\** *filename* **/s** (which looks through all directories from the root).

**A truly undocumented command.** This is a secret voodoo trick. There's an undocumented TRUENAME command to use if you've used SUBST, ASSIGN or JOIN and are confused about which directory a file is in. Just type

```
truename filename
```

at the DOS prompt, and DOS will respond with the path to where it's located!

You have to have used SUBST, JOIN or ASSIGN for TRUENAME to work correctly, however; if you haven't used those commands, TRUENAME just parrots the name of the file you entered. But if you ever get lost after substituting a shorthand drive name for a long path name, TRUENAME can really work magic!

**Shorthand for resetting the time.** You can use the abbreviations **a** (for AM) and **p** (for PM) when you reset the time. Don't bother with seconds or milliseconds. For example, to set the time to 4:55 PM, enter **time 4:55p**.

## Chapter 9: Arcane Commands

**Don't use wildcards with EXPAND.** If for some reason you have to go back to your DOS distribution disks to expand any compressed files (files with an underline (_) in their extensions), don't try to use EXPAND with any wildcards (like **expand \*.\***). It won't work.

You'll need to expand a compressed file if, for instance, there's a disk error as you're installing DOS and the file isn't written correctly to your hard disk. Or, if you purchase a different monitor, you'll need to expand its .VI_ and .GR_ files. (But there's a way around this; see "You can expand those compressed files individually," in Chapter 1.)

**Packed file corrupt?** This enigmatic message appears sometimes with very much older programs that can't use the extra memory that DOS 5 and 6 offer. There's a little-known LOADFIX command that tells DOS to run the program in the old area of memory.

If you get a "Packed file corrupt" message while trying to run a program, restart it this way:

```
loadfix command used to start the program
```

Be sure to include the path to the program, if it's not already in your path.

**Running older programs with SETVER.** There's another obscure command SETVER that fools older programs into thinking they're running under an older version of DOS. To use it, put the following line in your CONFIG.SYS file:

```
device=c:\dos\setver.exe
```

Then, if you have an older program that requires an earlier version of DOS, add that program to the version table with this command:

```
setver program.exe version number
```

For example, if a program named DOIT.EXE needs DOS 3.3, add it to the version table this way:

```
setver doit.exe 3.3
```

Restart your system for the change to take effect, and from then on your program will "think" it's running under DOS 3.3 whenever you run DOIT.EXE.

**Change the date and time format to another country's system.**
If you prefer European date and time formats, put the code of the country whose format you want to use in your CONFIG.SYS file (you can find the codes in the DOS manual or in other manual-type books). For example, to use the French format, put the following line in your CONFIG.SYS file:

    country=033,,c:\dos\country.sys

To reset your system dates and times back to the U.S. version, use this line:

    country=001,,c:\dos\country.sys

## MOVING ON

With this bag of tricks now written in your book of spells, you can begin to do some abstruse DOS wizardry.

In Chapter 10, we'll discuss ways to tweak DOS to handle memory more efficiently. If your computer is a 386 or higher, you *need* to check out Chapter 10. There are also tricks for managing memory with 286 (AT-class) computers, and even some for those of you with XTs and their clones.

# Chapter 10
# Managing Memory

If you upgraded to DOS 5 or 6, you probably had one good reason: memory. These versions of DOS very politely load themselves into high memory and free space your other programs (especially Windows, that notorious memory eater) can use. They also have advanced memory-management features. DOS 5 and 6 let you do all sorts of things to make more memory available to your programs. In particular, DOS 6 has a new MEMMAKER command that automatically optimizes memory for you.

You'll find many useful tips in this chapter for managing memory—whether you have a 386 or higher computer, a 286 (like an AT), or even an old XT-style computer. Try one trick at a time, restart your computer, and keep that bootable floppy disk handy. But first, let's look at memory.

There are several different types of memory. Here's a quick review:

- *Conventional memory* is the first 640k of RAM. The original IBM PC (using the Intel 8088 processor) and most DOS programs today use only the part of this first 640k of memory that's not used by the operating system.

- *Expanded memory* is obtained by using an expanded-memory board (also called a card) that conforms to the Lotus, Intel and Microsoft software interface (called the LIM standard or the

Expanded Memory Specification, or EMS). With expanded memory, a special device driver, the *expanded-memory manager*, swaps 16k "pages" of memory into an unused memory space between 640k and 1 megabyte (mb). This 384k area of memory between 640k and 1mb is called *reserved memory*. Much of it is reserved for routines in read-only memory (such as ROM BIOS) and hardware subsystems (such as video adapters). All PCs, from the original Intel 8088 (XT class) computers to all subsequent PCs and clones, can use expanded memory. But it requires both the memory-expansion card and the expanded-memory manager device driver. In addition, 286 and higher computers can emulate expanded memory by using another type of memory called *extended memory*.

- *Extended memory* above 1mb is available on 286 and higher computers, like IBM ATs and their clones. Extended memory is controlled by the *extended-memory manager*, a program whose principal job is to keep two or more programs from using the same memory at the same time. DOS 5 and 6 come with two extended-memory managers, HIMEM.SYS (for 286 and higher computers) and EMM386.EXE (for 386 and higher computers).

- Basically, you want to clear out as much conventional memory as possible, to allow programs to run there. *DOS runs programs only in conventional memory*. Although programs can *use* extended memory and expanded memory for temporary storage, they can't *run* there. (The exception is Windows, in 386 Enhanced mode.) The bottom line is to put DOS itself in high memory and to load as many device drivers and terminate-and-stay resident (also called memory-resident) programs into upper memory as you can; and to do this, you need to have a 386 or higher computer.

- This is a slightly oversimplified explanation, of course, but with voodoo you don't need to know how everything works. The important thing is to get the most from your system. And the first step is to find out what kind of memory it has.

**Use the MEM command to see how your system uses memory. If your computer has extended memory, you'll be able to see how much it has.** On a computer that has 2mb of extended memory, you'll see something like this:

```
   655360   bytes total conventional memory
   655360   bytes available to MS-DOS
   617600   largest executable program size
  2097152   bytes total contiguous extended memory
        0   bytes available contiguous extended memory
  2031616   bytes available XMS memory
MS-DOS resident in High Memory Area
```

This means that you have 640k of conventional memory (655,360 divided by 1,024, or one k) and 2mb (2,048k) of extended memory (2,097,152 divided by 1,024). (XMS memory is a type of extended memory.) So 603k is available for your programs—it's the "largest executable program size."

 **The difference between "available" and "usable" memory.** If you see this message:

```
  2097152   bytes total contiguous extended memory
  2097152   bytes available contiguous extended memory
```

you'll think everything is fine because the memory is "available." You'll be wrong. "Available" memory isn't *usable* unless an extended-memory manager is controlling it. You want to see this line:

```
        0   bytes available contiguous extended memory
```

It means that all your extended memory is being used as extended memory.

**Switches that tell more about memory.** Type **mem /c** to see a detailed report of how every program you run is placed in conventional and high memory. Don't run MEM /C from the Shell, though, it will give you the wrong answer! You can also type **mem /p** (for program) or **mem /d** (for debug) to get even more detailed listings.

**New switches in DOS 6.** DOS 6 adds a couple of new switches to the MEM command. MEM /F (for Free) shows the free areas of upper and conventional memory, and MEM /M *program-name* shows how a program is using memory. Here's what MEM /F can show you:

```
C:\>mem /f
Free Conventional Memory:
 Segment         Total
  01040             80      (0K)
  02A37            256      (0K)
  02A47          88368     (86K)
  03FDA         393808    (385K)
 Total Free:   482512    (471K)
Free Upper Memory:
 Region  Largest Free    Total  Free     Total    Size
    1     78848  (77K)   94576  (92K)   158832  (155K)
```

And here's how memory was being used during my recent session with WordPerfect:

```
C:\>mem /m wp
WP is using the following memory:
 Segment  Region      Total           Type
  02A37                 256    (0K)   Environment
  02A47              372448  (364K)   Program

 Total Size:         372704  (364K)
```

**What can you do about memory?** If, like me, you're always getting confused between extended and expanded memory, you're probably not sure what you can and cannot do to tweak your system's memory with DOS 5 and 6. Here it is, in a nutshell.

Managing memory depends on what kind of computer you have.

- If you have a 386 or higher computer, you can control extended memory with two extended-memory managers: HIMEM.SYS and EMM386.EXE. They let you load DOS into high memory (with the DOS command) and also put TSR (terminate-and-stay resident) programs and device drivers into high memory with the commands LOADHIGH and

DEVICEHIGH. You can also create a RAM disk with RAMDRIVE.SYS, and a disk cache with SMARTDRV.SYS.

- If you have a 286 or higher computer (like an IBM AT or clone), you can put DOS in high memory with HIMEM.SYS. You can also create a RAM disk with RAMDRIVE.SYS, and a disk cache with SMARTDRV.SYS. But you can't use the EMM386 memory manager (EMM386.EXE) and you can't load device drivers and TSRs into upper memory.

- If you have an 8088-type machine, like an IBM XT or clone, you can create a RAM disk (if you have expanded memory) and a disk cache, but you can't load DOS or TSR programs into high memory with HIMEM.SYS or EMM386.EXE.

- This chapter contains many memory tips. The numbers 8088+, 286+ or 386+ next to each tip and trap refer to the type of computer you have. Skip the tips that don't relate to your computer.

### (8088+) Make a bootable floppy before you experiment with memory.
Just in case something goes awry during the trial-and-error process of tweaking your system's memory for maximum performance, make yourself a bootable floppy disk as described in Chapter 1, "Beyond Magic." It should at least have, in addition to the system files, your current and working AUTOEXEC.BAT and CONFIG.SYS files.

You can use the bootable floppy disk in either of two ways. If you are comfortable experimenting, keep it handy to restart your computer in case it locks up from some memory conflict generated as you change your AUTOEXEC.BAT and CONFIG.SYS files. You can always copy your original CONFIG.SYS and AUTOEXEC.BAT files back onto your hard disk from this floppy disk.

But if you're not sure what you're doing, edit the AUTOEXEC.BAT and CONFIG.SYS files on the floppy disk and use that to start your computer until you've got memory managed the way you want it. *Then* copy the edited CONFIG.SYS and AUTOEXEC.BAT files onto your hard disk. (When you edit the files on the floppy disk, be sure to use the drive letter and full path name to where your device drivers are stored [usually in C:\DOS], or you'll get error messages when you start your computer.)

No matter which method you use, follow two basic rules. First, test your bootable floppy to make sure it works. Put it in drive A and restart your computer. Second, make only one change at a time to your AUTOEXEC.BAT and CONFIG.SYS files and restart your computer each time to try it out. That way, if there's a problem, you'll know what it is. Then you can delete that line from your file and try again. If you're using DOS 6, make use of its new interactive start feature that lets you debug AUTOEXEC.BAT and CONFIG.SYS on startup (see Chapter 1).

It's a good idea to make copies of your AUTOEXEC.BAT and CONFIG.SYS files and store them in your DOS directory under slightly different names, like AUTOEXEC.KAY and CONFIG.KAY, just so you'll know there are untouched, unedited working copies somewhere that you can get back and rename AUTOEXEC.BAT and CONFIG.SYS if things really go wrong. (By the way, it's a good idea to do this even if you aren't experimenting with memory.)

Also, remember that because your AUTOEXEC.BAT file is a batch file, you can execute it simply by typing **autoexec** at the DOS prompt. For changes in your CONFIG.SYS file to take effect, however, you have to restart your computer with Ctrl-Alt-Del. DOS has to read the CONFIG.SYS file at boot time to see what's in it.

In all the following tricks, I'm assuming that your device drivers are stored in C:\DOS. If your DOS directory has a different path, be sure to use it instead of C:\DOS.

**(286+) Make sure you're set up to use upper memory.** If you have a 286 or higher computer, you normally will see a message like this when your computer starts:

```
HIMEM: DOS XMS Driver, Version 2.77 - 02/27/91
XMS Specification Version 2.0

Copyright 1988-1991 Microsoft Corp.
Installed A20 handler number 1.
64K High Memory Area is available.
```

If you don't see a message like this, and DOS isn't reporting that you already have an extended-memory manager installed, check your CONFIG.SYS file. It needs to contain this line:

```
device=c:\dos\himem.sys
```

Ordinarily, the HIMEM.SYS line should come first in your CONFIG.SYS file. The one exception to this is when you're using a device driver like SpeedStor (SSTOR.SYS) or OnTrack (DMDRVR.BIN) that allows DOS to use partitions larger than 32mb. If you see something like that on the first line of your CONFIG.SYS file (and everything else is working right), keep it there and put the HIMEM.SYS line second.

### (286+) Can't access high memory? It may be the A20 handler.

The A20 handler provides access to the high memory area (HMA). Computers use different kinds of A20 handlers. Usually, HIMEM.SYS can tell which type of computer you have and will adjust the A20 handler accordingly. If you get a message that DOS can't access the high memory area, change the HIMEM.SYS line in your CONFIG.SYS file to add the /MACHINE: switch, followed by the special code for your computer (you can find it in the manual). Also, to find any additional codes that may have become available after the manual went to press, check the README.TXT file on your DOS distribution disk set.

### (286+) You can load DOS itself into high memory.

DOS does not *have* to be in high memory. It runs just fine in conventional memory. Getting it into high memory simply frees more memory for your programs.

To load part of DOS into high memory, making about 50k of conventional memory available for your programs, the second line of your CONFIG.SYS file should look like this:

```
dos=high
```

If you have a 386 or higher computer, the UMB switch gets DOS ready to create upper memory blocks, where you can load your device drivers and TSRs, as you'll see later. It should look like this:

```
dos=high,umb
```

Now, when you restart your computer, you should see the following line:

```
MS DOS resident in High Memory Area
```

**DOS doesn't optimize itself on a 386 or 486 computer.** The Setup program that installs DOS doesn't automatically configure EMM386.EXE to manage the upper memory area on 386 and higher computers. EMM386.EXE can use extended memory to simulate expanded memory, and it lets you run device drivers as well as TSR programs in upper memory, which frees up even more conventional memory.

To use EMM386.EXE on a 386 or higher computer, you'll need to add this line to your CONFIG.SYS file, right after the DOS=HIGH,UMB line:

```
device=c:\dos\emm386.exe
```

There are two switches you can use with EMM386.EXE: RAM and NOEMS. Use NOEMS, as illustrated in the line below, if you want to provide access to the upper memory area but don't want to emulate expanded memory with extended memory:

```
device=c:\dos\emm386.exe noems
```

You won't be able to use expanded memory if you use NOEMS, but that probably won't matter since most programs nowadays use extended memory instead of expanded memory.

If you do have programs that need to use expanded memory, change NOEMS to RAM, as shown:

```
device=c:\dos\emm386.exe 640 ram
```

This tells DOS to use 640k of extended memory as expanded memory and to provide access to the upper memory area. If you don't specify an amount of expanded memory, DOS assumes you want 256k. You can specify almost as much expanded memory as you have extended memory in your computer (DOS needs about 64k of it).

Now, when you restart your computer, you should see something like this on the screen (with DOS 5):

```
MICROSOFT Expanded Memory Manager 386 Version
4.20.06X
Copyright Microsoft Corporation 1986, 1990
```

These lines are followed by a detailed list of available expanded memory and total upper memory.

**(80386+) Optimize memory painlessly with DOS 6.** DOS 6 includes a new command, MEMMAKER, that sets up your AUTOEXEC.BAT and CONFIG.SYS files (and SYSTEM.INI, too, if you're running Windows) so that your memory-resident programs take up less conventional memory, which is then available for your programs to use. This command is wonderful because you don't have to figure out what's high memory and what's upper memory and which device drivers and programs can go where, as so much of this chapter has tediously tried to explain. Just let MEMMAKER take care of all that.

To run MEMMAKER, you'll need a 386 or higher computer. To start, you should be at the DOS prompt. That means the "raw" DOS prompt; don't exit to DOS temporarily from the Shell or from Windows. Then type **memmaker** and press Enter. Follow the instructions on the screen. To have MEMMAKER optimize your memory *completely* automatically with no input from you, start it at the command line by typing **memmaker /batch** so that is runs in batch mode.

MEMMAKER does the work for you, so there aren't many tricks you can use with it as long as you use "Express optimization," the default choice. There is a Custom optimization option, though, that lets you specify what you want to put in upper memory. If you have a VGA or EGA monitor, for example, you can use the monochrome region (which EGA and VGA monitors don't use, but monochrome and SVGA monitors do) for device drivers and memory-resident programs, which saves a little RAM. Or, if you don't run non-Windows programs (such as WordPerfect 5.1 for DOS) under Windows, you can specify that upper memory not be optimized for use with Windows. The advanced options you can use with Custom optimization are just that: fairly advanced. Most people will do just fine with Express optimization. If you decide to try Custom, though, you can get help with the advanced options by pressing F1 when you're at the Options screen, after you've started MEMMAKER.

**Check your AUTOEXEC.BAT before you run MEMMAKER.** MEMMAKER doesn't deal with TSRs that are loaded by a batch program in your AUTOEXEC.BAT. If you've set up a batch file to load any programs into high memory, you'll get better memory optimization from MEMMAKER if you change that batch file so that the TSRs are loaded into conventional memory. Take a look at any batch file you CALL in your AUTOEXEC.BAT and see if there are LOADHIGH or LH commands in it. If there are, take those commands out. (For an example of what one of these lines looks like, see the tips "Now you're ready to use upper memory" and "Load TSRs manually if you run into trouble.")

**(80386+) Change your mind? You can undo the changes MEMMAKER makes.** After MEMMAKER's done, you'll see a screen showing what your memory allocation was like before and after MEMMAKER performed its magic. If you don't like what you see, you can undo its last changes. Even later, when you're not looking at the MEMMAKER screen, you can undo its changes by typing **memmaker /undo** at the command line.

If you have trouble after MEMMAKER runs, usually it's just one memory-resident program or device driver that's causing the trouble by not wanting to run in upper memory. Before you undo all the changes MEMMAKER makes, try changing DEVICEHIGH commands in your CONFIG.SYS file, one by one, to DEVICE commands and see if you're still having a problem. Do the same with any LOADHIGH commands that load memory-resident programs into upper memory and see if you can isolate the culprit.

**If you've changed your AUTOEXEC.BAT and CONFIG.SYS files, you may need to edit them again.** If you've made any changes to your AUTOEXEC.BAT and CONFIG.SYS files after running MEMMAKER, and you decide to undo MEMMAKER's changes, those changes won't be in the original AUTOEXEC.BAT and

CONFIG.SYS files that MEMMAKER restores. You may need to edit those files again to put the changes you made back in them. Copy the AUTOEXEC.BAT and CONFIG.SYS files onto a floppy before you undo MEMMAKER's changes if you want to compare the "before" and "after" versions.

**(386+) Use DOS 6's improved Help facility to find out more about memory.** DOS 6 comes with extensive Help screens covering all the memory commands, such as EMM386. Before you struggle with a complex memory problem, check out the Help on it by typing at the command line **help emm386, help devicehigh, help loadhigh, help himem.sys** ... you get the idea. Check out all the help for the memory commands. Better yet, run DOS 6's MEMMAKER program and let it take care of everything for you. See the tips on MEMMAKER earlier in this chapter.

**(386+) Got a Weitek math coprocessor?** Be aware that EMM386.EXE doesn't normally support a Weitek math coprocessor. Add the /W=ON switch to the EMM386.EXE line in your CONFIG.SYS file if you want to be able to use the coprocessor all the time, or enter the command **emm386 /w=on** at the command line each time you use it if you just occasionally need it.

**(386+) Now you're ready to *use* upper memory.** If you've experimented with the previous tricks (and restarted your computer each time to make sure everything is still working), you've prepared upper memory for use. Now you can load device drivers (with the DEVICEHIGH command) and TSRs (with the LOADHIGH command) into upper memory, which will really clean out conventional memory for your programs. Remember, programs run only in the 640k of conventional memory (unless you're using Windows).

You either can load TSRs like Doskey "manually," with this line

```
loadhigh c:\dos\doskey
```

or, to start them automatically, put the memory-resident program you want to load into high memory in your AUTOEXEC.BAT file, as shown in the line above.

**DOS 6 lets you specify which memory region you want to load programs and devices into.** In DOS 6, both LOADHIGH and DEVICEHIGH have new /L switches that let you specify exactly which region of memory you want to load programs and devices into. Of course, you'll have to know beforehand a lot more about memory than I do if you want to use these switches, since there are many different regions of memory. If, say, you wanted to load Doskey into region 1, you'd do it like this:

```
loadhigh /l:1 c:dos\doskey
```

**(386+) Load TSRs manually if you run into trouble.** If a TSR is giving you problems or error messages after you've loaded it (with LOADHIGH), load the program the old-fashioned way: start it with the command at the DOS prompt or run it from the Shell. (Take the command for it out of your AUTOEXEC.BAT, if it's there.) Some programs won't run right in the rarefied air of the upper memory area because they're just not designed for it.

**(386+) What memory-resident programs can you load high?** The DOS memory-resident programs you can load into upper memory are DOSKEY.COM, DOSSHELL.COM, GRAPHICS.COM, KEYB.COM, MODE.COM, NLSFUNC.EXE, PRINT.EXE and SHARE.EXE. You can also load other third-party TSRs, like Borland's SideKick or a pop-up calculator program.

**(386+) Here's how to tell which of your programs are TSRs.** To see what TSRs you have before you try to load them into upper memory, use MEM /C. Your memory-resident programs will be listed after the line that says COMMAND, as below:

```
Name            Size in Decimal      Size in Hex
MSDOS           14272   ( 13.9K)     37C0
SSTOR            6496   (  6.3K)     1960
HIMEM            2896   (  2.8K)     B50
EMM386           8400   (  8.2K)     20D0
SETVER            400   (  0.4K)     190
COMMAND          2624   (  2.6K)     A40
SNAP           105872   (103.4K)     19D90
MOUSE           12784   ( 12.5K)     31F0
ALAP            12256   ( 12.0K)     2FE0
PSTACK          29648   ( 29.0K)     73D0
NETPRINT        32416   ( 31.7K)     7EA0
PAPOVL           9648   (  9.4K)     25B0
KEYINT           6464   (  6.3K)     1940
FREE               64   (  0.1K)     40
FREE               64   (  0.1K)     40
FREE               64   (  0.1K)     40
FREE              128   (  0.1K)     80
FREE           410448   (400.8K)     64350

Total FREE:    410768 (401.1K)
Total bytes available to programs :
               410768        (401.1K)
Largest executable program size :
               410448        (400.8K)


 655360    bytes total EMS memory
 262144    bytes free EMS memory
3145728    bytes total contiguous extended memory
      0    bytes available contiguous extended memory
2719744    bytes available XMS memory
           MS-DOS resident in High Memory Area
```

In this configuration, the TSR candidates for moving to upper memory are a big screen dump program (SNAP), a mouse, a Sitka/TOPS network (ALAP and PSTACK) and a network printer driver (NETPRINT) and the devices following it.

As before, load only one at a time so you can tell which one is causing any trouble. Use MEM /C again to make sure your programs were successfully transferred to upper memory.

### You get more information with MEM in DOS 6.
DOS 6 adds more information to what the MEM command shows. For example, it shows the amount of memory available on any add-in boards you may have installed, such as a video adapter board:

```
C:\>mem /c /p
Modules using memory below 1 MB:
  Name         Total          =  Conventional  +  Upper Memory
  MSDOS        15341   (15K)     15341   (15K)         0   (0K)
  HIMEM         1152    (1K)      1152    (1K)         0   (0K)
  EMM386        3120    (3K)      3120    (3K)         0   (0K)
  DBLSPACE     44352   (43K)     44352   (43K)         0   (0K)
  COMMAND       2912    (3K)      2912    (3K)         0   (0K)
  SNAP        106000  (104K)    106000  (104K)         0   (0K)
  WP          384224  (375K)    384224  (375K)         0   (0K)
  COMMAND       3216    (3K)      3216    (3K)         0   (0K)
  SETVER         816    (1K)         0    (0K)       816   (1K)
  PCACHE       12304   (12K)         0    (0K)     12304  (12K)
  SMARTDRV     28800   (28K)         0    (0K)     28800  (28K)
  MOUSE        17088   (17K)         0    (0K)     17088  (17K)
  SHARE         5248    (5K)         0    (0K)      5248   (5K)
  Free        189344  (185K)     94768   (93K)     94576  (92K)

Memory Summary:
Type of Memory    Total          =  Used             +  Free
Conventional      655360  (640k)    560592  (547K)     94768  (93K)
Upper             158832  (155K)     64256   (63K)     94576  (92K)
Adapter RAM/ROM   234384  (229K)    234384  (229K)         0   (0K)
Extended (XMS)   7340032 (7168K)   2514944 (2456K)   4825088 (4712K)

Total memory     8388608 (8192K)   3374176 (3295K)   5014432 (4897K)
Total under 1 MB  814192  (795K)    624848  (610K)    189344  (185K)

Largest executable program size            94672   (92K)
Largest free upper memory block            78848   (77K)
MS-DOS is resident in the high memory area.
```

### (386+) What device drivers can you load into upper memory?
Unlike LOADHIGH, which you can issue at the DOS prompt or put in your AUTOEXEC.BAT file, DEVICEHIGH has to be in your CONFIG.SYS file. You can't use it at the DOS prompt, and you have to restart your computer to see its effects (use MEM /C after each device driver is loaded).

The following device drivers can be put into upper memory: ANSI.SYS, EGA.SYS, DISPLAY.SYS, DRIVER.SYS, MOUSE.SYS, PRINTER.SYS, RAMDRIVE.SYS and (sometimes) SMARTDRV.SYS (see the next trick). Remember, all the device drivers you're using are named in your CONFIG.SYS file. If you're running DOS 6, you can use the DEVICEHIGH command to load DBLSPACE.UMB, INTERLINK.EXE and POWER.EXE into upper memory, too.

Your device drivers also appear *before* the command line in a MEM /C listing. In the displayed example in the preceding tip, they are SSTOR.SYS, HIMEM.SYS, EMM386.EXE and SETVER.EXE. Use MEM /C to check the size of your device drivers; make a list of them from largest to smallest. Load each one high, in the order of this list from largest to smallest. If you're running DOS 6, you can load DBLSPACE.BIN, INTERLINK.EXE into upper memory with the DEVICEHIGH command, too.

Check your CONFIG.SYS file and change to DEVICEHIGH= any of the lines (except HIMEM.SYS, EMM386.EXE or SETVER.EXE; see the next tip) that start with DEVICE= and are followed by a device driver that's listed before the command line (remember, one at a time, and restart!).

If you have any trouble (if your computer locks up, for instance), reboot from your other disk and change the DEVICEHIGH line for that particular device driver back to the simple DEVICE= line, which loads it into conventional memory instead of upper memory.

### Don't load HIMEM.SYS and EMM386.EXE into high memory.

It's easy to get carried away as you free up conventional memory and try to load everything into high memory. Don't try to put HIMEM.SYS, EMM386.EXE, COMMAND.COM or SETVER.EXE there, though, because they won't work right.

### (286+) Use the MEM command to see how memory is handled with HIMEM.SYS and EMM386.EXE.

Tweaking your system for maximum memory is a trial-and-error process (so be sure to keep that bootable floppy handy). There's no immediately obvious way to tell what effects your changes have. Use **mem /c | more** to see how HIMEM.SYS and EMM386.EXE are doing in managing memory.

Here's a "before" screen, showing only DOS 5 and MIRROR in high memory (these figures are for a configuration of 640k of conventional memory and 2mb of extended memory):

```
Conventional Memory :
Name                Size in Decimal      Size in Hex
MSDOS               14288  ( 14.0K)      37D0
SSTOR                6496  (  6.3K)      1960
HIMEM                2896  (  2.8K)      B50
EMM386               8400  (  8.2K)      20D0
SETVER                400  (  0.4K)      190
ANSI                 4192  (  4.1K)      1060
COMMAND              2624  (  2.6K)      A40
MOUSE               12784  ( 12.5K)      31F0
FREE                   64  (  0.1K)      40
FREE                  128  (  0.1K)      80
FREE               602800  (588.7K)      932B0

Total FREE:        602992 (588.9K)
Upper Memory :
Name                Size in Decimal      Size in Hex
SYSTEM             163840 (160.0K)       28000
MIRROR               6512  (  6.4K)      1970
FREE                  128  (  0.1K)      80
FREE                91600  ( 89.5K)      165D0

Total FREE:         91728  ( 89.6K)

Total bytes available to programs (Conventional+Upper):
        694720    (678.4K)
Largest executable program size :
        602800    (588.7K)
Largest available upper memory block :
         91600    ( 89.5K)

3145728   bytes total contiguous extended memory
0         bytes available contiguous extended memory
2894848   bytes available XMS memory

          MS-DOS resident in High Memory Area
```

Here's the "after" screen, showing that DEVICE= has been changed to DEVICEHIGH= for ANSI.SYS:

```
Conventional Memory :
Name                Size in Decimal     Size in Hex
MSDOS               14288   ( 14.0K)    37D0
SSTOR               6496    (  6.3K)    1960
HIMEM               2896    (  2.8K)    B50
EMM386              8400    (  8.2K)    20D0
SETVER              400     (  0.4K)    190
COMMAND             2624    (  2.6K)    A40
MOUSE               12784   ( 12.5K)    31F0
FREE                64      (  0.1K)    40
FREE                128     (  0.1K)    80
FREE                607200  (592.8K)    94320

Total FREE:         607200  (593.0K)
Upper Memory :
Name                Size in Decimal     Size in Hex
SYSTEM              163840  (160.0K)    28000
ANSI                4192    (  4.1K)    1060
MIRROR              6512    (  6.4K)    1970
FREE                128     (  0.1K)    80
FREE                87376   ( 85.3K)    15550

Total FREE:         87504   ( 85.5K)

Total bytes available to programs(Conventional+Upper):
        694704    (678.4K)
Largest executable program size :
        607800    (592.8K)
Largest available upper memory block :
        87376     ( 85.3K)

3145728    bytes total contiguous extended memory
0          bytes available contiguous extended memory
2894848    bytes available XMS memory

        MS-DOS resident in High Memory Area
```

As you can see, there's still a good bit of upper memory free; you can go ahead and load the mouse driver and even some other TSRs, like Doskey, into upper memory.

### (386+) You can put all sorts of things in upper memory.

DEVICEHIGH can be used with RAMDRIVE.SYS and SMARTDRV.SYS, too, so you can really run lean and mean. There's some debate about whether SMARTDRV.SYS works *well* in upper memory; try it on your system if you feel like experimenting.

To put RAMDRIVE.SYS in upper memory (for a 1mb RAM drive), put the following line in your CONFIG.SYS file:

```
devicehigh=c:\dos\ramdrive.sys 1024 /e
```

To put SMARTDRV.SYS in upper memory (for a 1mb disk cache), use this line:

```
devicehigh=c:\dos\smartdrv.sys 1024
```

See the tricks in the following "Using a Disk Cache and a RAM Drive" section for more about SMARTDRV.SYS.

### Don't load too much into upper memory if you're using Windows.

Windows wants all your extended memory for itself and its programs. If you fill up your upper memory area with device drivers and TSRs, you won't get the maximum performance from Windows.

### Upper memory and Microsoft Windows.

Windows has its own built-in expanded-memory manager. If you use the NOEMS switch with EMM386.EXE, you may have trouble running programs that use expanded memory from Windows. Instead, use the RAM switch in your CONFIG.SYS file, like this:

```
device=c:\dos\emm386.exe ram
```

### Don't load TSRs before Windows.

Some TSRs, like SideKick and SuperKey, need to be loaded *after* Windows starts. Don't automatically start them from your AUTOEXEC.BAT: put them in a Windows program group and start them from there.

## USING A DISK CACHE & A RAM DRIVE

If you don't have a 386 or higher computer, you may have just seen a lot of tips that you can't use. This next section, though, contains tricks that almost everybody can use. Learn how to speed up your computer with a disk cache and a RAM drive.

 **(8088+) Not a database user?** If you don't use a database, the following SMARTDRV.SYS tricks don't apply to you.

**(8088+) Creating a disk cache with SMARTDRV.SYS.** A disk cache is a part of your computer's memory that DOS uses to hold information about what has been done most recently on your disk. Using a disk cache reduces the amount of time DOS spends figuring out what's located where. A disk cache speeds up your work if you're working with programs, like databases, that constantly have to read your disk. DOS 5 and 6 come with slightly different disk-caching programs called SMARTDrive that you can use with extended or expanded memory.

It doesn't work in conventional memory, so you can't use it if you have an XT-style machine without expanded memory.

Here's how to use extended memory to create a 1mb disk cache. Put this line in your CONFIG.SYS file, right after the HIMEM.SYS line ("256" is an optional minimum size):

```
device=c:\dos\smartdrv.sys 1024 256
```

Note that the DEVICE= command for SMARTDRV.SYS must come *after* the memory manager command in your CONFIG.SYS file.

To create a 1mb disk cache using expanded memory, add an /A switch at the end of the line, like this:

```
device=c:\dos\smartdrv.sys 1024 256 /a
```

The first number is the amount of memory SMARTDRV.SYS uses when Windows isn't running, and the second is the amount used when it is running.

**(286+) Windows sets up its own SMARTDRV.** If you use Windows 3.0, edit your CONFIG.SYS file (delete the part of the path that leads to your WINDOWS directory) to use the SMARTDRV.SYS supplied with DOS 5 instead. For example, if your CONFIG.SYS file contains

    device=c:\windows\smartdrv.sys 2048 1024

change it to

    device=c:\dos\smartdrv.sys 2048 1024

If you're using Windows 3.1, you don't have to change the line, as the newer version of Windows uses the updated SMARTDRV.SYS. If there's some question, check the dates of all the .SYS files and use the most recent ones.

**(386+) With DOS 5 and Windows, use Windows' SMARTDrive.** There's one benefit you can get from Windows without using Windows itself if you're running DOS 5 and haven't upgraded to DOS 6 yet. That's using the SMARTDrive disk-caching program that comes with Windows. SMARTDrive speeds up your hard disk by storing in RAM data about the files you've accessed lately. This approach is a great improvement over DOS's FASTOPEN command, which you may have been using until now.

You'll find SMARTDRV.EXE in your Windows directory; put it and its path in your AUTOEXEC.BAT if it isn't already there. If you installed Windows, it may already be there. To see if you've got it, look at your AUTOEXEC.BAT; you should see this line:

    c:\windows\smartdrv.exe

Use the name of your Windows directory, of course.

Don't confuse the Windows 3.1 SMARTDrive with the one that came with Windows 3.0: the new one goes into your AUTOEXEC.BAT, not your CONFIG.SYS. The old SMARTDrive was a read-only cache; the new one caches reads and writes. The version 3.1 SMARTDrive is run from your AUTOEXEC.BAT as a program, so you can change its settings on the fly, without having to edit your CONFIG.SYS and restart your system. DOS 6 uses a SMARTDRV.EXE, which goes into your AUTOEXEC.BAT, instead of the older-style SMARTDRV.SYS that went into the CONFIG.SYS.

If your AUTOEXEC.BAT is showing SMARTDrive in the DOS directory, and you're running DOS 5 and Windows 3.1, edit AUTOEXEC.BAT to use the one in the Windows directory instead. If you're running DOS 6, leave SMARTDRive alone; you've got the good version.

To see what SMARTDrive's doing (either in DOS 5 or 6), type **smartdrv** at the DOS prompt. Type **smartdrv /?** to see the switches you can use with it.

**If you're using the Windows version of SMARTDrive with DOS 5, check your CONFIG.SYS file.** You may find leftovers from Windows 3.0 or DOS that direct DOS to use the equivalent SMARTDRV.SYS in the DOS directory. If you see DEVICE=C:DOS\SMARTDRV.SYS in your CONFIG.SYS, take it out, along with any commands that load SMARTDRV.SYS high, such as LOADHIGH or LH.

**Don't follow this advice if you've got a SCSI hard disk.** One exception: if your hard disk is a SCSI (small computer system interface) device, and you're running Windows 3.1 with DOS 5, you'll need to put SMARTDrive in your CONFIG.SYS instead of your AUTOEXEC.BAT, with this line:

```
device=c:\windows\smartdrv.exe /double_buffer
```

You may find this line in CONFIG.SYS already if Windows Setup figured out that your system needed double buffering, or if it couldn't figure out *what* it needed, in which case it put the SMARTDrive command there. To determine if you need double buffering, type **smartdrv** at the DOS prompt (assuming this line is in your CONFIG.SYS in the form shown above). You'll see a Buffering column (see Figure 10-1). If everything in that column is "no," you don't need double buffering and you can run SMARTDrive from your AUTOEXEC.BAT.

```
C:\COLL>smartdrv
Microsoft SMARTDrive Disk Cache version 4.0
Copyright 1991,1992 Microsoft Corp.

Cache size: 2,097,152 bytes
Cache size while running Windows: 2,097,152 bytes

              Disk Caching Status
    drive   read cache   write cache   buffering

     A:        yes           no           no
     B:        yes           no           no
     D:        yes           yes          no

For help, type "Smartdrv /?".

C:\COLL>
```

*Figure 10-1:* Checking SMARTDRive.

### (386+) What settings are best for Windows's Enhanced mode?

Windows's Setup program automatically adjusts the size of the SMARTDRV.SYS disk cache for your system's setup (256k is the minimum size), but it tends to allocate more memory to this disk cache than you really need. For DOS 5, Microsoft recommends the following sizes for a SMARTDRV.SYS disk cache and a RAM drive in a computer running in 386 Enhanced mode:

| RAM    | SMARTDRV | RAMDRIVE |
|--------|----------|----------|
| 4-6mb  | 1mb      | 1mb      |
| 7mb    | 1.5mb    | 1.5mb    |
| 8mb    | 2mb      | 2mb      |
| 9mb    | 2mb      | 2.5mb    |
| 10+mb  | 4mb      | 4mb      |

See if your settings fall within these guidelines.

If you have 3mb of RAM, only half a megabyte should go to your SMARTDRV.SYS, and you shouldn't be using a RAM drive. If you have less than 2mb of RAM, you aren't running Windows in 386 Enhanced mode anyway.

If you add more memory to your system later, you'll want to refer back to this table and adjust the cache size accordingly. If you're running DOS 6, use its MEMMAKER program to figure all this out for you. See the tips on running MEMMAKER in this chapter.

**Check to see how well SMARTDrive is doing.** If SMARTDrive was installed in your AUTOEXEC.BAT file when you installed Windows 3.1 or DOS 5 or 6, you'll see two numbers at the end of the SMARTDrive line. The first is the size before Windows starts (the InitCacheSize) and the second is the size after it starts (the WinCacheSize). When Windows starts, it switches to the smaller size so it can claim extended memory for its own applications.

If you have 2mb of RAM, the recommended sizes are an InitCacheSize of 1mb (1024) and a WinCacheSize of 256k. With 4mb of RAM, the first figure should be 1024 (1mb); and the second, 512. If you have up to 6mb of RAM, the first number should be 2048 (2mb); and the second, 1024. Beyond 6mb, you'll need 2mb (2048) for each. If you're not sure or don't want to experiment, leave the numbers off and let SMARTDrive figure out how big to set the caches. But be warned: SMARTDrive figures out which cache sizes to set based on how much memory you've got, not on how it's normally being used, so you may want to check out how SMARTDrive is doing and adjust the cache sizes based on how you work (you'll see how in the next paragraph). At any rate, don't be tempted to set up a SMARTDrive cache greater than 2mb because there's no improvement with a bigger cache, even if you have more RAM. And remember, the more memory you give to SMARTDrive, the less memory that's available for your programs.

To see how well SMARTDrive is doing, type **smartdrv /s** at the DOS prompt after you've been using your computer for a while. The screen will show the number of "hits" (times that the data was found in memory) and "misses" (times that your hard disk had to be accessed). Look at Figure 10-2 for an example. To figure out the percentage of the time that SMARTDrive is hitting, add the two numbers and then divide the number of hits by the total. If your score is less than about a B minus (80 percent or below), you may want to increase the cache size.

```
C:\COLL>smartdrv /s
Microsoft SMARTDrive Disk Cache version 4.0
Copyright 1991,1992 Microsoft Corp.

Room for 256 elements of 8,192 bytes each
There have been 7,615 cache hits
    and 4,620 cache misses

Cache size: 2,097,152 bytes
Cache size while running Windows: 2,097,152 bytes

            Disk Caching Status
drive    read cache    write cache    buffering
 A:         yes            no            no
 B:         yes            no            no
 D:         yes            yes           no

For help, type "Smartdrv /?".

C:\COLL>
```

*Figure 10-2:* Analyzing SMARTDrive's performance.

**Don't set too big a disk cache.** Be sure to leave room for your programs if you set up a disk cache. Remember, the bigger the disk cache, the fewer programs you can run: less memory is available to them. Use the MEM command to see how much additional memory you have. (For a detailed breakdown, use **mem /c | more**.)

**(8088+) Using a RAM drive.** A RAM drive (or disk) is also sometimes called a *virtual disk* because your computer uses RAM as though it were a disk drive. Accessing RAM is much faster than accessing a hard disk, so using a RAM drive can speed up your computer's performance.

Even XT-style computers can use a RAM disk, although some of DOS 5's other memory-management features can't be used. Be careful when you set up a RAM disk, though: if you don't have an expanded-memory card and you set too large a RAM disk, RAM will use (and perhaps use up!) conventional memory.

A RAM drive, which you set up with RAMDRIVE.SYS, isn't quite the same as the disk cache set up with SMARTDRV.SYS. A RAM drive has a drive letter and can be used just like a real hard disk; a disk cache is just a storage area that holds information about what you've been doing lately. The one big difference between a RAM drive and a real disk is that a RAM drive is temporary: it's lost when the lights go out!

**A RAM disk is only RAM, after all.** To get some use out of your RAM drive, you have to copy the files you're using to the RAM drive after DOS starts. When you're done, *copy them back to your real hard disk* or to a floppy disk. If you turn off your computer before you copy them back, your work is gone.

**(8088+) Should you use a RAM drive or a disk cache?** Either one can speed up your system, but a disk cache is usually safer to use than a RAM drive. Use both if you like. Just remember that each one does a slightly different job. A disk cache is a buffer that holds information about what you've done lately to the disk so DOS doesn't have to reread the whole hard disk to find out. A RAM drive is a super-speedy "virtual" disk that works just like a real drive (with the important limitation mentioned above).

An effective disk cache should be about 256k (which is the SMARTDRV.SYS default), but a RAM drive can be any size you like, as long as it can hold the files you intend to use it for.

If your computer has only conventional memory (such as an XT-class computer with no expanded memory card), you'll need to carefully balance your program's memory needs with the size of your RAM drive. (See the tip below, "How big a RAM drive do you want?")

**(8088+) Setting up a RAM drive.** If you have extended memory, by all means put your RAM drive in it. To set up a RAM drive that uses 640k of extended memory, add this line to your CONFIG.SYS file, just after the HIMEM.SYS line:

```
device=c:\dos\ramdrive.sys 640 /e
```

If you want a RAM drive that uses expanded memory, use the /A switch instead of the /E switch and put the line just after the line showing the name of your expanded-memory manager. If you don't specify a size, DOS will create a 64k RAM drive, but even that will speed things up.

To put the RAM drive in conventional memory, omit the /A or the /E switch.

DOS creates the RAM drive with the next available drive letter. If your last drive is drive C, the RAM drive will be drive D.

**(286+) Use extended memory instead of conventional memory for your RAM drive.** If you have extended memory, it's better to use it instead of conventional memory for your RAM drive.

**(8088+) A disk by any other name.** You can use a RAM drive just like any other disk except that you can't use the FORMAT command on it. You'll see RAM next to the disk's icon in the Shell, indicating that it's a virtual disk.

**(8088+) How big a RAM drive do you want?** A good rule to follow is to make a regular RAM drive big enough to accommodate your biggest program and the documents you create with it. Be generous.

Run CHKDSK or MEM /C | MORE (with no programs running) to see how much space DOS uses (read the number of bytes free). Subtract the memory your program needs (the documentation will tell you that) and then subtract a certain amount for your data. For example, assume you have 640k of RAM. DOS takes up 48k, Lotus 1-2-3 (Version 2) uses 179k, and you want to work with a 40k spreadsheet; you'll be able to create a 373k RAM disk. But, just to be on the safe side, make it about 300k to make sure you don't run out of memory.

**(8088+) RAMDRIVE.SYS and VDISK.SYS.** Use VDISK.SYS instead of RAMDRIVE.SYS if you're running versions of PC-DOS on a real IBM computer. It does the same thing.

**(286+) Sending temporary files to your RAM drive.** These next two tricks are tagged for 286 and higher machines because they require a larger RAM disk than you can comfortably create in conventional memory.

If you swap back and forth between programs a lot, create a RAM drive and set an environmental variable *temp* to reference it. If no environmental variable is assigned to *temp*, the DOS Shell automatically swaps programs to the drive that DOSSHELL is on. With *temp* in the RAM drive path, programs that are switched out of memory will go to that RAM drive until you're ready to activate them again.

For example, set up drive D as a 1mb RAM drive by putting this line in your CONFIG.SYS file:

```
device=d:\dos\ramdrive.sys 1024 /e
```

The /E switch tells DOS to use extended memory, so this assumes that your computer has extended memory.

Then, run this command:

```
set temp=d:\
```

From then on, you'll find that swapping between programs will go faster.

Are there other ways to use a RAM drive? Some programs, like Ventura Publisher, let you specify a RAM drive for their overflow files. You can also put spelling dictionaries or thesaurus files on a RAM drive, as shown in the next trick.

**(286+) How to put your spelling utility in a RAM drive.** To really speed up spell-checking, put WordPerfect's spelling and hyphenation dictionaries and thesaurus in a RAM disk. I'm using a 386 machine, and this really speeds up the spell-checking process on my already fast computer. You'll be amazed. It's useful to get an idea of what's involved in this process, even if you use a word processing program other than WordPerfect.

First, use the Editor to add this line to your CONFIG.SYS file to create a RAM drive:

```
device=c:\dos\ramdrive.sys 1024 /e
```

The /E switch creates the RAM drive in extended memory; the /A switch creates it in expanded memory; and an absence of switches creates it in conventional memory. (Use DEVICEHIGH instead of DEVICE if you've got a 386 or higher computer that uses upper memory, as explained in previous tricks in this chapter.) Restart your computer to make sure this procedure worked, and then note which drive letter is assigned to your RAM drive (watch for the RAMDRIVE.SYS message).

WordPerfect 5.1's main American spelling dictionary is named WP{WP}US.LEX; its supplementary dictionary is WP{WP}US.SUP. Either add these commands to your AUTOEXEC.BAT file (but if you do, your startup process will be a little slower than usual) or make a batch file that will create a directory on your RAM drive and copy your spelling files to your RAM drive. If you only use the Speller from time to time, it's better to put these commands in a batch file SPELLER.BAT and run it before you use the Speller. The following is a batch file in which the RAM drive is drive E.

```
md e:\spell
xcopy c:\wp51\wp{wp}us.lex e:\spell
xcopy c:\wp51\wp{wp}us.sup e:\spell
```

Your spelling dictionaries will then be copied to your RAM drive when you start your computer. Just issue the **speller** command at the DOS prompt to use your Speller batch file whenever you want to use WordPerfect's Speller.

When you're done, copy WP{WP}US.SUP (the supplementary dictionary) back to your WordPerfect directory to retain the words added during the spell-checking process.

Putting the RAM drive at the end of the path can slow your computer down.

You created the RAM drive to speed things up, right? But if you put it at the *end* of your path, your system will search through all the other directories in the path before it goes to the RAM drive. Put it near the beginning of the path so it'll get accessed first.

## Chapter 10: Managing Memory

**(8088+) Use MEM after setting up a RAM drive.** Use the MEM command to see how much additional memory is left after you've set up your RAM drive. For a detailed report of how memory is being used, issue **mem /c | more**. You may need to reset the size of your RAM drive.

**(8088+)Too many open files?** Sometimes you get a message that too many files are open at one time. This is a DOS message, although you may think at first it's from the program you're working with. DOS 5's and 6's Setup programs check your system and guess at how many files you'll need to have open at once. Sometimes this guess isn't right, particularly if you're working with a program like Lotus 1-2-3 Release 3, which lets you have several files open simultaneously.

If you get a "Too many open files" message, check the line in your CONFIG.SYS file that says **files=** to see how many files DOS allows you to open at once. You can have up to 255 files open simultaneously; but don't do that! Check your Lotus or dBASE (or whatever) manual to see what settings the program recommends. Typical values are 30 or 40 files.

You may need to change the number of buffers, too. Check the **buffers=** line in your CONFIG.SYS file. You can have from 20 to 50 buffers, which work sort of as mini-disk caches (see the preceding tips for details about disk caches). If you've got a very large hard disk (say over 120mb), use 50 buffers; if it's less than 40mb, use 20 buffers; if it's in between, use 30 buffers.

To be on the safe side, check your program documentation for the largest number of buffers recommended for the programs you use. Too many buffers can slow your system down.

**(8088+) Accessing files quickly with FASTOPEN.** The FAST-OPEN command makes DOS remember which files you've recently used. Then DOS doesn't have to search your disk's subdirectories each time you need a file or run another program. If you use a database or compile programs, by all means use FASTOPEN.

Type **fastopen c:=50** at the command line to tell DOS to keep track of the last 50 files and subdirectories you've used. Type in the number of files you want DOS to remember.

Or, you can put the following command in your AUTOEXEC.BAT file to make your computer automatically keep track of a specific number of files (we'll use 50 in these examples, but you can enter the number appropriate for you):

```
c:\dos\fastopen.exe c:=50
```

You can also load FASTOPEN from your CONFIG.SYS file, like this:

```
install=c:\dos\fastopen.exe c:=50
```

Another option is to load FASTOPEN into upper memory (if you've done all the things described earlier to tell DOS to load programs into upper memory). If you've got upper memory, add the /X switch:

```
loadhigh=c:\dos\fastopen.exe c:=50 /x
```

If you want to get fancy, you can specify a different number of files for each drive:

```
fastopen c:=number d:=number e:=number
```

How many files should you FASTOPEN? Well, at least 10. Do more if you have more than three levels of subdirectories (like C:\WP51\DOCS\CHAPS). If you use the FASTOPEN command without specifying a number, the default is 48 subdirectories.

**Don't use FASTOPEN if you're running Windows.** Don't use FASTOPEN (or APPEND) if you're running Windows. Windows insists on being in control of just about everything.

**You don't need FASTOPEN if you're running DOS 5 or 6.** SMARTDrive is a vast improvement over FASTOPEN. If you're running DOS 5 or 6, use SMARTDrive instead.

**(8088+) Don't bother with FASTOPEN if you're using a disk cache.** If you're using SMARTDRV.SYS or a third-party disk-caching program, you don't need to use FASTOPEN. They do pretty much the same thing.

Don't use FASTOPEN when you're doing disk compaction or optimizing your hard disk.

**(8088+) Don't run FASTOPEN from the Shell.** If you run FASTOPEN from the Shell, your computer may freeze up.

## TO SUMMARIZE

Most folks find that getting DOS into high memory is good enough for what they want to do, and the Setup program should take care of that. Depending on whether you use disk-intensive programs like a database, however, you might want to set up a disk cache with SMARTDRV.SYS, too. And, if you use a spell-checker or other temporary files, you'll find that creating a RAM drive will really speed up operations.

Managing memory can get pretty complicated, but it's no big secret if you're willing to experiment. After you get beyond the basics of putting DOS in high memory, which will free up about 45k of conventional memory, memory management is at best a trial-and-error process. Remember to try one trick at a time, restart your computer, and keep that bootable floppy disk handy (or use one as your experimental disk). Or get DOS 6 and let MEMMAKER work its magic.

## A

A20 handler   243
Abbreviations for commands   227
Active Task List   39, 66-67
Adding lines to
   AUTOEXEC.BAT   160
Add Program dialog box   71, 74
Advanced options dialog box   79
All Files view   58
Alphabetical directory listings   101-2
Alt key shortcuts, in Shell   40, 85
Alt-F4, to exit Shell   85
ANSI.SYS   30, 33
Anti-Virus   12
APPEND   223-24
Archive attribute   59, 60-61
Arroyo, Gil   22
ASCII characters, using in
   file names   135-36
ASCII files   191
ASCII mode   54
ASSIGN   4, 224-25
Associating files and programs   65-66
ATTRIB   20-21, 61, 97, 155, 180
AUTOEXEC.BAT   241-42, 246-47
   and batch files   191
   bypassing and testing   14-17
   defined   1-2
   editing   156-61, 187-88
   and path   88
   protecting   204-5
Available memory   239

## B

Backslashes, in directory names   95
Backup utility, for DOS 6   8, 12
   *See also* MSBACKUP
Backup batch files   206-7
Backup tricks   162-74
Backups
   in Shell   146-47
   types of   166-67
   with DOS 6   166-74
Bad command or file
   name message   14
BAK files, as backups   162
Batch files   185-208
   creating at command line   89
   and program groups   77
   storing   141
   using in place of path   157-58
   vs. macros   216-17, 218-20

Batch Help files  21-22
Beeps, in batch files  199
Blank lines, in message
    files  197, 202-3
Bookmarks, in Editor  188-89
Bypassing AUTOEXEC.BAT  14-17
Bypassing CONFIG.SYS  14-17

## C

CALL  77, 197-98, 200
Canceling a command  85, 88
Capacities, of disks  112-13
Capitalization
    at command line  2, 84
    in Editor  189
    in passwords  73
    in searches  51
Catalog files, for backups  172-73
CD  95-96
Central Point Software  133
Changing directories  91
Changing the path  158
Checksum option, in MSAV  133
CHKDSK  3-4, 137, 225-26
    and backups  163-64
    and Shell  148
CHOICE  200, 203-4
Clearing text, in Editor  187
Colors, in the Editor  26
Colors, on screen  25-26, 28,
    31-32, 208
COM1  231
Combining files  176
Command line, using the  83-109
    commands  91-92
    going to, from Shell  83
    help on  17
    shortcuts  89-91
    switching to from Shell  47-48
Command names, and
    batch files  205-6
Command prompt, exiting to,
    from Shell  68

COMMAND.COM, protecting  155
Commands
    best at command line  44, 91-92
    best in Shell  43-44, 92
    canceling  88
    customizing  215-16
    displaying  86
    editing  214
    issuing multiple  210-11
    pausing  87
    recalling  211-12
    repeating  85-86, 87
    for startup floppy  7
    using wildcards with  106
COMMON block  27
COMP  228
Compare function, and backups  171
Comparing disks  227
Comparing files  227-28
Compressed drives
    defragmenting  125-26
    expanding  8-9
    on setup disks  6-7
Compressing a disk  11, 125-28
Concatenating files  176
CONFIG.SYS  2, 241-42, 246-47
    adding lines to  161
    bypassing and testing  14-17
    customizing  29
    and SMARTDRV  257
Confirmation prompts, in Shell  47, 54
Conventional memory  238, 262
COPY  94, 142-43, 160-61, 174-78
    vs. PRINT  177
COPY CON  55, 160-61, 192
Copying and renaming files  94
Copying disks  142-43
    in Windows  177-78
Copying files  20-22, 136,
    141-44, 174-78
    in Shell  53
    in Windows  178
    with wildcards  107
Copying program items  75
Creating directories  93
Creitz, Colin "Slug"  98

Custom configurations,
    setting up   159-60
Custom Help screens, making   19-21
Customizing DOS   23-34

# D

Damaged disks   138
Date and time format, changing   236
Date, putting in a batch file   206-7
DATE   229
*DBLSPACE   125-28
DEFRAG   125, 137-38
Defragmenting a disk   125
DEL   97
Delete Sentry   119-20, 122-23
Delete Tracker   119-20, 122
Deleted files, listing   124
Deleting DOS files   35-36
Deleting files   97, 137, 153-56, 213
Deleting items from groups   81
Deleting macros   221
Deleting previous DOS versions   34-35
Deleting program items   81
Deleting read-only files   60
Deletion-tracking files,
    in DOS 5   117-18
DELOLDOS   34-35
DELTREE   96
Densities, of disks   112-13
Deselecting files, in Shell   53
Dettwiler, Jim   195
Device drivers, for loading in
    upper memory   250-51
DEVICEHIGH   240, 248, 250-51
Dialog boxes
    in Editor   189
    using in Shell   41-42
Differential backups   166-68
DIR   99-104, 229
DIRCMD   229
Directories
    changing   91
    creating   93

deleting   96
    on floppy disks   139-40
moving   93, 95
renaming   56
undeleting   124
Directory listings   98, 99-104
    customizing   229
    printing   181-82
    sorting   99-102
Directory names   95
Directory Tree, in the Shell   38
Disk caches   255-60
    vs. RAM drives   261
*Disk compression   125-28
Disk copying   142-43
    in Windows   177-78
    *See also* DISKCOPY
Disk Full message   178
Disk space
    checking   3-4
    freeing   34-36.
    *See also* Disk compression,
        DBLSPACE
Disk Utilities group   80, 146-48
DISKCOMP   137, 227
DISKCOPY   137, 142, 162, 227
Disks
    care of   111-12
    copying   142-43
    defragmenting   125
    erasing   55
    formatting   112-19
    locking   135
    optimizing   125
    rereading   136
    unformatting   117-18
Displaying files in Shell   45-47
Displaying the last command   86
DMA buffer size, increasing the   168
DO   200
Documents, putting in
    program groups   73-75
DOS 6 Resource Kit   18
DOS files, deleting   35-36
Doskey   209-21
DOSSHELL.INI   25

Dot dot shortcut   89
Double buffering   257-58
Double DOS prompts   194
*DoubleSpace   11, 125-28
Dragging and dropping   64
Drive A   4
Drive C   4
Duplicating files   54

# E

ECHO   195-96, 199
Editing commands, in Doskey   213-14
Editor   25-26, 186-90
   customizing   190
   starting from command line   99
EDLIN   185
8088 computers, and memory   241
EMM386   240-41, 244-45, 251-53
Envelopes, addressing   182
Environment, in
   AUTOEXEC.BAT   150
Environmental
   variables   194, 206-7, 233
Erasing a disk   55
Error messages, and batch files   198-99
ERRORLEVELs, and MOVE   93-94
Exiting from the Shell   47
EXPAND   229-30
   and wildcards   235
Expanded memory   238
Expanding compressed files   8-9
Extended memory   238, 262
Extensions, and associations   65-66
External commands   64

# F

F1
   to repeat a command at
     command line   86-87, 88
   in Shell

F2
   at command line   86
   to edit Doskey commands   212
F3, to repeat commands at
   command line   85-87
F4, to delete commands at
   command line   86
F5, to bypass AUTOEXEC.BAT and
   CONFIG.SYS   15
F6, to insert Ctrl-Z   86
F7, to view history list   212
F8
   to select in Doskey   212
   to step through CONFIG.SYS   15
F9, to view commands in Doskey   212
FASTHELP   17-18
FASTOPEN   265-67
FC   228
FDISK   4-5, 149
File allocation table   5-6
File attributes   59-61
File display options, in Shell   45-46
File information   56-57
File List   38
File names   95
   for batch files   191
   forbidden   89
Filenames, and wildcards   107-8
Files
   combining   176
   copying   20-22, 136,
     141-44, 174-78
   copying and moving, in Shell   53
   deleting   137, 153-56, 213
   duplicating, in Shell   54
   finding   102-4, 178-80
   hiding   135-136
   maximum number in
     directory   140
   moving   92-94
   protecting and hiding   59-60
   renaming   55
   selecting, in Shell   51-53
   sorting   104, 108
   undeleting   119-24
   viewing contents of   56, 109

Filing systems, on hard disks
   vs. floppies   140-41
FIND   102-4
Finding files   102-4, 178-80
Floppy disk, making a
   bootable   7, 116, 128-29, 241-42
Floppy disks
   compressing   126-28
   installing DOS on   5, 9-10
FOR   200
FORMAT prompts, suppressing   147
Formatting a hard disk   149-50
Formatting disks   112-19
   in Shell   146
Formatting while backing up   165
Forney, James S.   207
Function keys
   at command line   86-87
   redefining   33-34

## G

General failure message   114
GOTO   200, 217
GOTO loops, avoiding   199
Graphics display, in the Shell   23
Graphics, printing   182

## H

Hallgren, Gus   140, 161
Hard disks
   formatting   149-50.
      *See also* FDISK
   speeding up   138
   working with   148-50
Help   17-23
   for anti-virus utilities   134
   at command line   88-89
   creating custom in Shell   79-80
   in Doskey   214
   in DOS 6   17-18
   on memory, in DOS 6   247
Help screen, creating with
   batch files   204
Hercules adapter   230-31
Hidden attribute   59
Hidden files   225
   displaying   58, 97-98, 101
Hiding files   60, 135-36
High memory area (HMA)   13
   leading DOS into   243-44
   running DOS in   13-14
HIGH   243-44
High-density disks   112-13
HIMEM.SYS   240-41, 243, 251-53
History list, viewing in Doskey   212
Hot key, with VSAFE   130
Hot keys help   22
Hot line, for virus updating   133

## I

IF   200
IF EXIST   200
IF NOT EXIST   200
IN   200
Incompatibility with drive A   7
Incremental backups   166-68
Indents, in Editor   188
Installing DOS   1-12
Interactive starts   14-17, 242
INTERLNK   135
International commands   228

## J

JOIN   225

## K

Keyboard, customizing   33-34
Keyboard shortcuts
    assigning to groups in Shell   72
    in Shell   39-40, 45, 49, 52.
        *See also* Shortcuts

## L

Labels, electronic   115
Laptops   135
    changing screen during
        backups   170
LASTDRIVE   145-46, 230
LOADHIGH   240, 247-48
Loading Doskey   210
Locating files, in Shell   49-51
Locking a disk   135
Logical drives   144-46
LPT1   231

## M

Macros
    and Doskey   215-21
    vs. batch files   216-17, 218-20
Main group   39
    adding programs to   70
Manual installation   5, 10-11
McMahon, Dennis   113
MD   95
MEM   216, 226, 239-40, 265
    and DOS 6   250
MEMMAKER   237, 245-47
Memory
    managing   237-67
    optimizing in DOS 6   245-47
Menu colors   28
Menu shortcuts, in Shell   39-40
MENUCOLOR   26-27
MENUDEFAULT   26-27
MENUITEM   26-27
Menus
    creating with batch files   200-1
    using in Shell   39-41
Messages, in batch files   196, 201-2
Microsoft Backup   166-74
Microsoft support number   15
Minimal installation   9-10
MIRROR   117-118, 124, 230
MODE   231
MORE   107, 109
*Mounting a compressed disk   127-28
Mouse, using a   44
MOVE command   92-94
Moving files, in Shell   53
MSAV   128, 131-34
MSBACKUP   166-74
MSHERC   230-31

## N

Naming program items   75-76
Num Lock, turning off   34

## O

OEM version disks   2-3
Optimizing disks   125
Overwriting files with MOVE
    and REN   93
Overwriting vs. undeleting   156

## P

Packed file corrupt message   235
Packing list, with DOS 6   9
Parallel ports   231
Parameters   84
Partitioning a disk   4-5, 148-49

Partitioning information,
    saving (DOS 5)   118
Passwords   232
    assigning in Shell   73
    and FORMAT command   115
Path   1, 157-59
    and batch files   192
    keeping DOS in   88
    length of   14
    shortcuts   90
Path names, using when copying   54
Pause After Exit   73
PAUSE   195, 200
Pausing a command   87
Period shortcut   90
Piping   109
Porter, Matthew   194
Ports   231
POWER   135
Previous versions of DOS   6, 7
Print buffer, increasing size of   183
Print queue, increasing size of   183
PRINT   176-77
Printing files   176-77, 180-84
Program files   56
Program groups, creating   69-81
Program items
    copying   75
    deleting   81
    naming   75-76
Program List   38
Programs
    creating startup prompts for   77-79
    running from Shell   63-81
    switching between   67-68, 76
Prompt, customizing   29-33, 208
Protecting files   59-60
Protecting your AUTOEXEC.BAT
    file   156-57

## Q

QBasic   190
Quick Formats   114-15

## R

RAM drives   260-65
    vs. disk caches   261
RAMDRIVE.SYS   262
Read-only attribute   59
Read-only files, deleting   155
Reading README files   205
    *See also* MORE
README.TXT file   13
Rebuilding a disk   117-18
RECOVER   138-39
    vs. UNDELETE   139
Redirection   108-9
Refreshing and repainting
    the screen   49
Regular density disks   112-13
REM   196-97, 199
REN   56, 174
Renaming files   55-56, 174
Renaming and moving   93, 174
Repeating a command   85-86, 87, 212
REPLACE   143-44
Replaceable parameters, in
    batch files   192-94
Replacing changes files   143-44
Rereading a disk   136
Reserved keys, avoiding   76
Responses, putting in
    batch files   154-55
RESTORE   162, 231
Restoring backed-up files   231-32
    with MSBACKUP   172-74
Returning to the Shell   48
Rice, Don   203
Root directory   1, 141
    in Shell   45
    shortcut   89
Run command, in Shell   48, 64

## S

Screen color, changing   31-32, 208
Screen, refreshing the   49

Scrolling, in Shell   50
SCSI disks   257
Search command, in Shell   50-51
Searching for files   178-80
Searching for text in Editor   188-89
Selecting across directories, in
    Shell   47, 52
Selecting files, in Shell   51-53
Serial ports   231
SERVER   235
SET   233
Setup files, for backups   169-70
Setup tips   2-12
Shell   37-61
    and command line, switching
        between   85
    graphics mode in   22-23
    help in   18-21
    starting the   3, 229
SHIFT   200
Shortcuts
    Alt key   40, 85
    command line   89-91
    in the Editor   186
    menu, in Shell   39-40
    for path   90
    for switching between
        programs   67-68
Shortening your path   14
Shorthand, using macros as   216
SmartDrive   255-60
SMARTDRV   255-60
SORT   107, 109
Sorting and finding   104
Sorting files   104, 108
SpeedStor   5
Spelling dictionaries, putting on
    RAM drives   263-64
Startup directory, using a   72
Startup disk, creating   5-7,
    116, 241-42
    with anti-virus   128-29
Startup menus, creating   26
Startup procedures   14-17
Startup prompt, creating

in Shell   77-79
Stealth viruses   132
Stewart, Jim   154
Stopping printing   184
Subdirectories, maximum levels of   141
SUBMENU   26-27
SUBST   4, 144-46, 224-25
Substituting one drive for another   224
SuperStor   5
Supplemental Disk ordering   18
Switches   84
    order of   98
Switching between
    programs   67-68, 76
Symbols
    in Doskey macros   220
    used with PROMPT command   30
Synonyms for commands   227
SYS   150
SYSEDIT   26
System attribute   59
System disks, creating   116
SYSTEM.INI   25
    and DMA buffer size   169

# T

Tab, using in Shell   41-42
Task Swapper   63, 66
Text files   191
Text mode, in Shell   23, 37
Text-only files, printing   181
386 computers, and memory   240-41
Tilton, Homer B.   161
Time, resetting the   234
Too many open files message   265
Tree menu   41
TREE   98, 234
TRUENAME   234
TSRs
    identifying   248-49
    loading manually   248
    and locked-up computer   13

and MEMMAKER 246
and Windows 254
286 computers, and memory 241
TYPE 109, 205

Virtual drives 144-46
Virus list, updating 133
Viruses 128-34
Volume labels 225
VSAVE 128-31

# U

UMB 243-44
Unconditional formatting 116
Undelete utility, in DOS 6 12, 120, 123-24
UNDELETE 120, 123-24
    and overwriting files 156
    vs. RECOVER 139
UNFORMAT 117-18
Unformatting a disk 116-18
Uninstall disk 5-7
Upgrading 2
Upper memory, using 242-43, 247-48, 250-52, 254
Uppercase vs. lowercase
    at command line 2, 84
    in Editor 189
    in passwords 73
    in searches 51
Usable memory 239

# W

Weitek coprocessor 247
Wildcards 104-7
    and deleting files 154
    and DELTREE 96
    using in a search 50-51
    shortcuts 91
    using *.* 97, 154
    using with EXPAND 235
    using with UNDELETE 124
WIN.INI 25
Windows 6, 177-78
    and APPEND 224
    and BACKUP 165
    and SMARTDRV 256-59
    and upper memory 254
    checking viruses from 134
    returning to Shell from 69
Windows Undelete 121, 124
Windows versions of
    DOS utilities 12-13

# V

VDISK.SYS 262
Verifying a copy 144
Version of DOS, setting 235
Video attributes, changing 30-31
Viewing files on a disk 57-59
    *See also* DIR
Virtual disks 260

# X

XCOPY 20-22, 55, 142-43, 162-63, 174-78, 232
XCOPY command 20-22
XT-style computers, and memory 241

From Ventana Press...

# More Companions For Creative Computing

  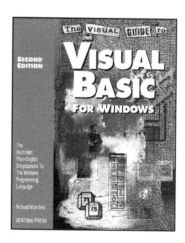

Available from bookstores or Ventana Press. Immediate shipment guaranteed. Your money returned if not satisfied. To order or for more information contact:

Ventana Press, P.O. Box 2468, Chapel Hill, NC 27515
800/743-5369 (orders only)   919/942-0220   Fax 919/942-1140

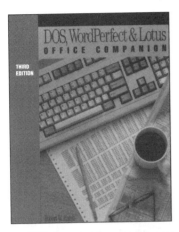

### Desktop Publishing With WordPerfect 6
$24.95
370 pages, illustrated
ISBN: 1-56604-049-3
The new graphics capabilities of WordPerfect 6.0 can save you thousands of dollars in design and typesetting costs. Includes invaluable design advice and annotated examples.

### Voodoo Windows
$19.95
282 pages, illustrated
ISBN: 1-56604-005-1
This one-of-a-kind guide offers a cauldron of Windows tips and tricks that will streamline daily tasks, solve problems and save time. An invaluable reference for beginners and experienced users alike.

### The Visual Guide to Visual Basic for Windows, Second Edition
$29.95
1400 pages, illustrated
ISBN: 1-56604-063-9
This graphics-oriented encyclopedia features thorough, helpful information on all commands, techniques and tools of this powerful programming language.

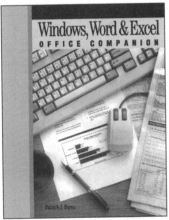

### DOS, WordPerfect & Lotus Office Companion, Third Edition
$21.95
435 pages, illustrated
ISBN: 1-56604-048-5
The bible for business software users is now updated and expanded to cover new versions of DOS (6.0) and WordPerfect (6.0). A three-in-one tutorial for all three programs to get you up and running quickly!

### Windows, Word & Excel Office Companion
$21.95
600 pages, illustrated
ISBN: 0-940087-99-5
Your Microsoft business bible. This three-in-one reference is organized as a quick course in each program. Chapters contain valuable information on basic commands and features, plus helpful tutorials, tips and shortcuts.

### The Official America Online for Windows Membership Kit & Tour Guide
$34.95
402 pages, illustrated
ISBN: 1-56604-013-2
This book/disk includes the AOL starter disk, 10 free hours of online time for new & current members (a $60 value!), a free month's membership plus your official AOL "tour guide."

# the Ventana Press

  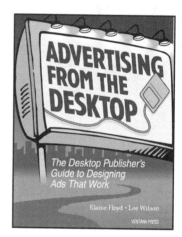

# Desktop Design Series

To order these and other Ventana Press titles, use the form in the back of this book or contact your local bookstore or computer store. Full money-back guarantee!

Return order form to:
Ventana Press, P.O. Box 2468, Chapel Hill, NC 27515
☎919/942-0220; Fax 919/942-1140

Can't wait? Call toll-free, 800/743-5369!

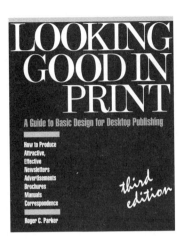

### Newsletters From the Desktop
$23.95
306 pages, illustrated
ISBN: 0-940087-40-5
Now the millions of desktop publishers who produce newsletters can learn how to dramatically improve the design of their publications.

### The Makeover Book: 101 Design Solutions for Desktop Publishing
$17.95
282 pages, illustrated
ISBN: 0-940087-20-0
"Before-and-after" desktop publishing examples demonstrate how basic design revisions can dramatically improve a document.

### Advertising From the Desktop
$24.95
345 pages, illustrated
ISBN: 1-56604-064-7
**Advertising From the Desktop** offers unmatched design advice and helpful how-to instructions for creating persuasive ads. This book is an idea-packed resource for improving the look and effect of your ads.

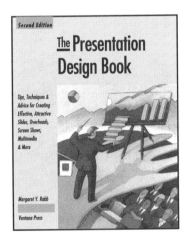

### Looking Good in Print, Third Edition
$24.95
424 pages, illustrated
ISBN: 1-56604-047-7
With over 200,000 copies in print, **Looking Good in Print** is looking even better, with a new chapter on working with color, plus sections on photography and scanning. For use with any software or hardware, this desktop design bible has become the standard among novice and experienced desktop publishers alike.

### The Presentation Design Book, Second Edition
$24.95
320 pages, illustrated
ISBN: 1-56604-014-0
**The Presentation Design Book** is filled with thoughtful advice and instructive examples for creating presentation visuals that have the power to communicate and persuade. For use with any software or hardware.

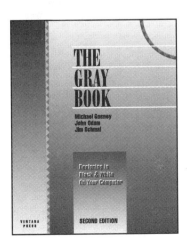

### The Gray Book, Second Edition
$24.95
272 pages, illustrated
ISBN: 1-56604-073-6
This "idea gallery" for desktop publishers offers a lavish variety of the most interesting black, white and gray graphics effects that can be achieved with laser printers, scanners and high-resolution output devices.

# WORK WONDERS WITH VENTANA VOODOO!

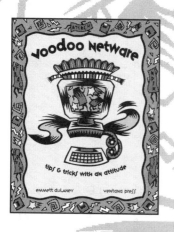

**VOODOO NETWARE**
$27.95
315 pages, illustrated
ISBN: 1-56604-077-9
Overcome network computing obstacles with insightful tips, tricks and shortcuts from *Voodoo NetWare*. This unique guide offers network managers an unparalleled collection of advice for troubleshooting, increasing user productivity and streamlining NetWare tasks. NetWare 4.0 users will find timely tips for a variety of commands and features.

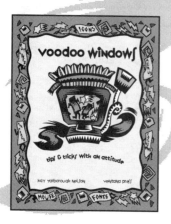

**VOODOO WINDOWS**
$19.95
282 pages, illustrated
ISBN: 1-56604-005-1
A unique resource, *Voodoo Windows* bypasses the obtuse technical information found in many Windows books to bring you an abundance of never-before-published tips, tricks and shortcuts for maximum Windows productivity. A one-of-a-kind reference for beginners and experienced users alike.

### VOODOO OS/2
$24.95
288 pages, illustrated
ISBN: 1-56604-066-3
Optimize OS/2 with this unique collection of never-before-published tips and shortcuts from *Voodoo OS/2*! Whether multithreading or multitasking, you'll find a variety of productivity-enhancing ideas to help streamline tasks and save time.

### VOODOO WINDOWS NT
$24.95
385 pages, illustrated
ISBN: 1-56604-069-8
Discover a cauldron of creative advice for mastering Microsoft's powerful new 32-bit operating system! A wealth of techniques for streamlining your work and increasing productivity is at your fingertips with time-saving tips, tricks and shortcuts for a variety of tasks. You'll find hundreds of hints for simplifying your NT tasks without having to wade through obtuse technical information

### VOODOO MAC
$21.95
340 pages, illustrated
ISBN: 1-56604-028-0
Whether you're a power user or a beginner, *Voodoo Mac* has something for everyone! Computer veteran Kay Nelson has compiled hundreds of invaluable tips, tricks, hints and shortcuts that simplify your Macintosh tasks and save time, including disk and drive magic, font and printing tips, alias alchemy and more!

**Special Offer: Buy all five books in the Ventana Press Voodoo™ Series Library and pay just $81.75, a 30% savings!**

**For faster service, order toll-free 800/743-5369.**
Ventana Press, P.O. Box 2468, Chapel Hill, NC 27515 (919) 942-0220; Fax: (919) 942-1140

**TO ORDER** additional copies of *Voodoo DOS* or any Ventana Press title, please fill out this order form and return it to us for quick shipment. Ask about other books in the *Ventana Voodoo*™ *Series*!

|  | Quantity | Price | Total |
|---|---|---|---|
| *Voodoo DOS, Second Edition* | _____ | x $21.95 = | $_____ |
| *The Official America Online for Windows Membership Kit & Tour Guide* | _____ | x $34.95 = | $_____ |
| *Voodoo Windows* | _____ | x $19.95 = | $_____ |
| *Windows, Word & Excel Office Companion* | _____ | x $21.95 = | $_____ |
| *Looking Good in Print, Third Edition* | _____ | x $24.95 = | $_____ |
| *The Gray Book, Second Edition* | _____ | x $24.95 = | $_____ |
| *Visual Guide to Visual Basic for Windows, Second Edition.* | _____ | x $29.95 = | $_____ |
| *Desktop Publishing With WordPerfect 6* | _____ | x $24.95 = | $_____ |
| *The Makeover Book* | _____ | x $17.95 = | $_____ |
| *Newsletters From the Desktop* | _____ | x $23.95 = | $_____ |
| *Advertising From the Desktop* | _____ | x $24.95 = | $_____ |
| *The Presentation Design Book, Second Edition* | _____ | x $24.95 = | $_____ |
| *Voodoo Mac* | _____ | x $21.95 = | $_____ |
| *Voodoo OS/2* | _____ | x $24.95 = | $_____ |
| *Voodoo NetWare* | _____ | x $27.95 = | $_____ |
| *Voodoo Windows NT* | _____ | x $24.95 = | $_____ |

Shipping: Please add $4.50/first book, $1.35/book thereafter; $8.25/book "two-day air," $2.25/book thereafter. For Canada, add $6.50/book. = $_____

Send C.O.D. (add $4.50 to shipping charges) = $_____

North Carolina residents add 6% sales tax = $_____

Total = $_____

Name _____

Company _____

Address (No PO Box) _____

City_____ State_____ Zip _____

Daytime Telephone _____

\_\_\_ Payment enclosed   \_\_\_VISA   \_\_\_MC   Acc't # _____

Expiration Date_____   Interbank # _____

Signature _____

Please mail or fax to: **Ventana Press, PO Box 2468, Chapel Hill, NC 27515**
☎ **919/942-0220, FAX: 919/942-1140**

# CAN'T WAIT? CALL TOLL-FREE ☎ 800/743-5369!

**T**O ORDER additional copies of *Voodoo DOS* or any Ventana Press title, please fill out this order form and return it to us for quick shipment. Ask about other books in the *Ventana Voodoo*™ *Series*!

| | Quantity | Price | | Total |
|---|---|---|---|---|
| *Voodoo DOS, Second Edition* | _____ | x $21.95 | = | $_____ |
| *The Official America Online for Windows Membership Kit & Tour Guide* | _____ | x $34.95 | = | $_____ |
| *Voodoo Windows* | _____ | x $19.95 | = | $_____ |
| *Windows, Word & Excel Office Companion* | _____ | x $21.95 | = | $_____ |
| *Looking Good in Print, Third Edition* | _____ | x $24.95 | = | $_____ |
| *The Gray Book, Second Edition* | _____ | x $24.95 | = | $_____ |
| *Visual Guide to Visual Basic for Windows, Second Edition.* | _____ | x $29.95 | = | $_____ |
| *Desktop Publishing With WordPerfect 6* | _____ | x $24.95 | = | $_____ |
| *The Makeover Book* | _____ | x $17.95 | = | $_____ |
| *Newsletters From the Desktop* | _____ | x $23.95 | = | $_____ |
| *Advertising From the Desktop* | _____ | x $24.95 | = | $_____ |
| *The Presentation Design Book, Second Edition* | _____ | x $24.95 | = | $_____ |
| *Voodoo Mac* | _____ | x $21.95 | = | $_____ |
| *Voodoo OS/2* | _____ | x $24.95 | = | $_____ |
| *Voodoo NetWare* | _____ | x $27.95 | = | $_____ |
| *Voodoo Windows NT* | _____ | x $24.95 | = | $_____ |

Shipping: Please add $4.50/first book, $1.35/book thereafter; $8.25/book "two-day air," $2.25/book thereafter. For Canada, add $6.50/book.                                = $_____

Send C.O.D. (add $4.50 to shipping charges)                                = $_____

North Carolina residents add 6% sales tax                                = $_____

                                                                    Total = $_____

Name _____

Company _____

Address (No PO Box) _____

City_____ State_____ Zip_____

Daytime Telephone _____

___ Payment enclosed   ___VISA   ___MC   Acc't # _____

Expiration Date_____ Interbank # _____

Signature _____

Please mail or fax to: **Ventana Press, PO Box 2468, Chapel Hill, NC 27515**
☎ 919/942-0220, FAX: 919/942-1140

# CAN'T WAIT? CALL TOLL-FREE ☎ 800/743-5369!